Secure Data Handling in
Science and Technology

Secure Data Handling in Science and Technology

RAFEAL MECHLORE

Readers Publications

CONTENTS

	INDEX	1
	INTRODUCTION	3
1	Chapter 1	18
2	Chapter 2	41
3	Chapter 3	65
4	Chapter 4	85
5	Chapter 5	106
6	Chapter 6	132
7	Chapter 7	154
8	Chapter 8	175
9	Chapter 9	197
10	Chapter 10	222
11	Chapter 11	248

CONTENTS

12 | Chapter 12 266

INDEX

Introduction

1. The Importance of Data Security in Science and Technology
2. Overview of the Book
3. Key Concepts and Terminology

Chapter 1: Fundamentals of Data Security
1.1 Definition of Data Security
1.2 Types of Data: Sensitive, Confidential, and Personal
1.3 The Threat Landscape: Cybersecurity Risks
1.4 Data Security Principles and Best Practices

Chapter 2: Data Privacy Laws and Regulations
2.1 Global Data Privacy Frameworks (e.g., GDPR, CCPA, HIPAA)
2.2 Compliance and Consequences

Chapter 3: Data Collection and Storage Security
3.1 Secure Data Collection Methods
3.2 Data Storage Solutions and Encryption
3.3 Data Retention Policies and Practices

Chapter 4: Data Transmission and Communication Security
4.1 Secure Data Transfer Protocols
4.2 Securing Data in Transit
4.3 Secure Messaging and Collaboration Tools

Chapter 5: Access Control and Authentication
5.1 User Authentication Methods
5.2 Role-Based Access Control

5.3 Implementing Multi-Factor Authentication
5.4 Access Control in Scientific Research Environments

Chapter 6: Secure Data Processing and Analysis
6.1 Data Anonymization and Pseudonymization
6.2 Secure Computation and Cloud Computing
6.3 Ensuring Data Security in Data Analytics

Chapter 7: Insider Threats and Social Engineering
7.1 Identifying Insider Threats
7.2 Preventing and Mitigating Insider Threats
7.3 Social Engineering Attacks and Countermeasures

Chapter 8: Vulnerability Management and Patching
8.1 Identifying and Prioritizing Vulnerabilities
8.2 Patch Management Strategies
8.3 Zero-Day Vulnerabilities and Their Implications

Chapter 9: Secure Collaboration and Data Sharing
9.1 Secure Collaborative Tools and Platforms
9.2 Secure Data Sharing Practices
9.3 Data Sharing Agreements and Data Access Control

Chapter 10: Incident Response and Data Breach Recovery
10.1 Developing an Incident Response Plan
10.2 The Anatomy of a Data Breach
10.3 Data Recovery and Business Continuity

Chapter 11: Ethical Considerations in Secure Data Handling
11.1 Ethical Principles in Data Science and Technology
11.2 Responsible Data Use and Governance

Chapter 12: Future Trends and Emerging Technologies
12.1 Quantum Computing and Data Security
12.2 AI and Machine Learning in Data Security
12.3 Blockchain and Secure Data Handling

INTRODUCTION

Data is the lynchpin that drives innovation, propels discoveries, and molds our future in the continuously changing landscape of science and technology. The gathering, processing, and dissemination of information are the three pillars upon which every achievement, every scientific endeavor, and every technological innovation are built. The digital age has drastically changed the way that we conduct research and develop in every subject, from genetics and artificial intelligence to astrophysics and renewable energy.

However, despite the fact that data is now the driving force behind technological advancement, it is also the focus of an ever-expanding number of risks. The rising digitization of scientific and technical processes has given rise to a complex web of vulnerabilities. These vulnerabilities range from the cyberattacks that endanger the security and integrity of research data to the ethical concerns that are related with the use of the data. There has never been a time when the management of data securely was more important in the fields of science and technology, nor has there ever been a time when it held such a weighty responsibility.

This book, which is titled "Secure Data Handling in Science and Technology," is devoted to deciphering the complexities of data security within these important fields of study. It is a thorough manual that takes the reader on a tour across the fields of science and technology, illuminating the significance of data security, privacy, and best practices along the way. In the pages that follow, we will delve into the essential components of this subject, covering everything from the fundamental concepts to the developing technologies that are reshaping the future of data protection.

At its most fundamental level, data security refers to the process of protecting information from being accessed, disclosed, altered, or deleted without permission. It involves the utilization of a wide variety of strategies and precautions, which, when combined, build a protective barrier around sensitive data. This data can take on many different forms in the field of science and technology, ranging from confidential research findings and proprietary algorithms to personal health records and financial information. The difficult task at hand is to secure these records while at the same time making it possible for researchers, developers, and tech innovators to make effective use of them.

It is necessary for us to first recognize the multifarious character of facts before we can appreciate the severity of the subject matter. Data can be deemed sensitive, confidential, or personal, and each of these classifications comes with its own unique set of concerns around privacy and safety.

It's possible that sensitive data relates to scientific breakthroughs, trade secrets, or intellectual property; these are the kinds of data that, if exposed, may be catastrophic for research projects or businesses. The need for increased degrees of security and control is necessitated by the fact that confidential data may include things like medical records, applications for research grants, or sensitive information from the government. Because personal data is frequently connected to the identities of individuals and to sensitive information, it is entitled to stringent privacy laws that prohibit its misuse.

The threat environment is equally complicated and is always changing to accommodate the development of new technology. A clarion call for heightened vigilance has been issued in recent years as a direct result of the surge in the number of cyber-attacks, data breaches, and information releases. Hackers, malevolent actors, and cybercriminals work diligently and are frequently successful in their attempts to exploit weaknesses in computer systems. The reasons for these assaults are just as diverse as the people or organizations that are being attacked, ranging from state-sponsored strikes to opportunistic hacking.

Throughout our voyage through this book, we will examine the fundamental principles that support data security in science and technology. Additionally, we will investigate the bedrock of best practices that should be embraced by individuals, companies, and institutions. We will delve into the world of data privacy laws and regulations, such as the General Data Protection Regulation (GDPR), the California Consumer Privacy Act (CCPA), and the Health Insurance Portability and Accountability Act (HIPAA), which not only establish the standards for data privacy but also determine the consequences for non-compliance with those standards.

But protecting sensitive information is not only an abstract idea. It is a task that involves active participation and hands-on work, as well as an in-depth knowledge of the data lifecycle. The earliest steps, which consist of collecting and storing data, are where the seeds of security are planted. In this lesson, we are going to get into the nitty-gritty details of secure data gathering methods, as well as the several data storage solutions that are currently available and the function that encryption plays in securing data while it is stored.

After being gathered and stored, data frequently needs to be conveyed and shared both within and across organizations. This can be done in a variety of ways. Protocols for the secure transfer of data, encryption while the data is in transit, secure communications and collaboration tools are all essential components during this phase. For the sake of protecting the information's honesty and privacy, it is essential to have a solid understanding of these components.

Mechanisms for access control and authentication are absolutely necessary in order to stop
unauthorized users from accessing sensitive data. We are going to investigate several ways of authenticating users, as well as the implementation of role-based access control and the advantages of using multi-factor authentication when it comes to constructing strong barriers against data breaches.

The processing of data and the analysis of that data are the engines that drive innovation in science and technology. Having said that, one must select one's tools and methods while keeping security in mind at all times. We will examine the anonymization and pseudonymization of data, safe computation, and the implications of cloud computing in data analysis, with the goal of ensuring that data security is ingrained into the very heart of the research processes.

Insider actors and social engineering attacks are two of the types of threats that can be among the most difficult to detect. Essential components of an effective data security plan include the ability to recognize the warning indications of insider threats, the ability to detect and mitigate those threats, and an awareness of the methodology behind social engineering assaults.

In the field of data security, the management of vulnerabilities and the application of patches are continual tasks. The issues posed by zero-day vulnerabilities, also known as unknown dangers that lurk in the shadows, will be discussed, along with the identification and prioritization of vulnerabilities, the tactics for patch management, and the patch management strategies.

Collaboration and the sharing of data are fundamental components of any forward movement in scientific research or technological development. This book discusses safe collaboration tools and platforms, recommended practices for securely sharing data, the significance of data sharing agreements and access control methods, and more.

Incidents and security breaches can affect any company or organization. It is essential to devise a plan for responding to incidents and have a solid understanding of the components that make up a data breach in order to reduce the amount of damage and get back on your feet more quickly. In the aftermath of an incident, we will also evaluate data recovery and business continuity measures. These are the kinds of precautions that can determine whether or not an organization is successful.

Although protecting sensitive information is primarily a technological challenge, it is also an issue of morality and responsibility.

The ethical implications of data management will be discussed in the book, along with the principles that guide responsible data use and governance, and real-world case studies that highlight ethical dilemmas in the area will be shared.

As we progress through the chapters, we will keep our eyes on the horizon and investigate new technologies that have the potential to alter the landscape of data security. In the fields of science and technology, quantum computing, artificial intelligence, and blockchain all stand on the cusp of ushering in sweeping changes to the way data is managed and protected.

This book will emphasize the practicality of data security measures by displaying both success stories and cautionary tales of data breaches through a series of captivating case studies. These case studies will be included in the book. These instances from real life will provide vital insight into the repercussions of both secure and unsecure data handling procedures, so keep an eye out for them.

1. **The Importance of Data Security in Science and Technology**

Data is not merely a consequence of scientific and technological endeavors in today's digital age; rather, it represents the fundamental core of progression itself. When it comes to driving innovation, bolstering research, and influencing the future, the fields of science and technology are significantly reliant on data. The massive datasets used in genetics and climate research, as well as the complicated algorithms that are the foundation of artificial intelligence, all point to the fact that data is the fields' most important resource. On the other hand, as our reliance on digital information continues to grow, there has never been a time when the need for strong data security has been more pressing. In the following paragraphs, we will discuss the tremendous significance of data security in the fields of science and technology, as well as its ramifications for academics, businesses, and society as a whole.

1. **Maintaining Honesty and Transparency in Research**
   The reliability of data is absolutely necessary for research in the scientific and technological fields. In the process of doing scientific research, hypotheses and conclusions are developed on the basis of data that is both accurate and dependable. Any breach of the data's integrity, whether it was caused by an accident or was the result of intentional manipulation, has the potential to result in incorrect conclusions, the misuse of resources, and a halt in the advancement of scientific knowledge.
   Consider, for instance, a study project on climate, which, in order to simulate weather patterns and anticipate changes in climate, relies on data collected over the course of decades.
   If these data were altered with or otherwise compromised, the entire research attempt would be rendered useless, which might result in inaccurate climate models and policies that are not based on accurate information. In order to maintain the reliability of research, data security is of the utmost importance.

2. **Safeguarding the Ownership of Intellectual Property**
   The protection of one's intellectual property (IP) is essential to maintaining a competitive edge in the field of technology and innovation. When companies want to produce innovative technology, goods, and services, they put a large amount of resources into research and development. This frequently entails the generation of confidential data that provides them with an advantage over their competitors. For example, a corporation that specializes in technology might make an investment in the creation of innovative algorithms for a brand-new product.
   This valuable intellectual property is at risk of being stolen or compromised if there is not effective data security. If a rival business or some other malevolent party were to obtain access to these sensitive data, they might recreate the product or the technology, which would result in monetary loss for the company that is doing the innovation. Data security acts as a barrier against these risks and ensures that an organization's intellectual property is kept confidential while also being safeguarded from prying eyes.
3. **Maintaining the Confidentiality of Private and Sensitive Information**
   The processing of private and confidential information is frequently required in the fields of science and technology. For example, patient records in the healthcare industry contain highly sensitive data, such as the patient's medical history as well as personal information. In a similar manner, the DNA information of individuals is processed and stored when genetic research is conducted. In many different jurisdictions, not only is there an ethical need to safeguard this private and sensitive information, but there is also a legal requirement to do so.
   Data breaches in these industries can have significant repercussions, including the theft of personal information, the provision of unlawful medical treatment, and the invasion of personal privacy. It is vital to implement stringent data security procedures in order to safeguard personal and sensitive information. This ensures that individuals may have faith that their data will be handled with the utmost care and responsibility.
4. **Compliance with the Laws and Regulations Regarding the Privacy of Data**
   The constantly shifting environment of data privacy laws and regulations places an increased premium on the significance of maintaining adequate data protection.
   For example, the General Data Protection Regulation (GDPR) in Europe and the California Consumer Privacy Act (CCPA) in the United States have both set stringent requirements for the management and protection of personal data. Both of these regulations were created in 2018. If you do not comply with these regulations, you could face significant fines as well as other legal consequences.

Compliance with these standards is absolutely necessary in the scientific and technological fields because international cooperation is commonplace and data is freely exchanged around the world. In order to achieve compliance with these regulations, data security policies need to be in line with their requirements, and companies and researchers need to keep themselves informed and on their toes.

5. **Lessening the Impact of Cybersecurity Dangers**

The scientific community and the technology community as a whole are becoming increasingly concerned about the dangers posed by cybersecurity threats. Organizations that have a lot of data are constantly being targeted by malicious actors, who can range from state-sponsored hackers to cybercriminals, with the intention of stealing, manipulating, or disrupting their data. These assaults can be carried out using social engineering techniques, ransomware, or distributed denial of service (DDoS) operations.

The repercussions of a breach in cybersecurity could have catastrophic effects. The unauthorized acquisition of data can result in monetary losses, damage to reputation, and legal penalties. In certain circumstances, manipulating data can lead to the making of incorrect decisions, which may even have dangerous consequences. In order to protect against these dangers and maintain business as usual, it is vital to implement stringent data security procedures.

6. **Making Certain That Data Is Accessible**

Not only does data security involve the safeguarding of data, but it also ensures that the data in question is accessible at all times. Experiments and observations in the field of scientific study generate enormous datasets, which are frequently irretrievable. In the field of information technology, day-to-day operations are dependent on data in the form of information on customers as well as financial records.

Particularly crucial is the availability of data in such industries as healthcare, where patient records are necessary for medical treatments and diagnostics. Data security procedures, such as backup and disaster recovery plans, assist ensure that data can still be accessed even in the event of unforeseen occurrences, such as malfunctioning technology, natural catastrophes, or malicious cyberattacks.

7. **Establishing a Foundation of Trust and Confidence**

In the realms of scientific research and technological development, trust is an indispensable commodity. Both academics and businesspeople need to work to win over the confidence of their contemporaries, colleagues, and the general public. This trust can be damaged when there is a data breach or a security incident, which can result in skepticism, reputational damage, and a loss of confidence.

On the other side, an organization's reputation can be improved by showing that it is committed to maintaining data security through the use of rigorous precautions and ethical business practices. It demonstrates that the organization handles data handling seriously and places a high priority on the confidentiality and safety of the stakeholders it works with.

8. **Considerations of an Ethical Nature**

   The need of maintaining a high ethical standard when it comes to data security cannot be stressed. The ethical obligation of ensuring that data, especially sensitive data, is handled with the highest care and respect falls on researchers and professionals working in science and technology. This applies to the manner in which data is gathered, stored, analyzed, and distributed as well. When handling data in an ethical manner, you ensure that individuals' privacy is maintained, that research is carried out in an honest manner, and that the risk of harm coming from data breaches or improper usage is kept to a minimum. When it comes to matters of science and technology, which have the potential to have a significant effect on society, ethical considerations are an essential component of data security.

9. **The Importance of Protecting User Data When Using New Technologies**

Emerging technologies such as quantum computing, artificial intelligence (AI), and blockchain are gaining significance in today's world of science and technology, which is continually shifting and adapting to new developments. These technologies open up new doors of opportunity while simultaneously posing new obstacles in terms of data protection.

For example, quantum computing has the ability to disrupt existing encryption methods, which makes the creation of encryption strategies that are resistant to quantum computing a must. AI may be used to improve data security by automating threat detection and response, but it can also be used by cybercriminals to launch more complex assaults. AI can be used to increase data security by automating threat detection and response. The decentralized and unchangeable nature of the data stored using blockchain technology is leading to a new definition of data security.

Understanding the ramifications of these evolving technologies and being able to react to them is essential for preserving data security in the scientific and technological fields.

B. Overview of the Book

The book "Secure Data Handling in Science and Technology" is an in-depth handbook that looks into the complex world of data security that exists within the realms of research and technology. This book serves as a guide for scientists, technologists, data analysts, and other professionals who are tasked with the protection of data. It sheds light on the crucial importance of data security, privacy, and best practices in the industry.

As we make our way through the pages of this book, we will investigate the various aspects of secure data handling in science and technology. We will learn about the fundamental concepts, ethical considerations, compliance with data privacy legislation, and the evolving threat landscape as we make our way through this journey. We are going to go into the more practical parts of data security, such as safeguarding the data collection and storage processes, as well as the data transmission and communication processes, access control and authentication, data processing and analysis, vulnerability management, and incident response. In addition to this, we will investigate the fundamentally important role that data security plays in developing technologies as well as the ethics that guide data management in these areas.

To better prepare you for what is to come, let's take a more in-depth look at the information presented in this book as well as its organization.

The Fundamentals of Data Security is Covered in Chapter 1.

The first step in the process is laying the foundation, which entails becoming familiar with the primary tenets of secure data storage. In this chapter, we will discuss the fundamentals of data security, including its definition as well as the many categories of data, such as personal, sensitive, and private information. We go into the threat landscape and conduct an analysis of the cybersecurity dangers that are encountered on a regular basis by scientists and engineers. At the end of this chapter, readers will have the knowledge they need to appreciate the vital role that data security plays in their job and will be armed with that knowledge.

Data Privacy Laws and Regulations Presented in Chapter 2

The privacy of one's data is not merely an idea; rather, it is a collection of laws and regulations that dictate the appropriate manner in which data should be handled. This chapter explores the global landscape of data privacy, with a particular emphasis on key legal frameworks such as the General Data Protection Regulation (GDPR), the California Consumer Privacy Act (CCPA), and the Health Insurance Portability and Accountability Act (HIPAA). We investigate the ramifications of compliance as well as the legal repercussions of breaches in data privacy.

Case studies based on the real world will provide insightful information regarding how important it is to comply with these standards.

Data Security during Data Collection and Storage (Chapter 3)

The protection of sensitive information is an ongoing process that starts at the very beginning of a dataset's existence. In this chapter, we will discuss the best practices for securing data gathering methods, the many data storage solutions that are now available, and the critical part that encryption plays in ensuring the safety of data while it is stored. One of the most important aspects of data security is gaining an understanding of how to protect data from the moment it is gathered onward.

Data Transmission and Communication Security is the Topic of Chapter 4.

Data does not often exist in a solitary state; rather, it is frequently transmitted, moved, and shared. This chapter delves into the world of data transmission as well as the protection of communication. We investigate the importance of secure data transmission methods, the role that secure communications and collaboration tools play, and the necessity of encryption while data is in transit. At the conclusion of this chapter, readers will have gained an in-depth understanding of how to maintain the data's secrecy and integrity while it is being transported from one location to another.

Access Management and Authentication Covered in Chapter 5

One of the most important aspects of data security is limiting unauthorized access to sensitive information. Access control and authentication are the topics that are discussed in Chapter 5. This chapter goes deeper into the topic by offering information on user authentication techniques, the implementation of role-based access control, and the benefits of multi-factor authentication. The only people who should be able to interact with sensitive data are those who have been given permission to do so, which can be prevented if one knows how to manage access to the data.

Data Processing and Analysis in a Secure Environment, Chapter 6

It is not enough to simply store data; it must also be processed and analyzed before it can be useful. In this chapter, we will discuss the methods of safe data processing and analysis that are essential to the domains of science and technology. Anonymization and pseudonymization of data, safe computation, and the ramifications of cloud computing in data analysis are all topics that are covered in depth here. The information presented here will help readers understand how to leverage the power of data while still maintaining the data's security.

Insider Attacks and Social Manipulation is the Topic of Discussion in Chapter 7.

Within an organization lies one of the most insidious dangers to the data security that might be encountered. This chapter identifies potential dangers posed by insiders and provides suggestions for preventing or mitigating such dangers. In addition to this, we shed insight on social engineering assaults, which involve exploiting vulnerabilities by manipulating human psychology. It is absolutely necessary to have a solid understanding of both the internal and external dangers in order to effectively protect against them.

Vulnerability Management and Patching is the Topic of Chapter 8.

Vulnerabilities are introduced into the landscape of technology and software as a result of its constant state of evolution, and these vulnerabilities can be exploited by bad actors. This chapter discusses the process of detecting and prioritizing vulnerabilities, tactics for patch management, and the persistent problem given by zero-day vulnerabilities, which are threats that are undiscovered and lying in the shadows of the internet. The successful management of vulnerabilities is an essential component of data security.

Secure Coordination and Data Exchange is the Topic of Chapter 9.

Collaboration and the sharing of data is frequently required in the scientific and technological communities. This chapter explores safe collaborative tools and platforms in order to meet the difficulty of enabling secure cooperation. In addition to this, we go over the most effective methods for safely exchanging data, as well as the significance of data-sharing agreements and access control systems. One of the most important aspects of data security is striking a balance between accessibility and protection.

Incident Response and Data Breach Recovery is the Topic of Chapter 10.

There is no security technique that can absolutely ensure protection. This chapter walks readers through the steps of building an incident response plan, which is critical for reducing the amount of harm caused by data breaches and quickly recovering from them. We investigate the components that make up a data breach, discuss potential strategies for data recovery, and investigate the function that business continuity planning plays in maintaining operations in the face of adversity.

Ethical Considerations in Secure Data Handling is the Topic of Chapter 11.

The application of data in areas of science and technology should always be guided by ethical standards as a moral compass. This chapter examines the ethical concerns that should be made while handling data, with a particular emphasis on the responsible use of data and governance. Real-world case studies will provide light on the ethical conundrums that might crop up in various disciplines, allowing readers to think on their own behaviors and the obligations they have in their respective practices.

Future Trends and New Technologies are Discussed in Detail in Chapter 12

Both the scientific and technological spheres are continuously undergoing change and development. This chapter takes a look into the future by analyzing how new technologies may affect data security in the near and far future. The methods of data management are on the cusp of being completely disrupted by developments in quantum computing, artificial intelligence, and blockchain technology. To maintain a competitive advantage in the field of data security, it is essential to have a solid understanding of these patterns and the ramifications they have.

Case Studies in Secure Data Handling is the topic of Chapter 13.

Both examples of accomplishment and cautionary tales can serve as instructive models for data security. This chapter includes a series of case studies that demonstrate both successful and unsuccessful attempts to handle sensitive data in a secure manner. The reader will get insights into the practical effects of secure and insecure data handling techniques by evaluating the examples taken from the actual world that are provided here.

Implementing Safe Data Handling Procedures in Your Organization is the Topic of Chapter 14.

The adventure comes to a close with a chapter that focuses on the actual application of safe data handling procedures within your firm. It is absolutely necessary to devise a data security strategy that takes into account the particular requirements and dangers of your industry. In addition to that, the creation of data security rules, training, and the significance of ongoing monitoring and improvement are all discussed in this chapter.

In the following chapters, we would like to welcome you on an adventure to discover the complex and ever-evolving terrain of secure data handling in research and technology. This book is intended to serve as an invaluable resource for scientists, technicians, data analysts, and other professionals who acknowledge the paramount significance of data security in the job that they do. You will be able to protect sensitive information, preserve the integrity of research, and ensure that data continues to be the driving force behind development and innovation in the domains of science and technology if you navigate through these pages and get the knowledge and insights necessary to do so.

C. Key Concepts and Terminology

It is absolutely necessary to have a thorough understanding of essential concepts and terminology in the realm of data security, which is constantly evolving. When it comes to securing sensitive information, the dangers and problems grow in tandem with the increasing sophistication and pervasiveness of data processing in scientific research and technological development.

This article provides professionals, researchers, and technicians with the information they require to traverse the complex terrain of data protection by examining important concepts and phrases that support the practice of data security in these fields.

1. **The Protection of Data**
   The technique of securing data against illegal access, disclosure, modification, or destruction is referred to as information security. Data security is another name for this aspect of information security. It includes a wide variety of strategies, procedures, and precautions that are intended to protect the privacy of the data while still ensuring its integrity and availability.

2. **Private Information**
   When we talk about sensitive data, we are referring to information that, if leaked or hacked in any way, has the potential to cause harm to individuals, companies, or even the nation's security. Research findings, confidential information, proprietary algorithms, and trade secrets are all examples of sensitive data that can be found in the fields of science and technology.

3. **Private and Discreet Information**
   Data that is both confidential and sensitive calls for additional layers of security to be implemented. Typically, it consists of non-public information pertaining to businesses, such as financial records, proprietary business information, and the results of confidential research that are not meant to be made public.

4. **Private Information**
   Individuals' names, addresses, social security numbers, and medical histories are

examples of the types of information that fall under the category of "personal data." It is vital to preserve personal data in order to protect the privacy of individuals and to comply with laws governing data privacy.

5. **A Breach of Data**
   A data breach takes place if sensitive, confidential, or personal information is either exposed to unauthorized parties or accessed by those parties. This might have been caused by a hack, an insider threat, or just plain old negligence.

6. **Protection against cyberattacks**
   The practice of preventing computer systems, networks, and data from being stolen, damaged, or accessed in an unauthorized manner is referred to as cybersecurity. It requires an integration of many aspects of technology, procedures, and social behavior.

7. **Codes and ciphers**
   The process of transforming data into a code in order to prevent unauthorized access is referred to as encryption. Encoding information requires the use of algorithms, and the information can only be decoded with the correct key.

8. **Validation of Authenticity**
   The process of confirming the identity of a person or system to determine whether or not they possess the appropriate credentials to have access to a particular set of data or resources is known as authentication. Passwords, biometrics, and multiple factors of authentication are all common forms of security measures.

9. **Regulation of Entry**
   Controlling who has access to specific data or resources is what we mean when we talk about access control. A person's job function or role in the organization determines the permissions that person is granted through role-based access control, which restricts access to only what is required.

10. **Protection of Personal Information**
    The protection of personal data involves ensuring that individuals have control over their own personal information and how it is gathered, utilized, and disseminated. Data privacy can be defined as the safeguarding of such information.

11. **Obligation to comply**
    Compliance is when a company ensures that it is in accordance with all of the laws and regulations that pertain to the data security business. Compliance in the fields of science and technology sometimes entails laws and regulations concerning data privacy.

12. **Regulation on the General Protection of Data (known as GDPR)**
    The General Data Protection policy (GDPR) is an all-encompassing data privacy policy in the European Union. It sets stringent penalties for non-

compliance and issues regulations regarding the manner in which personal data should be treated and secured.

13. **The California Consumer Privacy Act (often known as CCPA)**
The California Consumer Privacy Act (CCPA) is a law that goes into effect on January 1, 2020,
and it is a data privacy law that gives customers rights over their personal information and establishes requirements on corporations to protect this data.

14. **HIPAA, or the Health Insurance Portability and Accountability Act**
The Health Insurance Portability and Accountability Act of 1996 (HIPAA) is a law in the United States that regulates the privacy and safety of medical information.

15. **A digital assault**
A cyberattack is any intentional attempt to compromise the availability, confidentiality, or integrity of data or computer systems. Attacks using malware, phishing, and ransomware are some of the more common types.

16. **A Danger From Within**
An insider threat is a security risk that is posed by individuals working for or employed by an organization who have access to sensitive data and who have the potential to misuse that access. These dangers may or may not have been intentionally created.

17. **The Practice of Social Engineering**
Social engineering is a technique that is utilized by cybercriminals to trick individuals into exposing secret information, such as passwords or sensitive data, through the use of psychological manipulation. Social engineering is also known as "phishing."

18. **An exposure to risk**
A weakness or flaw in a system, software, or process is referred to as a vulnerability. Attackers
are able to take advantage of vulnerabilities in order to obtain unauthorized access or cause damage.

19. **Maintenance of Patche**
Patch management is the process of locating, testing, and deploying software updates (patches) in a timely way to resolve vulnerabilities and security risks. This process is also known as software update management.

20. **The Anonymization of Data**
The process of deleting or concealing personally identifying information (PII) from data, also known as data anonymization, helps safeguard individuals' privacy while still enabling data analysis to take place.

21. **The Anonymousization of Data**
The process of replacing personally identifiable information (PII) with

fictitious identifiers, also known as data pseudonymization, makes it significantly more difficult to connect the data to particular individuals.

22. **Vulnerability to Zero-Day Attacks**
A zero-day vulnerability is a security issue in software or hardware that is not known to the vendor and has not been patched because of this lack of knowledge. These vulnerabilities are exploited by attackers before their existence is recognized and they can be corrected.

23. **The Reaction to an Incident**
The phrase "incident response" refers to a methodical strategy for addressing and managing the aftermath of a security breach. The purpose of this strategy is to limit the amount of damage that occurs as well as the amount of time and money needed for recovery.

24. **Continuity of Business Operations**
In the event of a data breach, natural disaster, or any other type of disruption, it is essential to have a strategy and make preparations to ensure that essential operations and services can continue as normal.

25. **Computing on the Quantum Level**
Emerging technology known as quantum computing is based on applying the ideas of quantum physics to the process of carrying out complicated computations. It is possible that it will render the currently used encryption methods useless, which will make it necessary to build cryptography that is resistant to quantum computing.

26. **Artificial Intelligence (AI)**
In artificial intelligence (AI), the process of automating and improving data security, including threat detection and response, is accomplished through the use of algorithms and machine learning.

27. **Blockchain technology**
Blockchain is a decentralized and immutable digital ledger technology that may be used to increase data security by maintaining the integrity and transparency of transactions. Blockchain was developed by cryptocurrency pioneer and computer programmer Satoshi Nakamoto.

28. **Etiquette**
When it comes to data security, ethical considerations are of the utmost importance. These considerations help to guide responsible data handling methods and ensure that the utilization of data is in accordance with moral principles and societal norms.

29. **Conformity Assessment Frameworks**
Compliance frameworks provide firms with the standards and best practices they need to comply with regulations governing data security and privacy. Control frameworks such as NIST, ISO 27001, and COBIT may be included in this category.

30. **Policies for the Protection of Data**

Data security policies are organizational documents that explain the methods, rules, and practices for safeguarding data and ensuring compliance with relevant laws and regulations. These policies are intended to ensure that an organization is protecting its data in accordance with applicable laws and regulations.

To provide a solid groundwork for data security in the fields of science and technology, the first step in building a solid foundation is to have a solid understanding of these fundamental concepts and terms. To successfully traverse the complexity of data security and preserve the confidentiality, integrity, and availability of critical data assets, individuals and organizations need to be familiar with the words and principles outlined in this article.

Chapter 1

Fundamentals of Data Security

Understanding the principles of data security is certainly necessary in order to realize the complexities of protecting sensitive information in this day and age, given the prevalence of digital technology. It has never been more important to prevent illegal access to, manipulation of, and destruction of data, as data is becoming an increasingly important factor in driving growth and innovation across a variety of fields, including business and healthcare. These fields include science and technology. This article will go into the essential concepts and principles that form the foundations of data security. Its purpose is to provide readers with a comprehensive grasp of the fundamental aspects that are required to develop solid data protection policies.

1. **Having an Awareness of Data Security**
   Data security, at its foundation, refers to a collection of procedures and safeguards that are put in place to secure digital information from being stolen, corrupted, or accessed without permission. This entails putting in place a variety of controls, both technical and procedural, as well as administrative ones, in

order to guarantee the availability, integrity, and confidentiality of the data. The term "data security" refers to the protection of a wide range of different kinds of information, such as private and sensitive data, confidential corporate records, personally identifiable information (PII), intellectual property, and proprietary research data. Data security is an essential component of the operations of every company in the current day, as it has an impact on decision-making, risk management, and the organization's capacity to remain viable over the long term.

2. **The CIA Triad, which stands for Confidentiality, Integrity, and Availability**

    The CIA triad is a fundamental concept in data security that defines the three fundamental ideas that underpin efficient data protection measures. It was developed by the Computer Intelligence Agency (CIA). Maintaining data confidentiality ensures that it can only be accessed by authorized individuals or systems, hence avoiding unauthorized disclosure or access to the information. The term "integrity" refers to the process of ensuring that data is kept accurate and consistent throughout its entire lifecycle, while also preventing it from being changed or corrupted without proper authorization. When data is available, it is guaranteed that authorized users will have access to and be able to use the data whenever it is required. This helps prevent disruptions that could impede essential activities or services.

3. **Dangers to the Availability of Data**

    In today's ever-changing digital ecosystem, there are a myriad of dangers that pose serious threats to the confidentiality of data. Cyberattacks, such as malware, phishing, ransomware, and denial-of-service attacks, try to undermine data integrity and confidentiality by exploiting weaknesses in computer systems and computer networks. Data breaches can also be caused by insider threats, which are those that originate from the careless or malicious activities of workers or other trusted individuals working for a company. Another prominent risk that organizations need to protect themselves from is something called social engineering, which is a strategy that makes use of human psychology in order to coerce individuals into disclosing sensitive information.

4. **The Management of Risk**

Strong risk management methods are included into effective data security policies so that potential dangers and holes in protection can be identified, evaluated, and closed. In order to effectively manage risks, organizations need to undertake exhaustive risk assessments, comprehend the impact of a variety of dangers, and put in place suitable controls and remedies to reduce the possibility that their information security will be compromised. In addition to this, it requires the establishment of contingency plans and reaction systems to efficiently address security incidents and limit the impact these occurrences have on operations.

5. **The Encryption of Data**

Encryption of data is a fundamental strategy that is utilized to secure sensitive information from
being accessed or intercepted by unauthorized parties. It includes converting data into an unreadable format known as ciphertext, which can only be deciphered by using an encryption key. This process is carried out with the assistance of encryption algorithms. Encryption is essential during all stages of data processing, including data transport, storage, and processing, as it adds an extra layer of protection against unauthorized access to confidential information.

6. **Regulation of Access**

In order to ensure that only authorized users are able to access particular data or resources within an organization, access control techniques play an extremely important part in the data security process. The establishment of authentication and authorization processes are required for access control. These processes authenticate the identity of users and determine the level of access they are granted based on the roles and permissions that have been set. The purpose of role-based access control (RBAC) is to limit access to data and systems by assigning privileges to users based on their roles or responsibilities within an organization. These privileges are granted in accordance with the principle of least privilege.

7. **The Processes of Authentication and Authorization**

   The process of confirming the identity of a person or system that is attempting to gain access to data or resources is referred to as authentication. It requires the use of multiple authentication factors, such as passwords, biometric identifiers, security tokens, or multi-factor authentication (MFA), in order to guarantee that only those who are permitted to do so are able to access the resource in question. On the other hand, authorization is the process of defining the amount of access privileges that will be granted to users who have been authenticated based on the roles, responsibilities, and security clearances that they have.

8. **Transmission of Data in a Secure Manner**

   It is essential to protect data while it is being transmitted in order to prevent unauthorized parties from eavesdropping, intercepting, or otherwise manipulating the data. During connection between systems, secure data transmission protocols such as secure sockets layer (SSL) and transport layer security (TLS) encrypt data packets. This ensures that sensitive information is kept confidential and is shielded from being intercepted or manipulated in any way.

9. **Safekeeping of sensitive information**

   It is vital to protect data while it is "at rest," also known as while it is being stored, in order to prevent unauthorized access to critical information. establishing encryption for the data that is being stored, establishing access controls to limit data access to authorized persons, and adopting physical security measures to safeguard data storage devices from theft, damage, or removal without authorization are all components of secure data storage procedures. In the case of a system failure or an incident involving data loss, having secure data backup and recovery mechanisms in place is an additional important step to take toward assuring the availability and integrity of data.

10. **Methods for the Backup and Restoration of Data**

    The processes of data backup and recovery are necessary components of data security. They provide businesses with the ability to protect the data's integrity and guarantee the continuation of business operations in the event that data is lost or the system fails. The likelihood of experiencing data loss as a result of a hardware failure, a natural disaster, or a malicious assault is reduced when regular backups of the data are performed and either kept in a safe offsite place or on backup systems that are hosted in the cloud. Robust data recovery plans detail the actions and processes that must be carried out in order to return data and systems to the state they were in prior to the occurrence of a disruptive event or security breach.

11. **Procedures for Responding to and Managing Incidents**

    Protocols for incident response and management are absolutely necessary in order to address data breaches and security incidents in a prompt and efficient manner. It is absolutely necessary to develop a structured incident response plan that specifies the roles and duties of incident response teams, explains communication routes, and gives clear recommendations for containing security problems, eliminating them, and recovering from their effects. It is important to perform regular testing and review of the incident response plan using simulated security exercises or drills. This helps to ensure that the plan is functional and ready for use in real-world settings.

12. **Checks for Compliance and Audits of the Security**

    Evaluating the efficacy of data security measures and identifying potential vulnerabilities or holes in security policies both require regular security audits and assessments to be carried out. Compliance with industry-specific legislation and standards, such as the General Data Protection Regulation (GDPR), the Health Insurance Portability and Accountability Act (HIPAA), and the Payment Card Industry Data Security Standard (PCI DSS), can be evaluated through the use of security audits, which are helpful to organizations in determining whether or not they are in compliance. It is crucial to maintain compliance with relevant data security legislation and standards in order to protect the privacy of sensitive information and avoid the legal penalties that could result from noncompliance.

13. **Instruction and Education for Staff Members**

    It is essential, in order to cultivate a workforce that is aware of the importance of security, to spread a culture of security awareness and to provide extensive training for personnel. Employee training programs should educate staff members on the hazards of social engineering, phishing attacks, and other typical security threats. Additionally, employee training programs should include guidance on best practices for data handling, password management, and incident reporting. Regular security awareness campaigns and training sessions assist employees develop a proactive attitude toward data security and promote a shared responsibility for the protection of sensitive information.

14. **Privacy of Personal Information and Ethical Considerations**

    It is essential to preserve both trust and openness in the operations of a business that data privacy be respected, and that ethical data handling norms be upheld. Protecting the privacy rights of individuals should be a top priority for organizations, and these organizations should make certain that any data they collect, handle, or keep is done so in accordance with any applicable privacy legislation. Respecting the confidentiality of sensitive information is one of the ethical concerns that go into data security. Another is gaining informed consent before collecting and processing data. And finally, offering transparency regarding data usage and sharing policies is also an ethical factor.

15. **New Technologies and the Safety of Personal Information**

In the field of data security, the steady march of technological progress creates both new opportunities and new obstacles. New technologies, such as blockchain, artificial intelligence (AI), and quantum computing, usher in a plethora of innovative strategies for the security of data and the identification of potential dangers. For example, quantum computing has the ability to break existing encryption methods, which calls for the creation of encryption strategies that are resistant to the effects of quantum computing. While artificial intelligence can be used to improve data security by automating threat detection and response, blockchain technology provides data integrity and transparency through its decentralized and unchangeable ledger. AI can also be used to improve data security.

1.1 Definition of Data Security

In the context of the present digital landscape, protecting one's data should be of the utmost importance to oneself, one's organization, and even the government. It is a term that refers to a collection of policies, procedures, and techniques that are aimed to prevent digital data from being accessed, disclosed, altered, or destroyed without the owner's permission. It is common practice to refer to the three aspects of data security as the "CIA triad," which is an abbreviation for "confidentiality, integrity, and availability." The objective of data security is to guarantee all three of these aspects of data. In this essay, we will delve into the numerous layers of data security, analyzing its definition, major components, and the indispensable function that data security plays in today's linked world.

The Confidentiality, Integrity, and Availability Triad of the Central Intelligence Agency

The CIA triad, which specifies three basic principles, is considered to be the most important component of data security.

The notion of confidentiality ensures that only authorized people, computer systems, or business processes are able to access stored information. The process of protecting data from unauthorized access and preventing the disclosure of sensitive information to third parties who are not authorized to receive it is referred to as data security. No matter if it's private information, trade secrets, or classified government material, taking measures to maintain data's confidentiality is essential for protecting its privacy and keeping it secure.

Data integrity refers to the degree to which data is accurate, consistent, and reliable over its entire lifecycle. Integrity is a component of data quality. It entails guarding data against being altered or corrupted in a manner that is not authorized. A trustworthy and unaltered version of the data that has not been altered in any way, preserving both its original quality and content is what is meant by "ensuring data integrity." This approach is absolutely necessary for preventing illegal adjustments, the likes of which could result in inaccurate information or the manipulation of data.

Accessibility: Accessibility ensures that data may be retrieved and utilized whenever it is required to do so. It entails protecting data from being disrupted, unavailable, or otherwise made inaccessible as a result of technical failures, cyberattacks, or other incidents. It is vital for maintaining business continuity, disaster recovery, and continuous operations to ensure that data is available at all times. This is a crucial component of data security.

Data Security Components and Their Purposes

Encryption of Data: Encryption of data is an essential tool for the protection of sensitive information. Using encryption methods, the data are transformed into a format that cannot be read. This format is called ciphertext. It is only possible to decrypt the data with the associated encryption key, which ensures that only those who are permitted to do so can access the original data.

Control of Access: The techniques that comprise access control restrict users' access to data and resources on the basis of the principle known as least privilege. Authentication is the process of verifying the identity of users or systems, whereas authorization is the process of determining the level of access granted to individuals or systems based on the roles and permissions that have been set.

Secure Data Transmission: Protocols for secure data transmission, such as SSL and TLS, make certain that data does not become compromised while being transferred from one system to another. Data packets are protected from illegal access and modification thanks to these protocols' ability to encrypt them.

Safe Data Storage Safe data storage safeguards data while it is at rest, guaranteeing that it maintains both its confidentiality and its integrity. This entails utilizing encryption for the data that is stored, putting in place access controls, and protecting storage devices through the implementation of physical security measures.

Data Backup and Recovery: Procedures for data backup and recovery are vital for ensuring that the integrity of the data is maintained and for keeping corporate operations running smoothly. Regular data backups and recovery strategies can help reduce the likelihood of experiencing a loss of data as a result of faulty hardware, natural disasters, or malicious cyberattacks.

Response to Incidents and Incident Management: Incident response plans give systematic techniques for resolving and reducing the effects of data breaches or security incidents. These plans describe in detail the roles, duties, and procedures that must be followed in order to contain, eliminate, and recover from any security incidents.

Security Audits and Compliance: Conducting regular security audits and assessments is a helpful tool for companies in determining the efficiency of their data security policies and locating potential vulnerabilities. Avoiding legal penalties requires strict adherence to applicable data privacy legislation and standards, such as the General Data Protection Regulation (GDPR) or the Health Insurance Portability and Accountability Act (HIPAA).

Training and Awareness for Employees Employees are educated about common security dangers, best practices, and their roles in protecting data through training programs and awareness campaigns. These efforts promote shared responsibility for data security and help to cultivate a workforce that is aware of the need of data protection.

Privacy of Data and Ethical Considerations Maintaining trust and transparency requires a commitment to both the protection of individuals' privacy and the observance of ethical values. Protecting the privacy rights of individuals must be a top priority for organizations, and these organizations must also guarantee that data is gathered, processed, and stored in accordance with all applicable rules.

The Obstacles Facing Data Security

The danger landscape is always changing because hackers are always coming up with new methods and tools to breach data security. This causes the threat landscape to constantly evolve. Keeping one step ahead of newly surfaced dangers is a continual challenge.

Threats from Within Insider threats, whether they are deliberate or unintentional, constitute a substantial threat to an organization. Because employees who are malicious or negligent can circumvent security measures, it is absolutely necessary to put monitoring and reaction processes in place that are effective.

Regulations Regarding Data Privacy Data privacy legislation, such as the GDPR and the CCPA, bring about extensive compliance obligations. In order to avoid legal repercussions and secure customer data, businesses need to successfully traverse a maze of complicated regulations.

Emerging technologies, such as quantum computing, artificial intelligence, and blockchain, present both new potential and new concerns for the protection of sensitive data. For example, quantum computing may one day be able to decrypt data that was encrypted using more conventional methods.

The human element continues to be one of the most common points of failure in information security. Phishing scams and other forms of social engineering also abuse the psychology of their targets, which is why user education and awareness are so important.

The Importance of Securing Personal Information in Today's World

The relevance of maintaining data security in a society that is increasingly driven by data cannot be emphasized. It is essential to the protection of sensitive information, the maintenance of privacy and confidentiality, the upkeep of trust, and the guaranteeing of the continuity of business activities. It doesn't matter if you're in the commercial world, the medical field, the scientific community, or even the government; having strong data security standards is crucial to preserving the honesty and safety of digital data. The necessity of data security is a core principle in the digital age, and it will continue to be so as long as technology continues to improve and the digital world continues to become increasingly complicated. This principle shapes how individuals and businesses interact with and safeguard their most important asset: information.

1.2 Types of Data: Sensitive, Confidential, and Personal

Data is the driving force behind technological advancements, the basis for informed decisions, and the enabler of a vast number of facets of our day-to-day lives. However, not all data is created equal; therefore, it is essential to have a solid understanding of the many different types of data and the classifications that apply to each of them in order to adequately protect it. In this piece, we will discuss the three basic categories of data, namely personal data, sensitive data, and confidential data. We will throw light on the differences between the three forms of data as well as highlight the significance of safeguarding each category.

1. **Private Information**
1. **Intellectual Property:** This refers to information that is not publicly available, such as patents, trade secrets, and material that is protected by copyright laws. It is essential for companies and research organizations to protect their intellectual property in

order to preserve their competitive advantage and prevent the loss of their ideas.
2. **Health Records:** Health data is sensitive and subject to strong privacy requirements, such as the Health Insurance Portability and Accountability Act (HIPAA) in the United States. Health data can include medical history, treatment records, and patient identifiers.
3. **Financial Data:** The possibility of identity theft and financial crime makes financial information, such as banking records, credit card numbers, and financial transactions, particularly sensitive.
4. **Findings from Research:** In the fields of science, technology, and academia, research findings frequently entail seminal discoveries, ground-breaking innovations, or patented creations. It is absolutely necessary to keep these findings a secret in order to safeguard intellectual property rights and preserve the company's advantage over its competitors.
5. **Classified Information:** Both governments and security agencies deal with classified information, which is broken down into different levels of sensitivity and includes top-secret, secret, and confidential categories. Disclosure of classified information without proper authorization can have severe repercussions for the country's safety and security.
6. **Trade Secrets:** When it comes to gaining a competitive advantage, businesses frequently rely on trade secrets, which might include proprietary procedures, methods, or formulas. The importance of protecting a company's trade secrets cannot be overstated given their place in the success equation.

Encryption, access controls, and secure data handling procedures are all necessary components of an extensive security infrastructure for the purpose of protecting sensitive data. The failure to properly protect sensitive data can lead to monetary losses, the loss of a competitive advantage, legal repercussions, and even breaches in national security.

2. Private and Pristine Information

The scope of sensitive data is often narrower than that of confidential data, yet the two types of data share many commonalities. It refers to information that a company or other entity considers to be confidential because of the proprietary nature of the information or the potential value that it could have for competitors. The following are examples of several types of confidential data:

1. Business Plans and Strategies Strategic business plans, market strategies, and product roadmaps are all examples of sensitive material that companies carefully secure in order to preserve their advantage over the competition.
2. Financial Reports Detailed financial reports, projections, and budgets may contain confidential information that is essential for decision-making but must be secured from unauthorized access. This information must be safeguarded to ensure that it is not viewed by unauthorized parties.
3. **Information Regarding Employees:** Data regarding employees, such as wage information, performance evaluations, and disciplinary records, are frequently regarded as sensitive and need to be managed carefully in order to preserve employee privacy.
4. **Lists of Customers and Suppliers:** Lists of customers and suppliers, as well as business partners, are frequently deemed to be sensitive information, particularly in markets that are highly competitive.
5. **Internal Communication:** Confidential data includes communications such as emails, notes, and documents that disclose sensitive internal concerns. Examples of this type of communication include emails.

Even though confidential data might not always carry the same legal and regulatory ramifications as sensitive data, it is nonetheless extremely important to an organization's ability to succeed and remain competitive in the marketplace. Breach of confidentiality of data can result in negative ramifications for a business, including damage to its reputation, a loss of confidence, and adverse financial effects.

3. Private Information

1. **Name and Address:** Information that is regarded to be personal data, such as names, addresses, and phone numbers, is typically gathered by organizations and service providers.
2. **Social Security Numbers:** In the United States, social security numbers are extremely sensitive personal information that also function as unique identifiers.
3. **Medical Records:** Information pertaining to one's health, such as diagnoses, treatment histories, and the outcomes of medical tests, is considered personal data and is protected by stringent privacy restrictions.
4. **Financial Data:** Information pertaining to an individual's finances that is considered personal, such as bank account numbers, credit card details, and records of income, is considered to be personal data.
5. **Online Profiles:** Information obtained from a person's social media profiles, email accounts, and other online sources is considered personal data and can provide insight into the person's activities and interests.
6. Data Relating to Biometric Identifiers Individuals' fingerprints, retinal scans, and face recognition data are examples of biometric identifiers that are extremely personal and exclusive to them.

A key ethical and legal concept is to treat the privacy of individuals' personal data with respect. The General Data Protection Regulation (GDPR) in the European Union and the California Consumer Privacy Act (CCPA) in California are two examples of laws and regulations that have been enacted with the intention of protecting the rights of persons with regard to their personal data. If an organization is found to be in violation of these standards, they may be subject to monetary fines as well as other legal consequences.

1.3 The Threat Landscape: Cybersecurity Risks

In the linked world of today, the threat landscape is always changing, presenting a variety of sophisticated cybersecurity dangers that can put data security at risk, disrupt operations, and undermine the integrity of digital systems. These risks can be mitigated, but they are always present. The frequency, variety, and sophistication of cyberattacks against individuals, businesses, and governments all around the world have all increased in recent years. When it comes to building strong cybersecurity policies and putting effective measures in place to reduce potential risks, having a thorough understanding of the complexities of the threat landscape is absolutely necessary. This article will discuss the different hazards and threats to cybersecurity that are prevalent in the digital landscape, with a particular emphasis on the significance of preventative defense measures and maintaining vigilant at all times.

1. **Attacks Conducted by Malware**
   Malware, often known as malicious software, is one of the most prevalent and widespread threats to information technology systems. It encompasses a wide variety of malicious programs, such as viruses, worms, Trojans, ransomware, and spyware, which are meant to enter networks, steal sensitive data, or disrupt operations. Some examples of these programs are listed above. Because malware assaults frequently take use of weaknesses in software and operating systems, maintaining up-to-date software and installing security patches on a consistent basis are vital for protecting against these dangers.

2. **Social Engineering, also known as Phishing**
   Phishing and social engineering are two methods that use deception and psychological manipulation to deceive others into divulging confidential information or carrying out harmful acts. Phishing attacks often take the form of bogus emails, websites, or

messages that imitate legitimate institutions with the intention of stealing confidential data such as login credentials, financial information, or personal details. Social engineering techniques take advantage of people's trust and susceptibility, turning consumers into unknowing participants in data breaches or security vulnerabilities.

3. **Cryptolocker**

   In recent years, ransomware attacks have become increasingly common. These assaults target corporations as well as individuals, encrypting their data and demanding a ransom in exchange for decrypting it. These attacks have the potential to halt operations entirely, interfere with essential services, and result in significant financial losses. Because ransomware most commonly spreads through phishing emails, malicious links, or websites that have been hijacked, it is imperative that comprehensive backup and recovery techniques be implemented to reduce the negative effects of cyberattacks.

4. **Dangers Coming From Within**

   The acts or negligence of workers, contractors, or other trusted individuals working for or otherwise associated with an organization might provide a major danger to that business in the form of an insider threat. Unauthorized access to data, theft of data, or the intentional destruction of systems and networks can all fall under this category of threats. It is absolutely necessary, in order to reduce the risk of insider attacks, to put in place tight access controls, to monitor the activities of users, and to cultivate a culture of security awareness.

5. **Attacks Classified as Distributed Denial-of-Service (DDoS)**

   DDoS assaults are conducted with the intention of preventing users from accessing their preferred online services by flooding servers, networks, or websites with an excessive amount of malicious traffic. Because of these attacks, users may be prevented from accessing vital information or services, the affected services may become more sluggish, and service disruptions may occur. Implementation of effective network security measures, such as firewalls, intrusion detection systems, and content delivery networks, can help limit the effects of distributed denial of service (DDoS) assaults.

6. **The Zero-Day Vulnerability**

Exploits known as zero-days are designed to take advantage of flaws in software or hardware that have not been discovered or patched by the manufacturers. As a result of the frequency with which cybercriminals take advantage of these vulnerabilities to conduct sophisticated assaults before security patches or updates are available, organizations have a huge problem when dealing with zero-day exploits. To reduce the risks that are connected with zero-day exploits, it is necessary to do proactive monitoring, gather threat intelligence, and manage patches in a timely manner.

7. **Advanced Persistent Threats (also known as APTs)**

The goal of advanced persistent threats (APTs), which are a type of cyberattack that is both extremely sophisticated and targeted, is to infiltrate systems, remain undiscovered, and extract critical information over an extended period of time.

These kinds of assaults frequently make use of persistent and covert methods, such as sophisticated malware, social engineering, and lateral movement within networks. In order to detect advanced persistent threats and develop countermeasures against them, you will need capabilities for advanced threat detection, network segmentation, and continuous monitoring of network activities and behaviors.

8. **Potential Weaknesses in the Supply Chain**

Vulnerabilities in supply chains have arisen as a serious problem in recent years, particularly given the increasing dependence of businesses on interconnected networks of suppliers and service providers. It is possible for cybercriminals to get unauthorized access to valuable data or compromise vital infrastructure by exploiting weaknesses in the systems used by supply chain partners. It is absolutely necessary to implement supply chain risk management techniques, conduct frequent security assessments, and enforce stringent contractual security standards in order to reduce the likelihood of these hazards occurring.

9. **Vulnerabilities Associated with the Internet of Things (IoT)**
The growth of Internet of Things devices has led to the emergence of new cybersecurity threats. This is due to the fact that these interconnected devices frequently lack effective security mechanisms, which leaves them open to being exploited. It is possible for unauthorized access, data breaches, or the compromising of vital systems to result from vulnerabilities in Internet of Things (IoT) devices. For the sake of safeguarding Internet of Things devices and reducing the related risks, it is essential to put in place robust authentication procedures, industry-standard encryption practices, and routine firmware updates.
10. **Fraudulent credential use and theft of one's identity**

The fraudulent acquisition and use of an individual's personal information or login credentials is known as identity theft and credential stuffing. Both of these crimes fall under the umbrella of cybercrime. To obtain unauthorized access to accounts, systems, or sensitive information, cybercriminals use credentials that have been stolen from other users. When it comes to preventing identity theft and managing the dangers associated with credential stuffing attacks, it is essential to implement multi-factor authentication, robust password restrictions, and identity and access management solutions.

1.4 Data Security Principles and Best Practices

Within the context of the modern digital landscape, data is frequently referred to as the "new gold." For a wide variety of tasks, including but not limited to decision-making and interpersonal communication, individuals and businesses alike rely heavily on data. However, due to the great value that data possesses, it also draws the attention of hackers who intend to misuse it or steal it for nefarious reasons. The protection of sensitive data and the upkeep of trust have elevated the importance of data security to a position of preeminence.

In this piece, we will discuss some of the fundamentals of data security, as well as some of the best practices that individuals and businesses may implement in order to protect their data.

Acquiring Knowledge on Data Security

1. **The Classification of Data**

    There is not a uniform standard for all data. It is necessary to organize data in accordance with its level of sensitivity and significance. The proper allocation of resources and the implementation of appropriate security measures to protect an organization's most valuable assets are both made possible thanks to the classification of data. Data can be classified in a variety of ways, including as public, for internal use, confidential, or restricted.

2. **Restrictions on Access**

    Who can access the data and under what circumstances is decided by the access control systems. When the principle of least privilege is put into practice, it ensures that persons or systems only have access to the data that they require in order to carry out their duties. This reduces the likelihood of unauthorized access as well as data breaches occurring.

3. **Codes and ciphers**

    The use of encryption is essential when it comes to protecting sensitive data. It scrambles the data so that it can be read only with the correct decryption key, which can only be obtained after the data has been transformed. This prevents eavesdropping and theft of data both when the data is "at rest" (stored on devices or servers) and while it is "in transit" (moving across networks).

4. **Authentication & Authorization**

    Authentication is the process of confirming the identity of people or systems that are attempting to access data, and authorization is the process of deciding what activities those users or systems are permitted to take after they have been authenticated. Data security can be considerably improved by implementing multi-factor authentication (also known as MFA) and role-based access control (also known as RBAC).

5. **Perform Frequent Backups**
Data loss can be caused by a variety of factors, such as malfunctioning hardware, malicious cyberattacks, or simple human error. Regularly copying data to safe and distinct locations guarantees that it can be restored in the event that data is stolen or lost, hence reducing the amount of time the system is unavailable and the amount of possible damage that could occur.

6. **Management of Patches and Updates for Computer Security**
Cybercriminals often focus their attention on weak spots in computer programs, known as software vulnerabilities. It is absolutely necessary to stay up to date on all of the latest security updates and patches in order to guard against known vulnerabilities. A thorough patch management strategy guarantees that all of the software and operating systems are at their most recent versions.

7. **Training in the Awareness of Security Risks**
The human element is frequently the weakest link in the chain of data protection. It is important to educate both employees and users about best practices, phishing schemes, and any other potential security issues that may exist. Individuals who are well-informed can contribute to the prevention of data breaches through the actions they take.

8. **A plan for dealing with incidents**
In spite of an organization's best efforts to maintain data privacy and safety, data breaches are always a possibility. It is absolutely necessary to have a well-defined incident response plan already in place. This plan details how to quickly and efficiently identify

and contain data security issues, as well as recover from the effects of such occurrences.

9. **Security of Personal Information**

In order for an organization to comply with the principles of data privacy, such as those specified in rules such as the General Data Protection Regulation (GDPR) and the California Consumer Privacy Act (CCPA), the organization must first seek consent before collecting and processing any data. Maintaining the trust of one's consumers and protecting oneself from potential legal ramifications both require strict adherence to the standards in question.

Best Practices for the Protection of Data

1. **Set up a protective barrier (firewall)**
   The internet and other untrusted external networks are separated from a trusted internal network by firewalls, which operate as barriers between the two. They filter all network traffic, both incoming and outgoing, preventing potentially harmful traffic and protecting internal systems from threats originating from the outside.
2. **Covering Up of Data**
   Data masking, which is also known as data obfuscation, is the process of concealing sensitive data by substituting it in non-production situations with fictional values that are nevertheless plausible. Because of this, you may be assured that the data utilized for testing and development will not reveal any confidential information.
3. **Management of Mobile Devices (also known as MDM)**
   Because there are so many mobile devices now, businesses have no choice but to install MDM solutions in order to control and protect their mobile endpoints. MDM offers managers the ability to remotely delete data from devices, enforce security regulations, and protect data on mobile devices like smartphones and tablets.

SECURE DATA HANDLING IN SCIENCE AND TECHNOLOGY

4. **Safely Distributing Files**
Users are able to safely exchange data both inside and outside of the company when using technologies that provide secure file sharing. The protection of users' data is typically handled by such platforms through the use of functions like encryption, access limits, and audits.

5. **The Division of the Network**
When a network is segmented, it is divided into several smaller networks that are kept completely separate from one another. This prevents attackers from moving laterally across the network even if they get access to one section of the network. Because of this, a breach might not be able to spread throughout the entire network.

6. **Ongoing pen testing and security audits at regular intervals**
Audits and tests of penetration carried out on a regular basis are useful tools for determining
whether or not an organization's data security procedures have any flaws or vulnerabilities. These assessments ought to be carried out by specialists, and then remediation measures ought to be undertaken.

7. **Management of Risks Involved with Vendors**
Numerous businesses are dependent on the products and services provided by third-party vendors and providers. It is essential to evaluate the security procedures of these providers and make certain that they are up to the requirements you have set for the protection of your data. The inclusion of security clauses in contracts and service level agreements (SLAs) is highly recommended.

8. **Data Continuity and Regulatory Compliance**
The legislation and criteria concerning data residency might vary greatly from one country to the next. When it comes to keeping and processing data, companies have a responsibility to verify that they are in compliance with these requirements. Cloud service

providers in particular may make available data centers located in a variety of geographic areas to assist with regulatory compliance.

9. **Secure Development Lifecycle (SDL), also abbreviated as SDL**
It is absolutely necessary to incorporate security into the software development lifecycle in order to reduce the likelihood of vulnerabilities appearing in applications. Implementing secure coding techniques and carrying out code reviews are two methods that can assist in locating and fixing potential security flaws at an earlier stage of the development process.

10. **The Destruction of Data**

When data is no longer required, it should be deleted in a safe manner before being deleted. Shredding physical media and using secure data wiping on digital storage devices are two examples of ways that can be used to destroy data.

The process of securing data is a continual endeavor that calls for consistent attention and the ability to adjust to ever-evolving threats and technology. Individuals and organizations can dramatically lower the risk of data breaches, preserve sensitive information, and maintain the trust of their stakeholders if they adhere to the fundamental principles and best practices that are discussed in this article. Investing in data security at a time when information is a valuable commodity is not simply a good idea; it's a requirement for doing business in the modern digital world.

Chapter 2

Data Privacy Laws and Regulations

In this day and age, protecting one's personal data has evolved into one of the most pressing concerns. In response to the ever-increasing volume of personal and sensitive data that is generated and processed, governments and regulatory organizations all over the world have enacted a variety of rules and regulations in order to protect the rights of individuals and the data that pertains to them. This article examines the historical evolution, main components, and global influence of data privacy laws and regulations. It also includes a complete summary of data privacy laws and regulations.

Before we begin:

The idea of data privacy centers on the protection of individuals' personally identifiable information by requiring data controllers and processors to gather, store, and use data in an honest and open manner. Privacy laws are crafted with the intention of striking a balance between the promotion of data-driven innovation and the protection of individuals' rights to exercise control over the personal information that pertains to them. The necessity to address new problems to data privacy brought about by advancements in technology and the global nature of data flows is the impetus for the passing of these laws.

The Origins and Early Development of Privacy Regulations for Data

1. **1970: Passage of the Fair Credit Reporting Act (FCRA).**
   One of the earliest and most influential regulations in the United States pertaining to data privacy was the Fair Credit Reporting Act (FCRA). It gave individuals the right to see their credit reports and the ability to dispute any inaccuracies that they found within them, with the goal of ensuring that credit reporting is accurate and fair. It established the groundwork for subsequent privacy laws pertaining to data.

2. **1995: The Year of Adoption of the European Data Protection Directive**
   A structure for the protection of personal information across all member states of the European Union (EU) was put in place by the European Data Protection Directive. It demanded that nations pass legislation guaranteeing the confidentiality of individuals' personal data.
   In following years, this regulation was utilized as the foundation for the creation of the General Data Protection Regulation (GDPR), which will be further described below.

3. **HIPAA is an acronym for the Health Insurance Portability and Accountability Act of 1996.**
   In the United States, HIPAA is responsible for the introduction of data privacy standards that are specifically geared to the healthcare business. It established the right of individuals to access and control the information that pertains to their own health as well as created rules for the security of sensitive health information.

4. **Framework for Safe Harbor - Year 2000**
   The United States and the European Union came to an agreement known as the Safe Harbor Framework in order to streamline the

process of moving personal information from one zone to the other. It made it possible for organizations in the United States to self-certify their conformity with European data protection regulations. On the other hand, this framework was ultimately superseded by the EU-US framework. Privacy Shield, which will be covered in a later section and was ultimately ruled unconstitutional by the European Court of Justice in 2015.

5. **2018 marks the implementation date for the General Data Protection Regulation (GDPR).**

The General Data Protection Regulation (GDPR), which was established in the European Union, is among the most extensive data privacy legislation in the world. It does this by bolstering the rights of persons, by imposing stringent requirements on data controllers and processors, and by including significant consequences for noncompliance. The General Data Protection Regulation (GDPR) has had an effect on data protection regulations all over the world and has acted as a model for many.

Principal Elements Included in Data Privacy Laws

1. **The Rights of Data Subjects**
   Regulations governing the privacy of data give individuals specific rights over their own personal information. The right to access, rectify, erase, and port one's data is frequently included in this category of rights. Subjects of data may also have the right to object to the processing of their data and the right to receive information regarding the use of their data.
2. **Officers of Data Protection (also known as DPOs)**
   The appointment of a Data Protection Officer within an organization is a requirement imposed by a number of data privacy regulations.
   This officer is responsible for ensuring that the firm complies

with the rule. DPOs are frequently the authorities in charge of data protection and serve as their primary point of contact.

3. **Acceptance and assent**

    Consent is an essential component of the legislation that govern data privacy. In order for an individual's data to be processed, they must first grant their consent, which must be specific, informed, and voluntarily supplied. They should be able to change their minds at any time and withdraw their consent.

4. **Notification in the Event of a Data Breach**

    In the event of a data breach, it is frequently required by regulations that enterprises notify both the data protection authorities and the individuals whose data was compromised. Different jurisdictions have different mandated notification formats and different deadlines for reporting security breaches.

5. **Reduced amount of data**

    In order to comply with the principles of data minimization, companies are required to acquire and store just the minimum amount of data required to accomplish their goals. It is important to get rid of any unnecessary data in order to lower the risk that comes with keeping an excessive amount of information.

6. **Accountability and Administrative Oversight**

    Laws governing data privacy must be complied with, and data controllers and processors must provide evidence of their compliance. This includes carrying out adequate risk assessments, putting suitable security measures into place, and keeping detailed records of all data processing activities.

7. **Transfers of Information on a Global Scale**

    There are many legislation that include safeguards for international data transfers, which ensure that data is appropriately protected even when it is sent to countries that do not have adequate data protection laws. These kinds of transfers can be made easier through the use of mechanisms like Standard Contractual Clauses (SCCs) and Binding Corporate Rules (BCRs).

8. Sanctions for Disobedience or Failure to Comply

The failure to comply with the regulations governing data privacy typically results in financial fines and other consequences. These penalties, which can be quite severe, are intended to serve as a deterrent to businesses that do not sufficiently protect customers' personal information.

Important Privacy Protection Laws and Regulations All Around the World

1. **Regulation on the General Protection of Data (GDPR) of the European Union**
   The General Data Protection policy (GDPR) is an all-encompassing policy that oversees data protection inside the European Union (EU). It bestows significant rights upon data subjects, imposes stringent requirements upon data controllers and processors, and has the power to penalize noncompliance with fines of up to 4% of annual global turnover in the event of repeated violations. The General Data Protection Regulation (GDPR) has had an impact on the data protection regulations of a great number of other nations and areas.
2. **The California Consumer Privacy Act (CCPA) is a law that was passed in the United States.**
   The California Consumer Privacy Act (CCPA) is a groundbreaking piece of legislation in the United States. It gives people who live in California certain rights regarding their personal data, including as the right to view that data, the right to delete that data, and the ability to opt out of having their information sold. In addition to this, it mandates that companies establish transparent privacy policies and offer individuals with the means to exercise their legal rights.
3. **Act Respecting the Protection of Individuals with Respect to the Handling of Personal Information and Electronic**

Documents (PIPEDA) - Canada

PIPEDA is the Personal Information Protection and Electronic Documents Act of Canada. It regulates how organizations in the private sector can collect, use, and disclose individuals' personal information. It covers guidelines for getting people's consent, protecting their data, and notifying when there has been a breach of security.

4. **Act on the Protection of Personal Data (Personal Data Protection Act) of Singapore**

   The Personal Data Protection Act (PDPA) of Singapore lays forth guidelines for the acquisition, utilization, and disclosure of individuals' personal information by businesses. It contains procedures for getting consent, allowing for the portability of data, and appointing a Data Protection Officer.

5. **The Health Insurance Portability and Accountability Act (often known as HIPAA) is a law that was passed in the United States**

   The HIPAA law prioritizes the confidentiality and safety of patient information within the healthcare sector. It compels the notice of any data breach and establishes hefty fines for anyone who violate the law, as well as setting criteria for the protection of sensitive health information.

6. **Privacy Act, as it is known in Australia**

   The Privacy Act of Australia establishes guidelines for how organizations in the public sector and certain businesses in the private sector are to handle individuals' private information. It includes rules for notifying individuals in the event of a data breach as well as guidelines for the collection, use, and disclosure of personal information.

7. **Data Protection Bill being considered in India**

   When it becomes law, the Data Protection Bill in India will put limits on how individuals' personal data can be handled in the country. Consent, data subject rights, and the localization of data are some of the concepts that are incorporated into this measure.

8. **EU-U.S. (No Long in Use) Privacy Shield**
   The EU-U.S. Privacy Shield was developed with the intention of easing the process of transferring personal data from the EU to the US. The European Court of Justice ruled in 2020 that it was invalid because of concerns regarding the surveillance techniques of the United States government.

9. **The General Law on the Protection of Personal Data of Brazil (LGPD) - Brazil**
   The General Data Protection policy (GDPR) is an example of a comprehensive data privacy policy that can be compared to Brazil's LGPD. It provides data subjects with rights, mandates notification procedures for any data breach, and outlines penalties for those who do not comply with the regulations.

10. **Known in China as the Personal Information Protection Law (PIPL),**

The Personal Information Protection Law (PIPL) of China is an all-encompassing data privacy law that regulates the processing of personal data within the country. It contains provisions for gaining consent, protecting data subjects' rights, and transferring data internationally.

The Impact of Data Privacy Regulations on a Global Scale

1. **Increased responsibility and accountability**
   Regulations concerning the privacy of data have made it necessary for enterprises to have a more accountable attitude toward the handling of their data. For the purpose of demonstrating compliance, they are required to establish transparent rules and procedures, put in place rigorous security measures, and keep records of all data processing.

2. **Increased Protection for Individuals Who Provide Data**
   Because of the legislation governing data privacy, individuals have

more control over the information that pertains to them personally. They have the ability to exercise their rights, which include accessing their data, seeking the deletion of their data, and objecting to the processing of their data.

3. **Transfers of Data Around the World**

   In particular, the General Data Protection Regulation (GDPR) has become the standard for data transfers across international borders. Standard Contractual Clauses (SCCs) and Binding Corporate Rules (BCRs) are two examples of the kinds of safeguards that must be implemented by businesses all over the globe in order to guarantee the sufficient protection of data that is transferred to locations outside of the European Economic Area (EEA).

4. **Notification in the Event of a Data Breach**

   In many data protection rules, the duty to notify affected parties of a data breach has become standard. In order to contribute to increased transparency and knowledge of data security incidents, organizations are required to report breaches as soon as they become aware of them.

5. **Sanctions for Disobedience or Failure to Comply**

   In the event that data privacy regulations are violated, there is the possibility of incurring significant monetary fines. Because of this, corporations now have a powerful incentive to place a priority on the protection and security of their data.

6. **The localization of data**

   Some nations, under the influence of data privacy legislation, have enacted data localization requirements, which mandate that particular kinds of data must be stored and processed inside the borders of the nation. These policies have prompted the adoption of these requirements. This might provide difficulties for businesses operating on a global scale.

7. **Privacy Policies That Are Constantly Changing**

   The concept of "privacy by design" has emerged as an essential tenet in the creation of new products and services. There has been a recent uptick in the number of companies that are beginning to build in data protection measures from the very beginning of their development processes.

8. **Challenges in Legal and Regulatory Compliance**

Multinational corporations are required to traverse complicated legal landscapes and comply with a wide variety of data privacy standards, many of which have specific and detailed criteria. This can be a particularly difficult challenge for businesses that operate in a number of different nations.

Disputes and Obstacles to Overcome

1. **Both complex and variable in nature**
   The increase in the number of countries with their own data privacy legislation has led to increased complexity and unpredictability. It is necessary for organizations to be able to navigate different rule sets and adapt to ever-changing requirements.
2. **The Costs of Compliance**
   Particularly pricey for small and medium-sized businesses is the process of ensuring that they are in compliance with data privacy legislation. To ensure compliance, you will need to make expenditures in the training of your people, in technology, in legal help, and in continuous monitoring.
3. **Finding a Happy Medium Between Innovation and Regulation**
   It is an ongoing challenge to find a happy medium between facilitating data-driven innovation and safeguarding the rights of individuals whose personal information is being collected. The development of new technologies could be stifled by overly stringent rules, while lax restrictions could put individuals' privacy at risk.
4. **The localization of data**
   The limitations of data localization might cause disruptions in

the flow of information and restrict the expansion potential of multinational businesses. It is common for people to view these actions as protectionist, particularly when they are motivated by political or commercial motives.

5. **Implementation of**

The manner in which data privacy legislation are enforced can be inconsistent and vary greatly from country to region. It's possible that some nations don't have the means or the political will to go after organizations that don't comply with the law.

Developing Tendencies in the Regulations Governing Data Privacy

1. **Increased Strictness in Enforcement**
   It is expected that regulatory authorities will take a tougher stance when it comes to implementing legislation regarding data privacy. The imposition of significant fines and aggressive legal action against corporations that do not comply will serve as examples for other businesses.

2. **Increasing People's Rights**
   The rights of data subjects may be increased further as a result of new rules that provide further
   controls over their data. These controls may include the right to have their data forgotten and the right to have their data portable.

3. **Convergence on a Global Scale**
   There will always be disparities between countries' data privacy legislation, but there is a growing movement toward global uniformity. In an effort to bring domestic legal systems into conformity with international standards, nations are rapidly adopting aspects of the General Data Protection Regulation (GDPR).

4. **New and Upcoming Technologies**
   Emerging technologies like artificial intelligence (AI), the internet of things (IoT), and biometric data processing will necessitate

that regulations be updated to account for them. The most important things to think about are going to be ethical and legal issues.

5. **The Responsibility of Businesses**
It is required of organizations to take on a greater level of responsibility for the protection of data and privacy. The concept of "privacy by design" and conducting data protection impact assessments will soon become industry standards for the development of new products and services.

6. **Awareness among the public**
The public's awareness of, and concern for, the privacy of their data will continue to expand. Because of this, there may be an increased desire for firms that handle personal data to demonstrate greater transparency and responsibility.

7. **Regulation of Large Tech Companies**

The actions of large technological corporations are coming under more scrutiny, which may lead to the development of legislation that are unique to their industry. Concerns over data monopolies, online advertising, and the surveillance of consumers are currently being investigated by regulatory bodies.

Individuals now have a greater degree of control over the information that pertains to them as a result of changes brought about by the enactment of rules and regulations pertaining to data privacy. They have become an indispensable part of the digital landscape, exerting an influence on corporate practices all over the world, the progression of technology, and individual rights.

In order for businesses to remain compliant with the ever-changing data privacy requirements, they need to maintain a high level of vigilance. It is not only a legal necessity, but also a way to protect personal data from breaches and misuse, as well as to develop trust with customers, to be proactive in learning and following to these requirements, and to comprehend what they are. The right to one's private information is one of the most fundamental of all human rights, and its significance is only going to increase in the years to come.

2.1 Global Data Privacy Frameworks (e.g., GDPR, CCPA, HIPAA)

Data privacy frameworks have become vital in this era, which is defined by significant data sharing and digital interactions. This is because it has become essential to secure the personal information of individuals and ensure responsible data processing. There have been multiple global data privacy legislation developed, each with its own set of distinctive characteristics and applications. The General Data Protection Regulation (GDPR), the California Consumer Privacy Act (CCPA), and the Health Insurance Portability and Accountability Act (HIPAA) are just a few of the global data privacy frameworks that will be discussed in depth within this all-encompassing research.

Before we begin:

Data privacy frameworks are legal standards and regulations that define how businesses are required to gather, process, and keep personal information as well as provide protection for it. These frameworks have the goal of striking a balance between the necessity for data-driven innovation and the rights of individuals to continue to exercise control over their personal data. In this lesson, we are going to investigate three important data privacy frameworks and analyze their essential components, impacts, and implications for enterprises all over the world.

The General Regulation on the Protection of Data (GDPR)

In a Nutshell:

The General Data Protection Regulation (GDPR) is one of the privacy regulations that has the biggest worldwide impact and is one of the most comprehensive in the world. Since it became law on May 25, 2018, it has been enforced in both the European Union (EU) and the European Economic Area (EEA), and it has fundamentally altered the way that personal data is managed while putting a significant emphasis on the rights and protections of individuals.

Principal Constituents:

1. **Rights of the Data Subject:**
   The General Data Protection Regulation (GDPR) gives individuals numerous rights, some of which are the right to access their data, the right to correct inaccurate information, the right to be forgotten, and the right to have their data moved from one location to another. Individuals now have more control over their personal data thanks to these rights.
2. **Data Protection Officers (often abbreviated as DPOs):**
   It is mandatory for companies to hire a Data Protection Officer if they handle considerable volumes of personal data or participate in high-risk activities. DPOs are the ones who are accountable for ensuring that the regulation is followed.
3. **Acceptance:**
   Before processing an individual's data, companies are required by the GDPR to seek their "clear and informed consent" from the subject. The provision of consent ought to be voluntary, particular, and open to revocation at any time.
4. **Notification in the Event of a Data Breach:**
   Notifications of data breaches are required to be made within 72 hours of becoming aware of a breach under the GDPR. This obligation increases transparency and makes certain that persons who are affected are informed in a timely manner.
5. **Reducing the Amount of Data:**
   Under the idea of data minimization, businesses are obligated to acquire and store only the minimum amount of information required to achieve a certain goal. It discourages the acquisition of an excessive amount of data.
6. **Obligation of Accountability and Corporate Governance:**
   The General Data Protection Regulation (GDPR) requires organizations to demonstrate their compliance with the regulation by implementing adequate security measures, conducting risk assessments, and preserving records. Additionally, they are required

to carry out data protection impact assessments for processing operations that pose a high risk.
7. **Transfers of Information Across International Borders:**
The General Data Protection Regulation (GDPR) contains provisions for transferring personal data outside of the European Economic Area (EEA). Standard Contractual Clauses (SCCs) and Binding Corporate Rules (BCRs) are both examples of methods that can be utilized by businesses in order to guarantee the confidentiality of data that is being transferred across international borders.
8. **Consequences for Violations of the Regulations:**

If an organization is found to be in violation of the General Data Protection Regulation (GDPR), they may be subject to monetary fines that can reach up to 4% of their global annual turnover or €20 million, whichever amount is greater.

Influence :

The General Data Protection Regulation has an impact outside of Europe. It has inspired

several nations to revise current privacy legislation and establish new ones, which has led to a global shift toward stricter data protection norms that have been driven by it. When interacting with people whose data is subject to the GDPR in Europe, businesses all around the world have been forced to modify their standard procedures.

Possible Consequences:

Regardless of where in the world their actual location may be, businesses that conduct trade with EU/EEA residents are obligated to comply with GDPR rules. This frequently calls for considerable modifications to the procedures that are used for managing data, such as mechanisms for consent that are more open and transparent, greater security precautions, and rigorous data subject rights processes.

Act to Protect the Privacy of California Residents (CCPA)
In a Nutshell:

The California Consumer Privacy Act, sometimes known as the CCPA, is a data privacy framework that was established in California, United States of America, and will go into effect on January 1, 2020. It gives people living in California more control over their personal information and how companies utilize it when they do business with them.

Principal Constituents:

1. **Rights of the Data Subject:**
   The CCPA grants residents of California many data subject rights, including the right to see their own personal data, the right to request that their data be deleted, and the right to opt-out of having their data sold to third parties.

2. **Acceptance:**
   Under the terms of the CCPA, businesses are required to get the opt-in agreement of individuals younger than 16 years old before collecting or selling their personal information. Additionally, it provides individuals with the opportunity to opt out of having their data sold.

3. **Notification in the Event of a Data Breach:**
   In the event that a data breach occurs, organizations that are subject to the CCPA are required to notify impacted persons as well as the Attorney General of California. Having to comply with this obligation increases both accountability and openness.

4. **Reducing the Amount of Data:**
   The California Consumer Privacy Act (CCPA) mandates that organizations acquire only the minimum amount of personal information that is required for the objectives that have been made clear to the individuals whose data is being collected. This provision is intended to encourage the minimization of personal data.

5. **Responsibility and Administrative Structure:**
   Even though the CCPA isn't quite as strict as the GDPR, it nonetheless requires businesses to put in place reasonable security

measures and procedures in order to safeguard their customers' personal information.

6. The Consequences of Failing to Comply:

In the event that the CCPA is violated in any way, shape, or form, there is the potential for a pecuniary penalty of up to $7,500 per intentional violation and $2,500 each non-intentional violation.

Influence :
The California Consumer Privacy Act (CCPA) has had an impact on the privacy legislation in the United States by establishing a model for robust data privacy rights.

There has been a recent uptick in the number of states in the United States that have sponsored or approved legislation that is analogous to this, contributing to the growing trend of data protection policies.

Possible Consequences:
Companies that gather or process the personal information of people living in California are required to ensure that they are in compliance with the CCPA. It's possible that this may need updating privacy rules, putting in place permission methods, and adopting data subject rights procedures.

HIPAA is an acronym for the Health Insurance Portability and Accountability Act

In a Nutshell:
The Health Insurance Portability and Accountability Act of 1996 (HIPAA) is a federal law in the United States that was enacted with the purpose of protecting sensitive health information. It is largely relevant to the healthcare sector, including health plans, healthcare providers, and healthcare clearinghouses, among other relevant entities.

Principal Constituents:

1. Rights of the Data Subject:

Patients are granted certain rights under HIPAA with relation to their health information; however, these rights are far more restricted when compared to those granted by GDPR or CCPA. Patients have the legal right to request corrections to their medical records as well as access those data themselves.

2. **Acceptance:**
The Health Insurance Portability and Accountability Act of 1996 (HIPAA) places an emphasis on the significance of getting patient consent before using or disclosing a patient's protected health information (PHI). On the other hand, the consent mechanisms that are required by GDPR and CCPA are more extensive than those that are required by HIPAA.

3. **Notification in the Event of a Data Breach:**
In the event that unprotected protected health information (PHI) is compromised, HIPAA requires that patients, the United States Department of Health and Human Services (HHS), and, in some instances, the media be notified.

4. **Reducing the Amount of Data:**
Covered entities are strongly encouraged by HIPAA to only collect and utilize the least amount of personally identifiable information (PHI) required for the specific purpose.

5. **Responsibility and Administrative Structure:**
The implementation of safeguards for the protection of protected health information (PHI), including administrative, physical, and technical measures, is required of covered entities by HIPAA. In addition to that, it calls for the designation of a Privacy Officer.

6. **The Consequences of Failing to Comply:**

Infractions of the Health Insurance Portability and Accountability Act (HIPAA) can result in both civil and criminal fines, depending on the seriousness of the infraction. According to the clause, annual civil penalties might run anywhere from $100 to $1.5 million.

Influence :
Because it mandates the confidential treatment of individuals' health information, HIPAA has had a substantial and far-reaching effect on the

healthcare sector. Even while it does not apply to all fields of business, it has motivated companies to implement more stringent data protection procedures.

Possible Consequences:

The standards of HIPAA must be adhered to in a stringent manner by healthcare companies. These obligations include conducting risk assessments, putting security measures into place, and verifying patient permission for data processing. Failure to comply with regulations may result in monetary fines and other legal repercussions.

Examination of Differences

Let's do a side-by-side comparison of these data privacy frameworks so that we may get a better understanding of how they differ from one another and how they are similar.

The remit for:

The General Data Protection Regulation (GDPR) applies to all businesses around the world that handle the personal data of inhabitants of the EU or EEA.

Businesses that collect personal data of California residents and meet certain conditions are subject to the requirements of the CCPA.

HIPAA is a law that was passed in the United States that applies to healthcare providers, health plans, and healthcare clearinghouses.

Rights of the Data Subject:

The General Data Protection Regulation (GDPR) gives individuals extensive rights, such as access, rectification, erasure, and the freedom to move their data.

The CCPA gives individuals the right to view their data, the right to delete their data, and the right to opt out of having their data sold.

HIPAA grants only a few rights, with the primary emphasis being placed on access and correction.

Affirmative action:

Consent for the processing of data must be given in an open and transparent manner, and the GDPR places a premium on opt-in processes.

The CCPA necessitates opt-in consent from minors and opt-out consent from those who wish to sell their data.

Patient authorization is necessary under HIPAA for the collection, use, or disclosure of protected health information.

Notification in the Event of a Data Breach:

GDPR requires that notifications of data breaches be made within three days.

The CCPA mandates that entities must provide affected persons and the Attorney General of California with notification.

The Health Insurance Portability and Accountability Act (HIPAA) mandates that affected patients, the Department of Health and Human Services (HHS), and even the media must be notified when a data breach occurs.

Reduce the amount of data:

The General Data Protection Regulation (GDPR) encourages data minimization and places an emphasis on the fact that enterprises should collect only the data that is essential.

The CCPA incentivizes data minimization by restricting data collection to only what is required for the objectives that have been specified.

The Health Insurance Portability and Accountability Act of 1996 (HIPAA) encourages covered businesses to use and disclose just the minimum amount of protected health information that is necessary.

Responsibility and leadership in governance:

GDPR mandates that enterprises demonstrate compliance with the regulation using a variety of methods, such as risk assessments and data protection impact assessments.

The CCPA requires businesses to have appropriate security measures and procedures for their employees and assets.

The Health Insurance Portability and Accountability Act of 1996 (HIPAA) mandates the establishment of privacy officers and other safeguards for patients' protected health information.

Sanctions for Disobedience include the Following:

The General Data Protection Regulation (GDPR) imposes fines of up to 4% of a company's annual global revenue or €20 million, whichever is greater.

The Consumer Credit Protection Act (CCPA) imposes monetary fines of up to $7,500 per intentional violation and $2,500 each non-intentional infringement.

Civil penalties imposed under HIPAA can range from $100 to $1.5 million per year, per provision, and there is also the possibility of criminal prosecution.

Frameworks for data privacy play an essential part in determining how businesses gather, manage, and safeguard individuals' personal information.

The landscape of legislation governing data privacy is complicated and constantly shifting, with just a few examples include the General Data Protection Regulation (GDPR), the California Consumer Privacy Act (CCPA), and HIPAA.

While some frameworks are designed to address issues that are applicable on a global scale, others are tailored to address concerns that are unique to particular sectors of the economy or geographical areas. Organizations that deal with personal information are required to not only comprehend the requirements of these frameworks, but also modify their operations in order to assure compliance, protect the rights of persons, and reduce the danger of incurring penalties for non-compliance.

As the worldwide landscape for data privacy continues to undergo transformations, businesses need to maintain vigilance, ensure that they are up to date on the latest regulatory changes, and make data protection a primary concern in all aspects of their operations. In the end, the objective is to find a middle ground that strikes a balance between data-driven innovation and the protection of the rights and privacy of individuals in a world that is becoming increasingly digital.

2.2 Compliance and Consequences

Compliance with rules is an essential component of responsible governance and operation for companies operating in a variety of fields, including but not limited to the financial industry, healthcare, the protection of personal data, and the preservation of the natural environment. The failure of an organization to comply with predetermined regulations can have serious repercussions, including adverse effects on the company's reputation, financial position, and legal standing. In this piece, we will discuss the significance of complying with rules and regulations, as well as the potential repercussions of failing to do so.

The Importance of Adhering to Regulations

1. **Obligations under the Law:**
   Laws and statutes are the source of the majority of rules, and businesses have a moral and ethical obligation to behave in accordance with these governing documents. Failure to comply may result in legal action, as well as financial fines and other consequences.
2. **Management of One's Reputation**
   Compliance is beneficial to the development and upkeep of a good reputation. Consumers, investors, and other stakeholders frequently look favorably upon businesses that can demonstrate a commitment to conducting themselves in an ethical and responsible manner.
3. **Risk Avoidance and Mitigation:**
   The risk of legal and financial penalties is decreased by complying with the regulations. Compliance with rules allows firms to reduce their risk of incurring legal liability and financial penalties.
4. **Protecting the Data:**
   Compliance, in the context of legislation concerning data security and privacy, helps protect
   sensitive information and maintains the trust of customers and partners. Data breaches caused by non-compliance can result in significant damage to a company's reputation.

5. **The impact on the environment**
   Environmental restrictions are absolutely necessary in order to keep natural resources in good condition and cut down on pollution. Compliance guarantees that firms take measures to reduce the negative impact their operations have on the environment.
6. **Factors to Consider From an Ethical and Moral Standpoint:**

The ideals of ethics and morality frequently align with compliance requirements. It demonstrates an organization's dedication to doing the right thing and making a meaningful contribution to society.

The Repercussions of Not Being in Compliance

1. **Consequences legals :**
   If an organization does not comply with the standards, it may be subject to legal action, which may result in financial penalties, civil litigation, or even criminal accusations. Legal fines like this can have a crippling effect on a company's finances and even force it to go out of business.
2. **A significant loss of money:**
   Failure to comply with regulations might result in significant monetary losses. The expenditure of resources on things like fines and legal expenses can have a negative influence on an organization's capacity to turn a profit and maintain its financial health.
3. **Harm Done to One's Reputation**
   Damage to one's reputation is among the most important repercussions that can result from failing to comply. A breach of compliance can cause a loss of trust and confidence in a company, which can result in the loss of clients, business partners, and financial backers.
4. **The loss of clients and business partners:**
   Customers and business partners are frequently hesitant to work with companies that do not comply with regulations, particularly those that are associated with the protection of personal

information and financial data. The failure to comply with regulations might result in the destruction of important relationships.

5. **Inspections by Regulatory Bodies:**
Failure to comply with regulatory requirements can result in heightened regulatory attention, which may include audits and investigations. This can be a drain on an organization's resources and cause disruptions to its normal operations.

6. **The costs of remediation**
Following a breach of compliance, firms frequently have to make investments in remediation initiatives. These measures can include obtaining legal counsel, enhancing security, making adjustments to processes, and conducting public relations efforts in order to reestablish trust.

7. **Ineligibility to Receive Funds From Grants and Contracts:**
Certain industries, including government contracting and grant giving, have particularly stringent compliance requirements. Failure to comply with regulations might result in a company being ineligible for lucrative contracts and funding opportunities.

8. **Charges for Criminal Activity:**
Individuals within an organization, including CEOs, may be subject to criminal prosecution in instances of extreme non-compliance or infractions of laws under certain circumstances. This could result in a lengthy prison sentence as well as considerable personal liability.

9. **Incapacity to Carry Out Activities:**
In certain circumstances, government authorities may refuse to renew an organization's licenses or permissions, rendering it legally unable to conduct business as usual.

10. **The Effect on Staff Members:**

Employees who do not comply with the rules may face repercussions, some of which include job insecurity and damage to their reputations.

Because of the organization's current financial predicament, it may potentially result in staff reductions and other forms of downsizing.

Maintaining compliance with rules is not just an obligation imposed by the law; it is also an essential component of doing responsible and ethical company. The effects of failing to comply with regulations can be far-reaching, having an effect on an organization's finances, reputation, and capacity to function normally. In order for enterprises to effectively minimize these risks, they need to give compliance efforts high priority, invest in the resources that are necessary, and keep abreast of increasing regulatory requirements. They are able to safeguard their interests, keep the confidence of stakeholders, and make a contribution to a more responsible and ethical manner of conducting business if they do so.

Chapter 3

Data Collection and Storage Security

In this day and age of digitization, data has emerged as one of the most precious assets for companies, organizations, and even individual people. Whether it's for the purpose of making decisions, doing research, or delivering services, the collecting and storage of data are essential components of day-to-day operations. However, due to the ever-increasing amount of data that is being produced and kept, maintaining the data's safety has become an issue of the utmost importance. The vulnerability of data has been brought to light as a result of data breaches, cyberattacks, and privacy violations, which highlights the essential requirement for effective data collecting and storage security measures. During this in-depth conversation, we are going to go into the area of data collection and storage security, discussing its significance, the difficulties associated with it, the best methods now available, and the upcoming trends in the field.

1. **The Significance of Safeguarding the Data Collection and Storage Process**
   1.1 The Importance of the Data

Data is frequently referred to as the "new oil" in the digital economy. It is essential to the process of fostering innovation, facilitating the making of well-informed decisions, and enhancing the effectiveness of corporate operations. Data is utilized by businesses for a variety of reasons, including the examination of markets, the creation of client profiles, the advancement of products, and the improvement of business processes. In this day and age of big data, an organization's potential to generate competitive advantages and insights directly correlates to the amount of data it is able to collect and analyze.

1.2. Compliance and Protection of Personal Information

Safeguarding data is not just a question of good business ethics but also a legal need as a result of the emergence of severe data protection rules such as the General Data Protection Regulation (GDPR) of the European Union and the California Consumer Privacy Act (CCPA) of the state of California. It is possible to incur significant fines and suffer damage to one's reputation if one does not comply with these requirements. When it comes to guaranteeing regulatory compliance and preserving the privacy rights of individuals, the security of data collection and storage are of the utmost importance.

1.3. Credibility and Professional Standing

Data breaches and other security incidents can do severe harm to a business's reputation and diminish the public's trust in that institution. Customers, partners, and other stakeholders have an expectation that the data they provide will be protected from unwanted access and handled with care. Because even a single data breach can result in a trust deficit that is difficult to overcome, maintaining data security is an essential component of effective brand management.

2. Obstacles Faced During the Process of Data Collection and Storage

2.1. Dangers to Computer Security

The constantly shifting panorama of cybersecurity risks is one of the most significant difficulties that must be overcome in the field of data protection. Hackers and other malicious actors, including state-sponsored agencies and other organizations, are always developing new methods and tools to circumvent data protections. Phishing, ransomware, malware, distributed denial of service attacks, and other types of cyberattacks are all examples of cyberthreats. These dangers have the potential to jeopardize the data's availability, integrity, and secrecy.

2.2. Data Security Violations

Security incidents are known as data breaches when they include the exposure or theft of sensitive data. They may be the consequence of a wide range of causes, such as insecure passwords, software that is prone to vulnerabilities, inadvertent exposures, or even insider attacks. Data breaches not only put the individuals who are impacted in danger, but they also have substantial repercussions for the organizations that are responsible, both financially and in terms of their reputation.

2.3 Dangers that Come from Within

A major cause for concern are the insider threats that might be posed by workers or other trusted individuals who have access to the data of a company. It's possible that these people will intentionally or unintentionally misuse their access in order to steal or compromise data. Implementing security controls and employee education programs are also necessary steps in mitigating the risks posed by insiders.

2.4. Compliance with the Regulations

Maintaining compliance with data protection standards may be a challenging endeavor, particularly for firms that operate on a global scale. It is crucial to have a full grasp of data protection regulations and to modify security measures accordingly. Compliance requirements can differ from jurisdiction to jurisdiction, thus it is important to have this expertise.

2.5 The Complexity of the Data

The proliferation of big data, the Internet of Things (IoT), and artificial intelligence (AI) has led to a tremendous expansion in both the kind and volume of available data. The administration and protection of extensive data collections that are complicated and unstructured present a significant problem for companies.

2.6. Online Storage in the Cloud

The cloud storage model has the advantages of scalability and cost-effectiveness, but it also comes with some new security issues. The security of data kept in the cloud could be compromised by threats provided by third-party service providers. A paradigm of shared responsibility between the cloud provider and the user is required in order to guarantee the safety of data that is stored in the cloud.

3. Industry Standards for the Protection of Data During Collection and Storage

3.1. Classification of the Data

First things first, determine how sensitive each piece of data actually is. The same level of security is not necessary for all of the data. Through the process of categorizing data, companies are able to apply suitable security measures to the information that is deemed to be the most vital, hence lowering the danger of overinvestment in areas that are not high priorities.

3.2. Encoding and Decoding

Encryption is an indispensable tool for ensuring the safety of data at rest as well as when it is in motion. The data should be secured by utilizing algorithms that are reliable, and the encryption keys should be kept in a safe manner. This method ensures that data is unintelligible to unauthorized users even in the event that it is stolen or otherwise compromised.

3.3. Controlling Who Can Enter

In order to guarantee that only authorized personnel are able to access particular data, implement stringent access restrictions.

Limiting access to only what is required for employees to fulfill their responsibilities can be accomplished by implementing role-based access control (RBAC) and the principle of least privilege.

3.4. Multi-Factor Authentication (also known as MFA)

In order to access critical systems and data, multi-factor authentication must first be completed.

MFA increases the level of security of a system by necessitating the use of more than one method of authentication, which can be something the user knows (such as a password), something the user owns (such as a smartphone), or something the user is (such as a fingerprint).

3.5. Perform Frequent Security Checks

It is important to carry out frequent security audits and vulnerability assessments in order to locate any flaws in the data gathering and storage systems and then correct them. An objective assessment of an organization's security posture can be obtained through the use of external audits as well as penetration testing.

3.6. Education and Awareness for Staff Members

Employees should be made aware of the importance of data security and the best practices in cybersecurity. Employees are frequently the first line of defense, and the level of awareness and information they possess can contribute to the reduction or elimination of security breaches.

3.7. Plan for Dealing with Incidents

Create a thorough incident response plan that details the actions to take in the event that there

is a breach in the system's security. A reaction that has been thoroughly prepared can reduce the amount of damage and downtime that occurs while also assisting with regulatory compliance.

3.8. Policies Regarding the Storage of Data

Putting in place policies for the storage of data and its eventual deletion will ensure that it is not kept for any longer than is required. Simplifying data management and lowering the attack surface can be accomplished by reducing the amount of data that is not necessary.

3.9. Management of Security Updates and Patches

Software and operating systems should have regular updates and patches applied to correct any known vulnerabilities. Unpatched software, which gives hackers the opportunity to exploit vulnerabilities, is the cause of many data breaches.

4. Emerging Trends in the Protection of Data During Collection and Storage

4.1. AI and ML (Machine Learning and Artificial Intelligence)

The use of artificial intelligence and machine learning is now being explored to improve data security. These technologies have the ability to recognize anomalous patterns or behaviors in data access, which assists companies in spotting potential security problems in real time.

4.2. The Technology of Blockchain

The application of blockchain technology, which is most well-known for its part in the functioning of cryptocurrencies, is also being investigated for its potential to improve data security. Due to the fact that it is decentralized and irreversible, it can give an additional degree of trust and ensure the integrity of data.

4.3. Technologies That Protect Individual Privacy

The use of technologies that protect users' privacy, such as homomorphic encryption and federated learning, is becoming increasingly common. These technologies make it possible to use and analyze data without revealing the underlying information, which helps protect the privacy of individuals.

4.4. Dangers Involved with Quantum Computing

The development of quantum computing presents a new challenge to the confidentiality of stored data. Since quantum computers have the ability to break conventional encryption systems, the development of encryption algorithms that are resistant to the effects of quantum computing is necessary.

4.5. Regulations Regarding Data Security

The legislation governing data protection are constantly being updated, and new laws are being enacted in order to accommodate the shifting environment. Organizations have a responsibility to maintain a level of awareness regarding these advancements and to keep their security procedures current.

In this day and age of information proliferation, the security of data gathering and storage is an important concern for individuals as well as businesses. It is vital to place a priority on data security due to the value of data, concerns over privacy, and regulations imposed by regulatory bodies. For the purpose of protecting digital assets in an increasingly linked environment, it is vital to have an understanding of the problems, put best practices into action, and maintain a level of awareness regarding developing trends.

The environment of data security will continue to shift as technological development proceeds, bringing with it both novel dangers and novel approaches to mitigating those dangers. In this day and age, where data reigns supreme, maintaining a proactive and adaptable stance with regard to data security is not only a responsibility but also a source of competitive advantage.

3.1 Secure Data Collection Methods

The gathering of data is an essential component of many procedures that are carried out in the modern world, including those that are carried out in the fields of business and research, healthcare, and government. Concerns regarding the safety of confidential information have been brought to light as a result of the growing reliance on digital data collection technologies. It is necessary to protect data while it is being collected in order to protect individuals' privacy, retain trust, and ensure compliance with rules governing data protection. During the course of this conversation, we are going to investigate the concept of safe data gathering methods, the significance of these methods, and the best procedures to follow in order to reduce the risks that are involved with data collection.

1. The Vital Role of Confidential Information Gathering

1.1. Data Privacy and Security

The right to one's own privacy is one of the most fundamental rights, and the methods used to acquire data must take this right into consideration. The collecting of sensitive information, such as personal data or confidential company data, requires highly secure data collection procedures in order to prevent the information from being leaked, misused, or otherwise compromised. Regulations pertaining to data privacy, such as the GDPR and the CCPA, highlight the significance of safeguarding data gathering processes in order to preserve the privacy of persons.

1.2. Credibility and Professional Standing

Companies that gather and handle data are required to acquire and keep the trust of their users, customers, or clients in order to be successful. A breach of data or violation of privacy can do significant harm to an organization's reputation, which can result in a loss of trust that is difficult, if not impossible, to repair. It is essential to implement trustworthy data collection procedures in order to maintain credibility and confidence.

1.3. Compliance with Legal Requirements and Regulations

In order for enterprises to remain compliant with the law, they are required to adhere to the standards governing data protection and privacy. Failure to comply with regulations may result in monetary fines and other adverse legal consequences. In order to achieve regulatory compliance, the first foundational step is to put secure data collection procedures into practice.

2. Methods for the Secure Collection of Data

2.1. Reducing the Amount of Data

A fundamental aspect of safe data collecting is the reduction of the amount of data being collected. Collect only the information that is required to accomplish the goal that is being set. Avoid gathering information that is either unnecessary or excessive if you want to cut your risk of exposure in the event of a breach.

2.2. Encoding and Decoding

Data should be encrypted not only while in transit but also while it is stored. The protocols known as Transport Layer Security (TLS) and Secure Sockets Layer (SSL) are frequently utilized in order to protect data while it is being transmitted. Strong encryption algorithms are used for data that is stored, so that even if unwanted access is gained, the data will still be protected. This is done so that it can be used later.

2.3. Protocols for the Secure Transmission of Data

Make sure that there is no risk of data being stolen during transmission. When transmitting data, only use channels that are encrypted, and stay away from unprotected networks and open Wi-Fi connections. It should be standard practice to use secure protocols, such as HTTPS for web traffic and SFTP for file transfers.

2.4. Authentication and Authorization Procedures

Put in place secure methods of authentication and authorization. Access to the data and the ability to acquire it should be restricted to only those personnel who are permitted. Make use of role-based access control, also known as RBAC, to limit data access based on the job roles and responsibilities involved.

2.5 Tools for the Secure Collection of Data

Choose safe data collection technologies and platforms that come with their own security protections already installed. These solutions ought to be able to encrypt data, authenticate users, and keep a record of who accessed what data at what times.

2.6. Safeguarded Collection Forms of Information

When using web forms or applications to collect data, it is important to ensure that the forms are secure. In order to protect against widespread web application security flaws, you should include CAPTCHAs to stop automated attacks and validate user input.

2.7. Auditing and Monitoring Conducted On a Regular Basis

Maintain constant vigilance over data gathering methods and do regular audits to identify any potential security flaws. Audits at regular intervals can point up areas of security that need improvement and provide chances to do so.

2.8. Classification of the Data

Put data into categories according to how sensitive they are. The same level of security is not necessary for all of the data. By classifying data, organizations are able to more efficiently deploy resources and apply strong security measures to the information that is deemed to be the most important.

2.9. Consent and Openness to Information

Get folks' consent after informing them of what you plan to do with the data you acquire from them. Ensure that the goal of the data collection, the intended use of the data, and the length of time it will be kept are all communicated very clearly. Building trust with data subjects requires full disclosure of all relevant information.

3. New Directions in the Accumulation of Confidential Information

3.1. Technologies that Protect Individual Privacy

Technologies that protect users' privacy are gaining more and more traction. The use of techniques such as homomorphic encryption and federated learning enables data to be analyzed without revealing the data on which the analysis is based, thereby maintaining individuals' right to privacy.

3.2. The Use of Blockchain for Collecting Data

The blockchain technology, which is well-known for being decentralized and unchangeable, is currently being investigated for potential applications in the field of secure data collection. It is possible for it to give records that are tamper-proof and transparent, which can boost the data integrity.

3.3. Security Based on Zero Trust

The zero-trust security approach operates under the presumption that no one, either from within or outside the company, can be trusted. It encourages continuous verification of identities and safe access controls, which makes it an appealing strategy for the protection of data collecting.

3.4. Authentication Based on Biometric Traits

The use of biometric authentication techniques, such as fingerprint and facial recognition, is becoming increasingly commonplace for the purpose of safe data collecting. They offer robust user authentication, making it difficult for unauthorized users to gain access to the data.

3.5. Anonymization of the Data

Anonymizing or pseudonymizing data before to collection is becoming more common practice among organizations in the interest of protecting individuals' privacy. This can be accomplished by erasing or encrypting any personally identifying information (PII) in the data in order to protect its privacy.

When it comes to safeguarding data privacy, trust, and regulatory compliance in this day and age of widespread digital data collecting, utilizing secure data collection methods is absolutely essential. The protection of sensitive information while it is being collected is not only a moral requirement but also a necessity from a business perspective. Organizations have a responsibility to remain proactive in adopting secure data gathering procedures and remaining ahead of emerging trends in light of the rapid advancement of technology and the ongoing evolution of the regulatory landscape. They can protect vital information and establish a foundation of trust with their stakeholders if they do so, which will ultimately ensure their long-term success and sustainability in a world that is becoming increasingly data-driven.

3.2 Data Storage Solutions and Encryption

The modern digital world is built on data, and individuals and businesses alike rely on massive amounts of information for vital decision-making, analysis, and other operational purposes. It is imperative that appropriate data storage systems and encryption methods be utilized in order to guarantee the confidentiality of this information. During the course of this conversation, we will investigate the realm of data storage solutions and encryption, their significance, and the various ways in which they might protect sensitive information in a society that is becoming increasingly data-driven.

1. **The Significance of Secure Methods of Data Storage and Encryption**

   1.1. The Importance of Data as an Asset

   In this day and age, data has become one of the most valuable assets that a person can own. Data can be collected, generated, and stored for a variety of objectives, including personal records, corporate intelligence, and research. This activity can be performed by both organizations and people. The implementation of data storage solutions and encryption is absolutely necessary for the purpose of preventing unwanted access to and breaches of this precious asset.

   1.2. Mandatory Compliance Requirements

   The General Data Protection Regulation (GDPR) and the Health Insurance Portability and Accountability Act (HIPAA) are two examples of rules that place stringent standards on how data must be handled. It is absolutely necessary to implement solutions for data storage and encryption in order to be in full compliance with these rules. If regulations aren't followed, there may be serious repercussions.

   1.3. Preventing and Repairing Data Breaches

   Data breaches are becoming increasingly widespread and have the potential to result in major financial losses as well as damage to reputation. It is possible to lessen the severity of the effects of data breaches by using a robust combination of secure data storage and encryption. This will prevent unauthorized access to sensitive information.

   1.4. Maintaining Your Privacy and Confidentiality

It is imperative that private information, financial documents, and intellectual property be kept secure and out of the public eye at all times. Encryption and other data storage options ensure that this information cannot be accessed or interpreted by anybody who is not allowed to do so, so preserving the privacy and confidentiality of the data.

2. **Options for the Storage of Data**

   2.1. Storage located on the Premises

   The storage of data on physical servers and other storage devices that are housed on the grounds of an organization is what is meant by "on-premises storage." Despite the fact that it provides control over data, it calls for a significant investment in infrastructure, maintenance, and safety precautions.

   2.2. Storage on the Cloud

   Cloud storage, which is made available by third-party service providers, provides scalability, cost-efficiency, and accessibility from any location in the world that has access to the internet. Cloud service companies including Amazon Web Services (AWS), Microsoft Azure, and Google Cloud Platform are among the most prominent. Encryption and other access controls are necessities for ensuring the safety of data stored in the cloud.

   2.3. NAS, which stands for network-attached storage

   The ability for numerous users to view data at the same time is made possible by NAS devices, which are specialized file storage servers that link to a network. NAS solutions provide centralized features for managing data, backing up data, and sharing files with other users.

   2.4. Storage Area Network (also known as SAN)

   SANs allow for high-speed data access at the block level to storage devices that are connected via the network. Applications in enterprise contexts that require quick and reliable data access, such as database management systems and virtualization software, frequently make use of these storage devices.

2.5. Object Storage and Management

Object storage is a type of data storage that was developed specifically for the purpose of storing unstructured data, such as pictures, videos, and documents. Because it is scalable and organizes data using metadata, it is an excellent choice for applications dealing with large amounts of data and content distribution.

3. Codes and ciphers

3.1. Encryption of the Data

1. **Data Encryption While in Transit:** This secures data while it is being encrypted while it is being transported via networks or the internet. Both Transport Layer Security (TLS) and Secure Sockets Layer (SSL) are examples of common protocols used for encrypting data while it is in transit.
2. **Data Encryption While It Is At Rest:** This method encrypts data while it is still stored on a storage device, such as a hard disk, cloud storage, or mobile device. Common approaches of encrypting data while it is stored include encrypting the entire disk as well as individual files.

3.2. Encryption Algorithms

The process by which data is converted into an encrypted format is determined by the encryption algorithms. The Advanced Encryption Standard (AES), the Secure Hash Algorithm (RSA), and the Triple Data Encryption Standard (3DES) are all popular encryption techniques. The choice of algorithm is determined by considerations such as the necessary level of data security and the desired level of performance.

3.3. Management of the Keys

Management of encryption keys is an essential component of encryption. It requires the generation of encryption keys, their storage, and their protection. Only users who are allowed to view and decrypt encrypted data are able to do so when proper key management is implemented.

3.4. Encryption from Start to Finish

End-to-end encryption, also known as E2E encryption, is a technology that ensures data is encrypted on both ends, beginning with the side of the sender and ending with the side of the recipient. It stops any intermediates, including service providers, from gaining access to data that has not been encrypted.

3.5. Encryption With Zero-Knowledge Keys

When using zero-knowledge encryption, service providers do not have access to either the encryption keys or the plaintext data. This type of encryption is used to protect users' privacy. This ensures that the data cannot be decrypted by the service provider, which protects the user's privacy.

IV. New Directions Being Taken in the Fields of Data Storage and Encryption

4.1. Encryption That Is Safe From Quantum Attacks

As the technology behind quantum computing continues to progress, it poses a possible danger to the encryption systems that are now in use. In order to protect data in a world where quantum computing is commonplace, quantum-safe encryption algorithms are currently in development. These algorithms are designed to survive quantum attacks.

4.2. Homomorphic Encryption

Homomorphic encryption makes it possible to execute computations on encrypted data without exposing the plaintext information that was originally stored. This technique has potential uses in the areas of safe cloud computing, data analysis, and machine learning that protects users' privacy.

4.3. Safe Computation Among Multiple Parties

Through the use of secure multi-party computation, many parties are able to jointly compute a function over their inputs while still maintaining the confidentiality of those inputs. This technology is utilized in settings when numerous parties wish to examine data without disclosing their individual inputs, such as in a collaborative research project.

4.4. Private and Secure Computing

The new paradigm of confidential computing assures that data is kept encrypted throughout the operation of the system, including when it is stored in memory. This technology can be helpful for safeguarding data that is currently being utilized, which is an essential step in the lifecycle of data.

4.5. Efficient and Safe Erasure of Data

Methods for the secure deletion of data are growing in relevance, particularly in light of the rules in data protection regulations pertaining to the "right to be forgotten." Because these approaches ensure that data is completely deleted when it is no longer needed, the risk of data breaches is significantly reduced.

Encryption and other data storage solutions are essential components in the overall strategy for protecting digital assets and meeting regulatory requirements for data compliance and privacy. Because of the constantly shifting nature of the threats that exist in the modern world and the growing significance of data in that world, businesses and individuals alike need to ensure that they are up to date on the latest developments, trends, and best practices in the areas of data storage and encryption. They are able to preserve sensitive information and maintain the trust of their stakeholders by deploying secure storage solutions and encryption techniques. This, in turn, contributes to the longevity and success of their operations in our data-driven era.

3.3 Data Retention Policies and Practices

Because we live in a digital age, data has evolved into a resource that is useful to individuals, businesses, and organizations alike. In spite of this, there is a compelling need to adequately manage and store this data as a result of the ever-increasing number of data that is being generated and gathered. Policies and procedures pertaining to data retention are essential for striking a balance between the requirement to keep information for operational, legal, and regulatory purposes, on the one hand, and the imperative to preserve privacy and keep data security in good standing, on the other. This conversation delves into the realm of data retention rules and procedures, examining their significance, illuminating some of the most effective approaches, and pointing out some new trends.

1. **The Importance of Having Policies and Practices in Place to Keep Data**

    1.1. Compliance with Legal Requirements and Regulations

    Policies on data retention are absolutely necessary in order to guarantee conformity with the numerous data protection and privacy standards that exist all over the world. The General Data Protection Regulation (GDPR), the California Consumer Privacy Act (CCPA), and the Health Insurance Portability and Accountability Act (HIPAA) all have stringent regulations about the amount of time that data must be stored and how it must be disposed of securely. In the event that compliance is not met, significant penalties may be imposed.

    1.2. Electronic discovery and the obligations imposed by the law

    In the course of judicial procedures, it is possible that organizations will be forced to produce pertinent data as evidence. Because data retention regulations ensure that all required records are kept, e-discovery can be conducted in a more timely and cost-effective manner.

    1.3. Effective Administration of the Data

    The administration of data is simplified by policies that are effective in data retention. Organizations may lessen the complexity of their data storage operations, improve their operational efficiency, and save money on storage costs if they determine what data to maintain and what data to get rid of.

    1.4. Protecting Individual Privacy While Using the Minimum Amount of Information

    The protection of sensitive information is a primary priority.

Keeping data that is no longer required can put an organization at danger of experiencing a data breach, as well as misuse of the data and infringement of its users' privacy. The goal of data minimization is to save only the minimum amount of information necessary to achieve a specific goal. Data retention policies contribute to this goal.

2. **Recommended Procedures for the Data Retention Policy**

   2.1. Establish Unambiguous Objectives

   Your first order of business should be to establish the goals of your data retention policy. Gain a thorough understanding of the legal obligations, operational requirements, and privacy concerns that are unique to your firm. The formulation of your policy should be based on these aims.

   2.2. Categorize the Data

   Create categories for the data depending on its significance, level of sensitivity, and level of criticality to the organization. Not all data is created equal, and different types of data may have varying requirements about how long they should be kept. Data pertaining to operations, data pertaining to customers, financial records, and so on could all fall under this category.

   2.3. Compliance with Legal Requirements and Regulations

   Maintain a level of familiarity with the legal and regulatory requirements that are applicable to your sector and location. In order to ensure compliance, the data retention policy you use should be consistent with these standards.

   2.4. Determine What the Retention Periods Are

   Clearly describe the periods of retention for each of the distinct categories of data. The legal requirements, operational requirements, and industry standards ought to serve as the basis for determining these times. For instance, the duration of time that financial records are required to be kept may be longer than that of marketing data.

   2.5. Access Controls and Safeguards for Precious Items

The information that is kept must be stored safely. Install access restrictions to guarantee that only authorized personnel will be able to view the data that has been retained. Access can be restricted by using role-based access control, also known as RBAC. This takes into account job duties and roles.

2.6. Getting Rid of and Destroying Your Data

Establish policies and procedures for the disposal and destruction of data. When the data has served its purpose or is no longer required, the data should be deleted from the storage medium in such a way that it cannot be recovered in a safe and secure manner.

2.7. Audit Trails and Documentation

It is important to maintain a record of all operations related to the retention of data, including what data was retained, when it was retained, and when it was disposed of. Transparency and accountability can both be ensured with adequate documentation.

2.8. Rights of the Data Subject

The right to erasure, sometimes known as the "right to be forgotten," is one of the rights that must be respected in accordance with GDPR. Ensure that the processes necessary to fulfill these rights within the allotted timeframes are in place before moving further.

3. Evolving Tendencies in the Policies and Practices Regarding the Storage of Data

3.1. Policies of Automatic Expiration

Some businesses are moving toward the adoption of automated data retention rules, which reduce the danger of data over-retention by allowing data to expire automatically after a period of time that has been defined.

3.2. Blockchain for Tracking the Origin of Data

Investigations are currently being conducted into the use of blockchain technology for data provenance and retention policies. A tamper-proof record of data creation, access, and alteration can be provided by the transparent and immutable ledger that blockchain technology uses.

3.3. Pseudonymization and Anonymization of Data

Data anonymization and pseudonymization are two approaches that businesses are implementing in order to keep data without disclosing personally identifiable information (PII), which is one of the ways that companies are working to improve data privacy.

3.4 The Application of Artificial Intelligence to Policy Management

Artificial intelligence (AI) is currently being utilized as a tool for the purpose of more effectively managing data retention policies. Artificial intelligence has the ability to recognize different types of data, determine how important they are, and automatically impose retention periods.

3.5. Safe and Reliable Erasure Technologies

In this day and age, when people are increasingly concerned about their privacy, technologies that delete data securely are becoming more advanced. Tools and processes that ensure data is erased in a way that cannot be recovered are growing in relevance.

Policies and procedures pertaining to the storage and preservation of data are an essential component of appropriate data management in the modern day. The difficulties that arise when trying to strike a balance between the obligation to safeguard data privacy and security and the requirement that data be retained for operational, legal, and regulatory purposes are complicated, but they are necessary for guaranteeing an organization's longevity and reputation. Organizations are able to design data retention policies that respect individual privacy rights while promoting compliance, efficiency, and data security by adhering to best practices and staying updated about emerging trends. These policies can be developed by adhering to best practices and remaining informed about emerging trends. In today's data-driven world, these rules not only protect sensitive information but also contribute to the overall performance and reputation of enterprises.

Chapter 4

Data Transmission and Communication Security

Data transmission and communication are essential to the functioning of modern society since we live in an increasingly interconnected environment. Information is transmitted without interruption throughout the entire planet, providing the fuel that drives commercial operations, personal connections, and the digital ecosystem as a whole. Nevertheless, this comfort is accompanied by a severe drawback in the form of an inherent susceptibility of the data as it travels from the sender to the receiver. In this day and age, when information can be both a powerful tool and a dangerous threat, it is essential that data be safeguarded while it is being transmitted in order to maintain privacy, integrity, and secrecy.

This in-depth discussion digs into the area of data transmission and communication security, analyzing its relevance, the challenges it confronts, the best practices to mitigate those risks, and the developing trends that shape the ever-evolving landscape of secure data transmission. Specifically, it examines best practices to mitigate threats, best practices to prevent threats, best practices to prevent threats, and best practices to prevent threats.

The Building Blocks of a Secure Data Transmission and Communication Infrastructure

The protocols of communication

The rules and conventions that control how data is sent and received in a network are referred to as the communication protocols that govern that process. HTTP, HTTPS, TCP/IP, and UDP are some examples of protocols. Choosing the appropriate communication protocol is often the first step in the process of transmitting data securely. This is because different communication protocols offer differing degrees of security and efficiency.

Cryptography as well as Authentication

The transmission of confidential data must always begin and end with authentication and encryption. Encryption is the process of encrypting data in such a way that it cannot be understood by anyone who is not allowed to view it. Authentication checks to see if the parties involved in a conversation are really who they say they are. Together, these safeguards keep data from being spied on or assumed to be something they're not.

SSL and TLS stand for Secure Sockets Layer and Transport Layer Security, respectively

Both the Secure Sockets Layer (SSL) protocol and its successor, Transport Layer Security (TLS), are examples of cryptographic protocols that ensure confidential communication over a computer network. They ensure the secrecy of the data as well as the integrity of the data by establishing a secure connection between a client and a server. SSL and TLS are popular protocols that are used to secure a broad variety of applications, including online traffic, email, and others.

The acronym VPN stands for "virtual private networks"

VPNs, or virtual private networks, are extremely useful tools for guaranteeing the security of data transfer, particularly in settings that involve public or remote networks. They extend a user's private network across the internet by constructing encrypted tunnels between the user's device and a remote server. Virtual private networks (VPNs) are increasingly popular tools for protecting sensitive data and preserving anonymity.

Standards for the Secure Transmission of Data

The transfer of secure data is a primary emphasis of a variety of industry-specific standards and methods. As one illustration, the financial industry makes use of a protocol known as the Payment Card Industry Data Security Standard (PCI DSS) to protect customer credit card information during the course of transactions. In a similar manner, healthcare providers must comply with the Health Insurance Portability and Accountability Act (HIPAA) in order to ensure the safe transmission of patient records.

Threats and Obstacles to Overcome

The Nature of Online Dangers

The landscape of the cyber threat is defined by a wide variety of potentially harmful actors, strategies, and vulnerabilities that are constantly evolving. Hackers, assaults sponsored by states, malicious software, ransomware, phishing, and distributed denial-of-service (DDoS) attacks are all examples of potential dangers. These attackers are continually adapting new strategies and coming up with new ideas, which presents a substantial challenge to the security of data transfer.

Interception of data and listening in on conversations

The theft of information by unauthorized parties while it is in transit constitutes a significant risk.

Attackers have the ability to listen in on communication that is not encrypted as well as exploit any flaws in the encryption protocol. This can lead to the theft of sensitive information, such as financial data, intellectual property, and personal facts about the individual.

Attacks Employing a "Man in the Middle"

Attacks known as "Man in the Middle" (MitM) occur when an adversary eavesdrops on communication taking place between two parties. The data that is being communicated can be altered, intercepted, or eavesdropped on by the attacker. Attacks using a man in the middle can frequently be made easier by exploiting weak authentication or encryption mechanisms.

Attacks on the Data's Integrity and Those Who Tamper With It

Attacks that include data tampering involve changing data while it is being transmitted in order to jeopardize its integrity. In order to cause disruptions in operations or to fool recipients, attackers may introduce malicious code, modify the details of a transaction, or manipulate data. It is necessary to defend oneself against these dangers by ensuring the data's integrity while it is being transmitted.

Phishing and Social Engineering to Gain an Advantage

Phishing and other forms of social engineering are designed to trick people into divulging sensitive information or login credentials so that the attackers can gain access. These kinds of assaults frequently concentrate on the human component of the communication chain in order to circumvent technical safeguards.

Security Standards for the Transmission and Communication of Data Best Practices

Security-Grade Encryption

For the purpose of protecting data while it is in transit, you should make use of robust encryption techniques like Advanced Encryption Standard (AES). This guarantees that the data is safe from anybody listening in on the conversation and that its confidentiality is maintained.

Proof of Authenticity

Put in place reliable authentication systems, including multi-factor authentication (MFA), if at all possible. Strong authentication is helpful in preventing illegal access as well as Man in the Middle attacks.

Administration of Certificates

The SSL/TLS security infrastructure cannot function without accurate handling of digital certificates. It is critical to do routine updates on certificates, check their validity, and maintain a safe environment for private keys.

Patching and updating on a regular basis

Always make sure that your software and communication protocols are up to date with the latest security fixes. Attackers are able to take advantage of vulnerabilities that exist in old software.

Separation of Network Traffic

You can restrict the damage that could be done by possible assaults by segmenting your network. The network can be segmented in order to assist contain breaches and stop attackers from moving laterally within the system.

Training and Education for Staff Members

Employees should go through training to learn how to identify social engineering and phishing attempts. A considerable reduction in the likelihood of successful assaults that breach communication security can be achieved through the implementation of awareness programs.

Plan for Dealing with Emergencies

Create a comprehensive incident response plan that explains the actions to take in the event that there is a breach in the system's security. Damage and data exposure can be reduced to a minimum with a prompt and structured reaction.

Trends That Are Just Starting To Emerge In The Field Of Data And Communication Security

Model of Security Based on Zero Trust

The traditional method of protecting a network is taken to task by the Zero Trust security paradigm, which operates under the presumption that no one, either from within or outside the company, can be trusted. It encourages the ongoing verification of identities as well as the implementation of safe access controls.

Security at the Edge of Computing

Computing at the edge, in which data processing takes place closer to the data source, provides a unique set of difficulties to data security. As new security practices and solutions are developed, the protection of data at the edge of the network is becoming an increasingly critical task.

Safe for Quantum Computing Encryption

Existing methods of encryption may be vulnerable to attack if quantum computing becomes widespread.

In order to protect data transmission in a post-quantum computing age and withstand quantum attacks, quantum-safe encryption techniques are now in the process of being developed.

Technologies for the Secure Erasure of Data

The clauses in data protection rules that provide individuals the "right to be forgotten" have contributed to the development of more secure data erasure technology. One of the most important aspects of secure communication is making certain that old data is deleted completely once it is no longer required.

5G and Internet of Things Security

New vulnerabilities being found as 5G networks and the Internet of Things (IoT) continue to grow in popularity. Protecting the ever-increasing volume of data requires the implementation of strategies that ensure the confidentiality of data transmissions in 5G networks and Internet of Things devices.

The digital ecosystem relies heavily on secure data transfer and communication as two of its most important building blocks. As data travels across networks, it is more important than ever to protect its validity, integrity, and secrecy. Protecting sensitive information in a globally networked society needs individuals and organizations to maintain vigilance, implement best practices, and be open to emerging trends in order to keep up with the always shifting threat landscape. In this day and age, maintaining privacy, trust, and the integrity of data is just as important as ensuring that communications are secure. This is a commitment that must be maintained throughout time.

4.1 Secure Data Transfer Protocols

Within the context of the modern digital environment, the use of secure data transfer protocols is very necessary to guarantee the integrity and privacy of the information that is passed from one party to another. The requirement for stringent safety precautions is becoming increasingly obvious as the transmission of data grows both more common and more important. The core of these safeguards is comprised of procedures for the secure transfer of data, which protect information while it is in transit from sender to receiver. During this conversation, we will go into the realm of secure data transfer protocols, investigating their significance, the issues that they solve, the methods that are considered to be their best, and the developing trends in the field.

1. **The Importance of Private and Confidential Data Transfer Protocols**

   1.1. Keeping Private Information Private and Secure
   Protocols for the secure transfer of data are absolutely necessary in order to protect sensitive and secret information while it is in transit. The risk of unauthorized access to data as well as the risk of data being intercepted or tampered with is a serious worry in today's environment, which is marked by the ongoing evolution of cyber threats. Protocols for secure data transfer offer some kind of reassurance that the data will continue to be safeguarded.

   1.2. Compliance and Protection of Personal Information
   Data privacy legislation such as the General Data Protection Regulation (GDPR) and the Health Insurance Portability and Accountability Act (HIPAA) dictate that enterprises take necessary precautions to secure personal and sensitive data while it is being transmitted. These regulations may be found in the EU and the United States, respectively. One of the most important steps in achieving regulatory compliance is to utilize secure transfer protocols.

   1.3. The Integrity of the Data
   Maintaining data integrity during transmission ensures that the data has not been tampered with
   in any way. The use of secure transfer protocols helps to maintain data integrity by preventing information from being altered or tampered with by third parties that are not allowed to do so while it is in transit from sender to recipient.

1.4. Credibility and Professional Standing

A strong data transfer security system is essential to the upkeep and preservation of trust and reputation. Those individuals and organizations that do not adequately protect data while it is being transmitted run the risk of not only facing legal and financial repercussions, but also suffering damage to their credibility and reliability.

2. Protocols for the Secure Transfer of Data

2.1. Hypertext Transfer Protocol Secure (also known as HTTPS)

The protocol that is utilized for the process of data transmission over the internet is known as

HTTP. The secure version of HTTP is known as HTTPS. It protects the connection between the user's browser and the web server by using encryption, which is often in the form of SSL or TLS. HTTPS is widely used for transferring data securely in a variety of online contexts, including financial transactions, email communication, and other areas.

2.2. The Secure File Transfer Protocol, also known as SFTP

SSH, or Secure Shell, is an encryption mechanism that is used by SFTP, or the Secure File Transfer mechanism, to protect data while it is in transit. It is widely utilized for the purpose of securely sharing files either over the internet or within a local area network. The Secure File Transfer Protocol (SFTP) is well-known for the robust encryption and authentication techniques it offers.

2.3. File Transfer Protocol Secure (also known as FTPS)

FTPS is yet another protocol for the secure transfer of files, but instead of SSL or TLS for encryption, it utilizes FTPS. It is an extension of the standard File Transfer Protocol (FTP), adding capabilities for secure data transfer while keeping compatibility with existing FTP clients and servers.

2.4. SCP, which stands for "Secure Copy Protocol"

SSH is used for encryption and authentication in the SCP protocol, which allows for the safe transfer of files via the SCP protocol. Users are granted the ability to safely copy files between a local host and a remote host using this functionality. SCP is frequently used in the operations of securely backing up and transferring data.

2.5. AS2 (Applicability Statement 2)

In the context of business-to-business (B2B) data exchange, often known as Electronic Data Interchange (EDI), AS2 is a protocol that is frequently implemented. Encryption, digital signatures, and non-repudiation are some of the methods that are utilized to ensure the safety of structured data that is sent from one trade partner to another.

3. **The Obstacles Confronted and Overcome by Secure Data Transfer Protocols**

3.1. The Interception of Data

Secure data transfer methods encrypt the data while it is in transit to protect it from being intercepted by unauthorized parties. Because the data are encrypted in this way, even if the transmission is intercepted by a malicious party, the data will not be readable.

3.2. Access Granted Without Permission

Authentication techniques in secure transfer protocols ensure that data can only be accessed and transmitted by authorized parties. This aids in preventing unwanted access as well as breaches of data.

3.3. Manipulating the Data

Encryption and checksums are two methods that secure protocols use to preserve the integrity of data. During transmission, these safeguards protect the data from being changed or tampered with by anyone who is not allowed to do so.

3.4. Transfer of Files in a Secure Manner

Protocols for the secure transfer of files, such as SFTP and FTPS, provide a solution to the problem of safely transferring files, which is especially problematic when dealing with huge amounts of sensitive data.

3.5. Assurance of Conformity with the Data Protection Regulations

When it comes to complying with data protection requirements, the use of secure transmission methods is absolutely necessary. These procedures ensure that personal and sensitive data is appropriately protected at all times, including when it is being sent, thereby satisfying the obligations imposed by the law.

4. Recommended Methods for Carrying Out the Implementation of Secure Data Transfer Protocols

4.1. Make Sure You Use Secure Encryption

Make sure that the secure data transfer protocol you choose has robust encryption techniques (like AES) to protect data while it is being sent from one location to another. The use of robust encryption is essential to the process of securely transmitting data.

4.2. Put a Secure Key Management System Into Place

A reliable key management system is required for the secure transfer of data. It comprises generating encryption keys, storing them securely, and exchanging them with other parties. Keys should be updated on a consistent basis, and strong authentication techniques should be used.

4.3. Identify and Verify the Parties

For the purpose of verifying the identities of the parties involved in data transfer, strong authentication methods, such as multi-factor authentication (MFA) or public key infrastructure (PKI), should be utilized.

4.4. Maintain Consistent and Regular Software and Protocol Updates

Make sure that your software, operating systems, and secure transfer methods are all up to date with the latest patches and updates for security. Attackers are able to take advantage of vulnerabilities that exist in old software.

4.5. The Segmentation of the Network

You can restrict the damage that could be done by possible assaults by segmenting your network. The segmentation of a network helps to stop breaches from spreading and stops attackers from moving laterally within the network.

4.6. Use Digital Signatures

Use digital signatures to assure non-repudiation and data integrity in situations where the validity of the data is extremely important, such as in business-to-business transactions.

5. New Developments in the Field of Secure Data Transfer Protocols

5.1. Architecture Based On Zero Trust

Traditional methods of network security are challenged by the Zero Trust security paradigm, which operates under the presumption that no one, either from within or outside the company, can be trusted. Continuous verification and stringent access management are prioritized in architectures that employ zero trust.

5.2. Encryption That Is Safe From Quantum Attacks

The development of quantum computing poses a possible risk to the encryption systems that are now in use. In order to protect data transmission in a post-quantum computing age and withstand quantum attacks, quantum-safe encryption techniques are now in the process of being developed.

5.3. Safe Data Transfer in the Internet of Things

The Internet of Things (IoT) is becoming more widespread, which means there is a growing demand for secure data transfer protocols that are specifically adapted for IoT devices. These protocols need to meet the one-of-a-kind issues posed by the transmission of IoT data.

5.4. Data Security When Transferring It Over 5G Networks

The rollout of 5G networks brings about new concerns regarding data protection and privacy. It is vital to develop strategies for securing data transmission in 5G networks in order to protect the ever-increasing amount of data that is carried over these networks.

The protection of data while it is being transmitted relies heavily on the use of secure data transfer protocols. They play an essential part in protecting the data's confidentiality and integrity, resolving issues such as data interception, unauthorized access, and data manipulation as they arise. Because the digital landscape is always shifting, businesses and individuals alike need to make it a priority to implement industry standards and educate themselves on developing tendencies if they want to maintain data privacy in an increasingly linked world. Not only are secure data transfer protocols a technological need, but they are also an essential component of upholding trust, compliance, and data integrity in the digital age.

4.2 Securing Data in Transit

The transmission of data is an essential component of the current digital world since it paves the way for the flow of information across various networks and systems. Although the transfer of data makes communication, collaboration, and the sharing of data more efficient, it also creates issues in terms of data security. It is of the utmost significance to safeguard sensitive information from being eavesdropped on, intercepted, or tampered with while it is in transit from the sender to the receiver. This can be accomplished by securing the data in transit. During the course of this conversation, we are going to investigate the necessity of safeguarding data while it is in transit, the methods and technologies that are utilized, best practices, and emerging developments in this extremely important subject.

1. **The Importance of Protecting Information While It Is in Motion**

    1.1. Personal Space and Confidential Information

    It is absolutely necessary to protect data while it is in transit in order to maintain privacy and confidentiality. The confidentiality of sensitive information, such as personal data, financial records, and trade secrets, must be maintained at all times while the information is in transit. A breach in security and an invasion of privacy could result from unauthorized access to these records.

1.2. The Integrity of the Data

The integrity of the data guarantees that it will not be changed or corrupted while it is being transmitted. Attackers have the potential to change or tamper with data while it is in transit, which could result in erroneous information, unlawful transactions, or operational disruptions if suitable security measures are not implemented.

1.3. Compliance with Legal Requirements and Regulations

In order to comply with data protection rules such as the General Data Protection Regulation (GDPR) and the Health Insurance Portability and Accountability Act (HIPAA), businesses are required to encrypt sensitive information while it is being transmitted. Maintaining compliance with these standards is absolutely necessary in order to stay out of legal trouble.

1.4. Credibility and Professional Standing

Maintaining trust and a good reputation requires having data transmissions that are adequately protected from unauthorized access. Not only do businesses run the risk of facing regulatory penalties for failing to protect data while it is in transit, but they also risk having their integrity and the trust of their customers harmed.

2. Techniques and Instruments for the Protection of Data While It Is in Motion

2.1. The Use of Encryption

Encryption of Data in Transit: This technique safeguards data while it travels from one system to another or from network to network. When it comes to protecting data while it is being transmitted over the internet, Secure Sockets Layer (SSL) and Transport Layer Security (TLS) are two of the most popular protocols.

Encryption that occurs while the data is held on a storage device, such as a hard drive or a database, is referred to as "data at rest" encryption. Full-disk encryption and encryption at the file level are both used to ensure that data is kept secure even while it is not being actively used.

2.2. Protocols for Safe and Private Communication

Encryption and secure authentication are two methods that are utilized by safe communication protocols, such as HTTPS, SFTP (Secure File Transfer Protocol), and SCP (Secure Copy Protocol), respectively, to protect data while it is in transit. During the transport of data, these protocols will protect its privacy, maintain its integrity, and authenticate its recipients.

2.3. Electronic Signatures and Seals

Digital signatures offer a method for determining whether or not the data that has been transferred is authentic. They do this by utilizing several cryptographic algorithms in order to generate a one-of-a-kind digital signature for each individual piece of data. The presence of this signature verifies that the data has not been altered in any way and originates from a reliable source.

2.4. Virtual Private Networks (VPNs), also known as

VPNs are virtual private networks that generate encrypted tunnels for the transport of data, so shielding it from the possibility of being monitored or intercepted. Using a virtual private network, or VPN, to secure data transmissions across public networks or to gain remote access to private networks is an especially beneficial application of this technology.

2.5 Safeguarding of the Key Management System

The successful management of keys is absolutely necessary for ensuring the safety of data while it is in transit. It is imperative that keys, which are utilized in both encryption and decryption, be safely generated, kept, and traded. Strong key management guarantees that encryption continues to serve its intended purpose.

3. Best Practices for the Protection of Data While It Is in Motion

3.1 Always Make Use Of Robust Encryption

Protecting data while it is in transit requires the utilization of robust encryption techniques such as Advanced Encryption Standard (AES). A secure encryption method protects the confidentiality of the data and makes it resistant to any attempts to decrypt it.

3.2. Put an Authentication System Into Place

To authenticate the identity of the parties engaged in data transfer, strong authentication mechanisms should be implemented. Examples of such techniques include multi-factor authentication (MFA) and public key infrastructure (PKI).

3.3. Maintain Consistent and Regular Software and Protocol Updates

Make sure that all of your software, operating systems, and secure communication protocols are up to date with the latest patches and upgrades for security. Attackers are able to take advantage of vulnerabilities that exist in old software.

3.4 Be on the Lookout for Any Abnormalitie

Install monitoring and alerting systems in order to identify unusual occurrences or behaviors that seem suspicious while data is being transmitted. The swift action that can be taken in response to possible security breaches is enabled by their prompt identification.

3.5. Segmentation of the Network

Separate different parts of the network to reduce the effectiveness of any possible attacks. The segmentation of a network helps to stop breaches from spreading and stops attackers from moving laterally within the network.

3.6. Education and Awareness for Staff Members

Employees should go through training to learn how to identify social engineering and phishing attempts. Programs that raise people's awareness have the potential to greatly cut down on the risk of successful assaults that undermine data security while it is being transmitted.

4. New Directions in Protecting Data While It's in Motion

4.1. Model of Security Based on Zero Trust

The traditional method of protecting a network is taken to task by the Zero Trust security paradigm, which operates under the presumption that no one, either from within or outside the company, can be trusted. It encourages the ongoing verification of identities as well as the implementation of safe access controls.

4.2. Encryption That Is Safe From Quantum Attacks

Existing methods of encryption may be vulnerable to attack if quantum computing becomes widespread. In order to protect data transmission in a post-quantum computing age and withstand quantum attacks, quantum-safe encryption techniques are now in the process of being developed.

4.3. Safe Data Transfer in the Internet of Things

There is a growing demand for secure data transfer protocols that are specifically designed for IoT devices, as the Internet of Things (IoT) continues to expand its scope. These protocols need to meet the one-of-a-kind issues posed by the transmission of IoT data.

4.4. Safe Transmission of Information in 5G Networks

The rollout of 5G networks will bring forth new difficulties in terms of cybersecurity. It is vital to develop strategies for securing data transmission in 5G networks in order to protect the ever-increasing amount of data that is carried over these networks.

In this day and age, ensuring the safety of data while it is being transmitted from one location to another is an essential component of data protection. As information travels through a variety of networks and systems, the need to protect its authenticity, integrity, and confidentiality becomes increasingly important. To guarantee the safety of data transmission in today's hyperconnected world, businesses and individuals alike need to implement data security best practices and keep up of current industry developments. The protection of data while it is in transit is not solely dependent on technological advancements; rather, it is an essential component of maintaining trust, compliance, and data integrity in our data-driven world.

4.3 Secure Messaging and Collaboration Tools

In a world that is becoming more interconnected, individuals and organizations need to have access to secure messaging and collaboration technologies in order to function effectively. These tools make communication more effective, encourage collaboration among users, and boost overall productivity. Nevertheless, the proliferation of digital communication has also given rise to worries regarding the privacy and security of data. The protection of sensitive data both while it is being transmitted and while it is stored has become a high issue. In this conversation, we will investigate the significance of secure messaging and collaboration platforms, as well as the difficulties they address, best practices, and emerging developments in the field of data protection.

1. **The Importance of Confidential and Private Messaging and Collaboration Tools**
    1.1. Improvements in Productivity
    Regardless of where members of a team are physically located, they are able to collaborate effectively thanks to secure communications and collaboration technologies. They make collaboration on documents possible, as well as real-time communication, file sharing, and management of projects. The improved productivity and accelerated response times that result from this greater efficiency are a direct result.
    1.2. Flexibility in Geographical Areas
    The workforces of modern companies are frequently dispersed across a variety of locales and time zones. Secure messaging and collaboration solutions enable teams to interact as if they were physically present in the same room, breaking down geographical barriers in the process. This flexibility encourages a healthy

balance between work and life, which in turn boosts employee satisfaction.

1.3. Safety of the Data

It is imperative that stringent safety precautions be taken whenever these tools are used to facilitate the transfer of sensitive corporate information, intellectual property, or personal data. Tools for secure messaging and collaboration provide data encryption, access controls, and authentication techniques in order to safeguard information from being accessed in an unauthorized manner and from being compromised.

1.4. Essential Conditions for Compliance

Many different types of businesses are required to comply with various regulations regarding the privacy and safety of their customers' data. In the healthcare industry, compliance with the Health Insurance Portability and Accountability Act (HIPAA) is required, whereas compliance with the Gramm-Leach-Bliley Act is required for financial institutions. By ensuring that sensitive data is protected, secure messaging and collaboration technologies make it easier to satisfy these compliance standards.

2. The Obstacles Confronted That Are Overcome By Tools For Secure Messaging And Collaboration

2.1. The Privacy of Your Data

When it comes to protecting one's data, the use of messaging and collaboration applications presents a big difficulty. It is of the utmost importance to prevent unauthorized access to important corporate data, as well as personal data and information about customers. Tools that offer robust encryption and privacy features are helpful in protecting users' personal information.

2.2. Data Loss and Disclosure

When information that is considered private or proprietary is shared, the risk of data leakage
increases. Secure messaging systems provide features such as digital rights management (DRM) and content control to prevent

unauthorized sharing or printing of sensitive data. DRM stands for "digital rights management," while content control restricts what users can view or print.

2.3 Dangers to Computer and Network Security

Messaging and collaboration platforms have the potential to become targets for several types of assaults, including phishing, the dissemination of malware, and social engineering. In order to protect users from these dangers, secure software typically includes a number of sophisticated security features, such as anti-phishing filters, anti-malware scans, and user authentication.

2.4. Encryption from Start to Finish

When it comes to preventing data from being stolen while in transit, end-to-end encryption is absolutely necessary. End-to-end encryption is a method that is utilized by secure messaging applications. This method ensures that the communications can only be decrypted and read by the intended receiver.

2.5. Adherence to the Requirements of the Regulations

Regulations regarding data protection, such as the General Data Protection Regulation (GDPR) and the California Consumer Privacy Act (CCPA), must be complied with by organizations. solutions for secure messaging and collaboration help assure compliance by providing features that protect personal data and give audit trails for regulatory reporting. These solutions are helpful because they offer these features.

3. Guidelines for the Proper Operation of Secure Communication and Coordination Tools

3.1. Select the Appropriate Instruments

Choose communications and collaboration solutions that place a premium on data protection. Think about things like encrypting the data, authenticating the users, and providing privacy options. Evaluate the tool's history of handling sensitive data as well as its reputation for providing a secure environment.

3.2 Make Sure Encryption Is On

Always enable encryption for both the data that is stored and the data that is being transferred. Check to see that the data protection technology you're using employs robust encryption techniques to prevent unauthorized access. When it comes to messaging apps, end-to-end encryption is of the utmost importance.

3.3. Establish Controls for Gaining Access

Establishing access controls allows you to limit who can see, edit, or distribute data. Make advantage of role-based access control, also known as RBAC, in order to delegate permissions to users in accordance with the roles and responsibilities they play inside the business.

3.4. Inform and Instruct Users

Users should be made aware of the significance of maintaining their data's privacy and security. Instruct them to spot phishing attempts, social engineering strategies, and secure data exchange methods, and train them to avoid falling victim to any of these. Awareness of security risks is an essential component of any cyber defense strategy.

3.5. Ongoing and Frequent Updates

Always make sure that the tools for communicating and collaboration have the most recent upgrades and patches for their security. Attackers are able to take advantage of software flaws, making timely updates absolutely necessary.

3.6. Authentication That Is Robust

To ensure that only authorized users are able to use the tools, strong authentication techniques should be implemented. Some examples of such methods include biometrics and multi-factor authentication (MFA). MFA offers an extra layer of protection on top of the one provided by usernames and passwords.

4. Recent Developments in the Field of Secure Messaging and Online Collaboration Tools

4.1. Architecture Based On Zero Trust

A security approach known as "zero trust" operates under the presumption that no one, either from within or outside the organization, can be trusted. This strategy places a strong emphasis on continuously verifying the identities of users and implementing safe access controls; as a result, it is becoming an increasingly viable option for messaging and collaboration applications.

4.2. Safe Cooperation Within Decentralized Financial Institutions (DeFi)

Decentralized finance, often known as DeFi, is a relatively new industry that operates on the back of blockchain technology and smart contracts. When it comes to maintaining the safety of data in this sphere, having secure collaboration solutions that are also compatible with DeFi systems will be absolutely necessary.

4.3. Improved Capabilities Regarding Privacy

As the number of people concerned about privacy continues to rise, it is expected that messaging and collaboration technologies will provide heightened privacy options in the form of self-destructing texts and private chat rooms.

4.4. Integration with Private and Secure File Sharing

The integration of secure messaging and collaboration tools with secure file sharing platforms will become more common in the future. This will enable users to share files and documents while maintaining a higher level of security.

solutions for secure messaging and collaboration play an important role in the modern workplace. These solutions make communication and collaboration more efficient while also addressing concerns about data privacy and security. In today's hyper-connected world, businesses and people alike need to implement data security best practices and ensure they are up to date on the latest industry developments if they want to keep their information secure. The utilization of these solutions not only increases productivity and efficiency but also guarantees that sensitive information continues to be kept safe and secure, thereby reinforcing trust and regulatory compliance in this digital age.

5

Chapter 5

Access Control and Authentication

Controlling who has access to sensitive information and verifying their identities are essential parts of information security. The need of protecting sensitive data and systems cannot be overstated in light of the fact that our world is becoming increasingly digital and networked. The topics of access control and authentication are investigated in depth throughout this extensive paper, which goes into the significance of these concepts as well as their underlying ideas, methodologies, and real-world applications. In addition to this, it analyzes how the landscape of these security measures is changing in response to the problems that are provided by an environment that is both dynamic and linked.

Before we begin:
Information is one of the most precious assets in today's digital landscape, which has become increasingly digitalized. There has never been a time when it was more important to protect one's data and systems from being accessed by unauthorized parties, whether the context is professional or private. Access control and authentication are two of the most important foundations of information security. They are crucial

for the protection of sensitive information as well as the maintenance of the integrity and privacy of digital resources.

This essay investigates the realm of access control and authentication, looking into their respective functions, concepts, and approaches, as well as the fluid nature of these security measures in the context of a technological environment that is constantly changing. After finishing this conversation, readers will have a comprehensive understanding of how access control and authentication function, the significance of these concepts in modern life, as well as the tactics and technology that are utilized to execute them.

1. The Importance of Understanding the Concept of Access Control
   1. An Explanation of What Access Control Is
      The process of defining and managing who or what is allowed to access particular resources or data within a given system is referred to as access control. This process is also known as authorization control. As a result of its role as a barrier that prevents unlawful entry, it is an essential component of security in both physical and digital settings. Access control mechanisms are created with the purpose of successfully enforcing policies, managing user permissions, and mitigating potential security vulnerabilities.
   2. The Importance of Having an Access Control System

   Keeping Private Information Private and Safe
   Controlling who has access to sensitive data is of the utmost importance. It restricts the ability of unauthorized individuals to read, modify, or delete vital information. For businesses, this involves protecting their trade secrets, customer data, and proprietary research; for people, this means protecting the privacy of their personal data. For businesses, this means protecting their trade secrets, customer data, and proprietary research.

   Reducing the Dangers to Our Security

Unauthorized access can result in a wide variety of security problems, such as the loss of data, the introduction of insider danger, and cyberattacks. Access control serves as the first line of defense since it restricts entry to only those who are permitted to do so, hence lowering the probability that a security breach would occur.

Both compliance and accountability are essential.

Certain categories of data must comply with the legal and regulatory standards applicable in many different sorts of businesses. Access control plays an essential part in assisting companies in meeting the requirements of these rules and ensuring that they continue to be compliant with the requirements. In addition to this, it helps preserve accountability by producing an audit trail that shows who accessed which resources and at what time.

II. Access Management Theory and Practice

1. **The Principle of Least Privilege (sometimes abbreviated as POLP)**
   According to the Principle of Least Privilege, persons or systems should only have the level of access that is required for them to carry out the responsibilities assigned to them. This reduces the amount of possible damage that could occur if an account were to be hacked or used inappropriately. The principle of "need-to-know" or "need-to-use" access is enforced by POLP. This ensures that users only have access to the resources that are pertinent to the jobs that they play.

2. **RBAC stands for "role-based access control"**
   A style of access control that is very common that assigns rights based on user roles inside an organization is called role-based access control, or RBAC for short. Users are categorized into roles according to the functions they do in their jobs, and specific access permissions are allotted to each role. This makes access control more straightforward by ensuring that the same permissions are always granted to users who have the same job.

3. **Access Control Lists, abbreviated as ACLs**
   Access Control Lists are a method that are based on rules and are utilized in the control of access to various resources. Access control lists, or ACLs, are used to define which users or other system entities are permitted to access particular resources and which are not. These lists are connected to specific resources, which enables access permissions to be fine-tuned and granularly managed.
4. **The acronym MAC stands for mandatory access control.**
   Access regulations are enforced according to labels and other security classifications when using mandatory access control. In the contexts of the government and the military, where information is classified according to various levels of sensitivity and users are given different clearance levels, this phrase is used frequently. Users who have the necessary level of security clearance are the only ones who are allowed to access the material thanks to MAC's protection.
5. **DAC stands for Discretionary Access Control.**

The owner of a resource is provided the ability to decide who has access to their resources as well as the level of access that is granted through the use of discretionary access control. It allows users the ability to decide whether to grant access to their own resources or to cancel access. If it is not handled correctly, DAC, despite the fact that it gives flexibility, can also result in inconsistent access control.

III. **Models for Controlling Access**

1. **DAC stands for Discretionary Access Control.**
   Within DAC, the owner of a resource has complete control over which users are permitted access to their resources. Users have the ability to grant permissions to one another, which can result in an access control system that is very flexible but also potentially complex. DAC is frequently used in environments that are less

hierarchical, such as personal computing, in which users handle their own files and directories.
2. **The acronym MAC stands for mandatory access control.**
   The Access Control Policies are enforced by MAC and are based on the security labels and classifications. It is frequently utilized in governmental and military situations, both of which place a high priority on the confidentiality of data. MAC makes certain that users with the required level of security clearance are the only ones who can access certain information, and it prevents resource owners from modifying access regulations.
3. **RBAC stands for "role-based access control."**
   RBAC is responsible for delegating responsibilities, or roles, to users, who are then given those roles. This paradigm streamlines the process of controlling access by categorizing users according to the duties or responsibilities of their jobs. It is especially useful in large organizations, where roles are clearly delineated and access must be regulated in a uniform manner.
4. **ABAC stands for attribute-based access control.**
   ABAC is an example of a dynamic access control paradigm that makes judgments on access based on the attributes of the user. User characteristics, property characteristics of resources, and environmental factors are all examples of attributes. ABAC is appropriate for use in contexts that are both complex and dynamic since it enables access control on a finer grain and is aware of its context.
5. **RBAC stands for Rule-Based Access Control.**
   RBAC is a flexible paradigm that determines access based on the application of rules or conditions. Access decisions are determined based on previously stated rules, which may take into account a variety of criteria. These factors may include user traits, resource attributes, and context. RBAC is widely implemented in web applications, Internet of Things platforms, and cloud service platforms.

6. Controlling access based on roles inside hierarchies, also known as RBAC-H.

The RBAC paradigm can be extended using RBAC-H, which introduces hierarchical roles. Because of this, more granular access control is possible, with roles able to inherit permissions and attributes from their parent roles. It is of particular value in establishments that have intricately layered organizational hierarchies.

IV. Authentication serves as the cornerstone of a secure access system.

1. A Definitive Exposition of Authentication
   Before allowing a user or other system entity access to a resource, authentication is the process of confirming that the user actually is who they say they are. It assures that only authorized users may access systems, apps, and data. This prevents unauthorized people from accessing sensitive information. To determine a person's identity, authentication methods require them to demonstrate that they know, own, or are something that only they should (referred to as the "knowledge," "possession," and "inherence" elements, respectively).
2. The Importance of Authentication in Today's World

   Keeping Unauthorized Access from Taking Place
   When it comes to preventing unwanted access, authentication is the first line of protection. Systems are able to restrict access to only those users who have the necessary credentials if they verify the identity of the users that attempt to log in. This is absolutely necessary in order to safeguard private information and valuable resources.
   Protecting Financial Transactions Conducted Online
   In this day and age, authentication is absolutely necessary to ensure the safety of online activities including banking, e-commerce, and

communication. It prevents fraud and identity theft by establishing beyond a reasonable doubt that users are who they claim to be.

Maintaining a Culture of Accountability

In addition, accountability can be enforced thanks to the use of authentication. Organizations have the ability to track and audit activities, which is crucial for compliance, incident response, and forensic investigations. This is accomplished by correlating actions and access with unique user identities.

V. Authentication Guidelines and Principles

1. **Something That You Are Aware Of**
   This authentication factor uses information that should only be known by the user, such as a password, a personal identification number (PIN), or a passphrase. Even though it's one of the most prevalent methods of authentication, it leaves users open to assaults if their passwords aren't strong enough or they've been compromised.

2. **Something That You Possess**
   This factor involves something the user holds, such as a smart card, a hardware token, or a mobile device. Other examples of this element include a fingerprint scanner. Because an attacker would have to physically steal the item in order to circumvent possession-based authentication methods, these methods offer an extremely high level of security.

3. **Something That You Constitute**
   The use of an individual's unique physical or behavioral features for the purpose of authentication is known as biometrics.
   This encompasses a wide range of biometric identifiers such as fingerprints, facial scans, iris scans, voice recognition, and more. Although they provide a high level of protection, biometrics may be difficult to deploy and may give rise to privacy worries.

4. **The acronym MFA stands for "multi-factor authentication"**
   Increasing the level of security by combining two or more

existing authentication elements is the purpose of multi-factor authentication. MFA (Multi-Factor Authentication) is a security measure that increases the level of protection against unwanted access by requiring various forms of authentication. The phrases "something you know" (password) and "something you have" (smartphone) are frequently used in conjunction, as are the phrases "something you are" (fingerprint) and "something you know" (PIN).

5. **The acronym "Single Sign-On" (SSO)**

The convenience-driven authentication mechanism known as single sign-on, or SSO for short, enables users to log in just once and then access various systems or applications without having to re-enter their credentials. While SSO makes user access more straightforward, it necessitates stringent security precautions to safeguard the central authentication mechanism.

VI. Various Methods of Authentication

1. **Authentication with Username and Password**
   One of the most widespread techniques is authentication through the use of a password. Users are required to log in with a username and password before being granted access. Passwords, despite their practicality, are vulnerable to a variety of threats, including brute force assaults, dictionary attacks, and password phishing.

2. **Two-Factor Authentication, also abbreviated as 2FA**
   By necessitating the use of two distinct authentication factors, Two-Factor Authentication (also known as 2FA) provides an additional degree of protection. For instance, a user may be required to submit a password (representing something the user is aware of) and get a one-time code on their smartphone (representing something the user possesses) in order to finish the authentication process.

3. **Authentication using Biometric Measurements**
   For the purpose of identity verification, biometric authentication uses observable traits, such as fingerprints, facial features, or voice patterns, as well as other bodily or behavioral characteristics.
   The use of biometrics can be difficult to execute, and there are privacy problems involved with the storing of biometric data. However, biometrics provide a high level of security.
4. **Cards and Tokens with Smart Technology**
   Users are the exclusive owners of the physical hardware that comprise smart cards and tokens. These devices produce or store credentials, and their normal deployment involves the usage of a PIN or password in conjunction with their use. In highly protected settings, such as government organizations and military bases, smart cards are a popular form of payment.
5. **PKI stands for "public key infrastructure."**
   The Public Key Infrastructure (PKI) is a sophisticated authentication method that makes use of digital certificates and asymmetric cryptography. Secure email, digital signatures, and the authentication of websites are typical applications for this technology. The Public Key Infrastructure (PKI) provides a high level of security but requires meticulous certificate management.
6. **Authentication using Mobile Devices**

Users' identities can be validated via mobile authentication by utilizing their smartphones. Push alerts, mobile apps, and SMS-based codes are some of the available methods. Because of the proliferation of smartphone technology, mobile authentication is gaining a larger percentage of the market share.

VII. Applications of Access Control and Authentication Technology in the Real World

1. **Security of Computer Networks**
   Controlling who can access a network and verifying their

identities are essential to its safety. They are put to use to control who has access to vital network resources including servers, databases, and routers among other things. User authentication is used to ensure that only authorized individuals are able to log in to networked devices and services. Access control lists (ACLs) are used by network administrators to define who can access what on the network.

2. **Computing in the Cloud**
   In this day and age of cloud computing, businesses now keep their data and apps running on remote servers that can be accessed through the internet. It is absolutely necessary to have robust access control and authentication measures in place in order to safeguard cloud-based resources. Cloud service providers typically make available a variety of authentication and authorization mechanisms, which enable users to safely manage their access to cloud-based services.

3. **Applications for the Web**
   Web apps are an essential component of modern life, playing a part in everything from online banking to social media. When it comes to protecting user accounts, personal data, and transactions, having a reliable access control and authentication system is absolutely necessary. A wide variety of web applications now make use of robust authentication procedures, such as multi-factor authentication (MFA) and Open Authorization (OAuth) for granting third-party access.

4. **IoT stands for "the Internet of Things"**
   The Internet of Things (IoT) is a network that connects various devices, such as smart thermostats and industrial sensors, to the public internet. Controlling access to these devices securely is essential in order to prevent unwanted users from gaining access to them and causing problems in the real world. Strong authentication is required in order to safeguard not only the devices themselves but also the data that they produce.

5. **Safety from harm to the body**
   Controlling access is not something that is unique to digital contexts; rather, it is just as important in the real world. The usage of physical access control systems allows for the restriction of admission into buildings, rooms, or other locations based on the verification of an individual's identity. To do this, key cards, biometric scanners, and personal identification numbers (PINs) are frequently used.
6. **Banking and Financial Services in the Final Category**

The authentication and access control processes are given a high priority in the financial sector. It ensures the secrecy and integrity of financial transactions by implementing numerous levels of security, some of which include biometrics, one-time passwords, and transaction verification.

VIII. Emerging Obstacles and Prospective Developments

1. **The Changing Nature of the Threat Landscape**
   The threat landscape, which includes access control and authentication, is always shifting and changing. Attackers are always looking for new ways to compromise user identities and access controls, which is contributing to the proliferation of increasingly complex cyberattacks. Organizations have a responsibility to maintain vigilance and be flexible in response to new risks.
2. **Authentication on a Continuous Basis**
   The practice of continuously monitoring and verifying a user's identification while they are actively making use of a resource is referred to as the trend of continuous authentication. This strategy provides an additional layer of protection because it is able to identify suspicious behavior or unauthorized access even after the user has successfully logged in.
3. **Authentication Without the Need for a Password**
   As an alternative to the more conventional practice of using a

login and password combination, passwordless authentication is quickly rising in favor. Users no longer have to rely on remembering their passwords, which are typically a security vulnerability, thanks to authentication methods such as biometrics, mobile device authentication, and cryptographic keys.

4. **AI and ML stand for "artificial intelligence" and "machine learning," respectively.**

   The use of AI and ML to improve authentication and access control is becoming increasingly common. These systems are able to examine user activity, device attributes, and network patterns in order to identify irregularities and uncover unwanted access. In addition to this, they contribute to the development of better biometric recognition systems.

5. **Identity that is not centralized**

   Users are supposed to have greater control over their personal data and identities when they adopt decentralized identification solutions. Users are able to manage their digital identities across several services, supplying only the information that is required for each contact in order to maintain their privacy and maintain a secure environment.

6. **Security Based on Zero Trust**

The Zero Trust security architecture operates under the presumption that danger can come from both inside and outside of the network. No matter where the users, devices, or resources are located, they are all subject to stringent identity verification and constant monitoring as a need.

Controlling who can access data and verifying their identities are the cornerstones of information security in a digital environment. They make certain that only authorized users are able to access resources, thereby protecting sensitive data, individuals' privacy, and the integrity of the system. The ideas and strategies that are discussed in this article reflect the breadth as well as the depth of these essential safety precautions.

Access control and authentication will continue to face new issues as the landscape of available technologies continues to shift, and new problems will require new approaches.

In this ever-evolving digital world, both organizations and individuals need to maintain a heightened state of vigilance and be open to adopting new technologies and best practices in order to safeguard their information and assets. As we learn to adapt to a threat landscape that is constantly shifting, the future of access control and authentication promises to be both inventive and safe. Examples of this include the use of biometrics and decentralized identities.

5.1 User Authentication Methods

Methods of user authentication are required for confirming the identities of users seeking access to a variety of systems, applications, or data. These methods are vital. These solutions offer essential security protections to guarantee that only authorized users can gain access, protecting critical information and resources in the process.

Users validate their identities by supplying a one-of-a-kind string of letters or phrases as part of the password-based authentication process, which is one of the user authentication methods that is utilized the most frequently. Even though it is frequently used, this approach can have its security breached if the passwords are either inadequate, leaked, or in some other way hacked.

Two-factor authentication, often known as 2FA, is another approach that is commonly used. This method provides an additional layer of protection by forcing users to present two distinct forms of identity. Combining something that the user knows (like a password) with something that the user possesses (like a smartphone or token) is the conventional method for accomplishing this.

Biometric authentication, which makes use of one's fingerprints, face recognition, or iris scans, among other distinctive physical or behavioral characteristics, is becoming increasingly popular due to the high level of security it provides as well as the simplicity it affords. Despite this, concerns over privacy and the likelihood of breaches in biometric data continue to exist.

In addition, smart cards and tokens, which users are required to physically carry, are employed for authentication reasons. These kinds of cards and tokens are often utilized in high-security situations, which place a significant emphasis on the control of physical access. Public key infrastructure, also known as PKI, is an additional advanced authentication mechanism that allows users to safely access a variety of digital services and information by utilizing cryptographic keys and digital certificates.

It is highly likely that user authentication methods will continue to develop alongside the progression of technology, eventually embracing forward-thinking solutions such as passwordless authentication, continuous authentication, and decentralized identity management systems. With these improvements, the focus will continue to be on striking the correct balance between ease and solid security in order to fulfill the expectations of a digital world that is becoming increasingly linked.

5.2 Role-Based Access Control

Within the field of information security, the paradigm of access control known as Role-Based Access Control, or RBAC, is one that is commonly used. It provides a method that is both organized and methodical for managing user access throughout an organization's many systems and applications. RBAC helps to simplify access management, improves security, and guarantees that users have the right amount of access based on the job duties and responsibilities they are responsible for. This is accomplished by structuring permissions around roles. This extensive essay dives into the fundamental ideas of RBAC, as well as its various components, benefits, and applications in the real world.

1. **The Foundational Concepts Behind Role-Based Access Control**

1. **An Approach Centered on Roles**
   RBAC is based on the fundamental premise that permits should be organized in accordance with roles rather than individual individuals. Within an organization, job functions, responsibilities, and tasks are used to establish roles. These roles are then assigned to employees. This method to access management is role-centric, which streamlines the process by grouping individuals with comparable access requirements together.
2. **The Position of Least Privilege**
   The principle of least privilege is followed by RBAC, which ensures that users are only permitted the bare minimal amount of access necessary for them to efficiently carry out the duties assigned to them in their jobs. This reduces the potential for damage that could be caused by compromised accounts and lowers the risk associated with having users with excessive privileges.
3. **The Assigning of Roles**
   RBAC replaces the concept of individually granted permissions with the assignment of roles to users. When a user is given a certain position, they automatically take on the permissions and responsibilities that are connected to that role. This makes it much easier to manage users, as changes to role assignments can now have an effect on several users at the same time.
4. **Separation of Duties (SoD) comes in at number three.**

RBAC contains the notion of Separation of Duties, which ensures that crucial responsibilities or permissions are not centralized in a single function. This is accomplished by preventing the accumulation of privileges. This is a precautionary safety measure that will avoid potential conflicts of interest and lessen the likelihood of insider attacks.

II. The Individual Elements That Comprise Role-Based Access Control

1. **Positions**

    The RBAC model is built on the foundation of roles. They are collections of permissions that are pertinent to particular job tasks within an organization, and they represent such collections. Some examples of roles include "HR Manager," "Financial Analyst," and "System Administrator."

2. **The Authorizations**

    The specific actions that a user is authorized to carry out within a system or application are outlined by its permissions. For instance, permissions may include actions such as "read," "write," "delete," or any other operation that is pertinent to the system. Roles are linked to their related permissions.

3. **Customers**

    Individuals who are given a role or many responsibilities within the RBAC system are referred to as users. Users obtain access to permissions as a result of the roles that have been assigned to them.

4. **The Hierarchy of Roles**

Certain RBAC implementations include role hierarchies, which enable lower-level jobs to pass along their permissions to more senior roles. This eliminates or greatly reduces the need for explicit role-to-permission allocations, which in turn makes access control administration much easier to handle.

III. The Numerous Advantages of Utilizing Role-Based Access Control

1. **Heightened Safety and Protection**

    RBAC encourages a preventative method of securing data by limiting user access to only those resources that are relevant to the functions they play within an organization. Users are unable to access data or systems beyond the scope of their responsibilities, which reduces the potential damage that could be caused by security breaches or threats from within an organization.

2. **Access Management That Is Easier to Use**

   The RBAC framework simplifies access management since it organizes permissions based on roles. Administrators are free to concentrate on the task of giving roles to users rather than managing users' individual permissions. It is possible to amend an employee's access by modifying their role assignments if there is a change in the employee's role.

3. **Observance of Regulations and Personal Responsibility**

   RBAC software will frequently keep a comprehensive record of all role assignments as well as access activity. This makes auditing easier and assures compliance with the restrictions imposed by regulatory agencies. In the event that there is a breach in security, businesses that utilize role-based access control are able to monitor and investigate the activities of their users.

4. **Scalability**

RBAC is capable of efficiently scaling along with the growth and change of organizations. Role-based access control can accept changes in roles or job functions without requiring a major increase in administrative overhead, and new employees can be given roles that enable the required access.

IV. Role-Based Access Control's Practical Applications in the Real World

1. **Environments Within Corporations**

   RBAC is frequently used in commercial environments, where it is put to use to manage access to a broad variety of resources such file systems, databases, email servers, and business applications. Access rights can be defined for certain job responsibilities by assigning users specific roles, such as "HR Manager," "Sales Representative," and "Marketing Specialist."

2. **Healthcare & Medical**

   When it comes to the healthcare industry, where data privacy and regulatory compliance are of the utmost importance, RBAC guarantees that medical professionals, administrative personnel, and healthcare providers have appropriate access to electronic health records (EHRs) and patient data. Controlling access is essential to ensuring that the confidentiality of patient information is preserved and that requirements such as the Health Insurance Portability and Accountability Act (HIPAA) are adhered to.

3. **Services Financiers et Monétaires**

   RBAC is used extensively within the financial services industry as a means of controlling access to sensitive financial data and information pertaining to customers.
   Permissions for roles such as "Loan Officer," "Financial Analyst," and "Branch Manager" are defined to correspond with certain job activities while still preserving data security and adhering to applicable financial requirements.

4. **The Government and the Armed Forces**

   RBAC is used by government agencies and military groups to manage access to secure locations, vital infrastructure, and classified information. In order to create a stringent security clearance structure, role hierarchies are frequently utilized. This helps to ensure that personnel may only access data and systems that are appropriate for their authorized security level.

5. **Cloud Computing Services**

RBAC models are implemented by cloud service providers so that enterprises may govern access to cloud resources such as virtual machines, storage, and cloud-based apps. In order to ensure that users and groups have the appropriate levels of access control, administrators provide users and groups specific roles and permissions.

V. Obstacles and Things to Take Into Account

1. **The Proliferation of Roles**
   The proliferation of roles in complex organizations can be caused by the introduction of a large number of roles, which in turn makes access management more difficult. In the process of designing roles, it is vital to find a happy medium between granularity and simplicity.
2. **Changing Conditions of the Environment**
   The fact that RBAC is static can be problematic in settings that experience fast environmental change. To ensure that roles and permissions continue to meet the requirements of the business even as job functions undergo change, they need to be evaluated and updated on a regular basis.
3. **Implementation of a Role-Based Access Control System**
   Planning thoroughly and establishing reliable access management solutions are necessities for a successful RBAC implementation. It is imperative that businesses think about integrating RBAC with a variety of applications and systems, providing their users with training, and conducting periodic audits.
4. **Control of Access for Entities Other Than Humans**

RBAC was conceived largely with human users in mind. It is possible that other access control models will be required in order to extend role-based access control to non-human entities such as software applications, gadgets, or bots.

VI. Upcoming Developments in the Role-Based Access Control System

Innovations in RBAC are being driven by both the progression of technology and concerns regarding security.

1. **Access Control Based on Attributes (also known as ABAC)**
   ABAC is an extension of RBAC that takes into account a wider variety of variables when making decisions on access control. These attributes include user traits, resource qualities, and

environmental factors. ABAC allows for more dynamic modifications to be made in response to shifting situations and provides access control that is more fine-grained and aware of context.

2. **Authorization Based on Dynamic Logic**
An variation of RBAC known as dynamic authorization enables real-time access control choices to be made on the basis of contextual data and user attributes. This trend is congruent with the requirement for dynamic environments to have adaptive security in the modern day.

3. **Integration with Existing Identity Management Systems**
Integration of RBAC into identity management systems is becoming more common as a means of streamlining the procedures of user onboarding and offboarding as well as authentication. Through integration of these systems, user lifecycle management can be improved while access control is preserved.

4. **RBAC that is hosted in the cloud**

RBAC (Role-Based Access Control) solutions are being made available as a service by cloud providers as more and more businesses migrate to cloud environments. This change enables companies to manage access to cloud resources in a manner that is more scalable and flexible when utilizing RBAC than was previously possible.

5.3 Implementing Multi-Factor Authentication

Implementing Multi-Factor Authentication, also known as MFA, is an essential step toward improving the safety of digital systems and preventing unwanted access to sensitive data. By requiring users to give various forms of identity before giving access to a system, application, or data, multi-factor authentication (MFA) provides an additional layer of security.

Organizations should adhere to a number of critical measures in order to successfully adopt MFA. First, they have to choose the suitable authentication factors that are in line with their needs for user ease and the level of security they require. Passwords, biometrics, hardware tokens, codes generated via SMS, and mobile authentication apps are all examples of common factors.

The next step for companies is to ensure that multi-factor authentication is integrated smoothly into their existing authentication procedures. In most cases, this requires making use of identity and access management (IAM) solutions that provide multi-factor authentication (MFA) capabilities. This integration ensures that multi-factor authentication is applied uniformly across all systems and apps that are pertinent.

In addition, enterprises should make user education and awareness a priority in order to enable a smooth transition to multi-factor authentication (MFA). Providing users with training on how to make efficient use of multi-factor authentication (MFA) and explaining the significance of this additional security feature will help reduce any resistance or confusion that may arise throughout the deployment process.

Additionally, it is essential to perform routine monitoring and testing of the MFA system in order to locate any potential vulnerabilities or weaknesses. The effectiveness of multi-factor authentication (MFA) should be evaluated on a regular basis so that companies may proactively remedy any security holes and improve their overall security posture.

5.4 Access Control in Scientific Research Environments

Controlling access in environments used for scientific research is extremely important for a number of reasons, including the protection of sensitive data, the upkeep of the experiments' integrity, and the fulfillment of legal obligations. Due to the fact that doing scientific research frequently requires the management of sensitive information, intellectual property, and classified data, effective access control mechanisms are required. This essay explores the significance of access control in scientific research environments, including its problems, best practices, and best practices overall, as well as its applicability in the actual world.

1. **The Importance of Permitting Only Authorized Individuals to Participate in Scientific Research**

1. **Privacy and Security Measures**
   Controlling who has access to the study data is absolutely necessary in order to prevent illegal access, alteration, or theft of the data. Integrity of data is of the utmost importance in scientific research since it helps to assure the validity and reliability of experimental results and analysis.
   The implementation of adequate access controls prevents unauthorized personnel from manipulating sensitive data or making inappropriate use of it.
2. **Protection of the Owner's Intellectual Property**
   The application of scientific research frequently results in the creation of novel technologies, goods, and procedures. By limiting who can see sensitive research findings, proprietary information, and commercial secrets, access control mechanisms protect intellectual property. This protection is absolutely necessary in order to preserve a competitive advantage and guarantee the economic viability of the results of research.
3. **Observance of All Regulations**

Particularly in industries like pharmaceuticals, biotechnology, and environmental science, the surroundings in which scientific research takes place are subject to a wide variety of regulatory standards and compliance requirements. Access control helps to reduce the likelihood of incurring legal liabilities and penalties by ensuring compliance with data protection rules, ethical norms, and industry-specific requirements.

II. Obstacles Encountered When Attempting to Establish Access Control in Scientific Research

1. **Complexity of the Requirements for Data Sharing**
   The conduct of scientific research frequently calls for cooperative efforts on the part of a number of researchers, institutions, and other stakeholders. It can be difficult to strike a balance between the requirements for data sharing and cooperation and the

necessity for tight access controls. It is absolutely necessary to put in place access restrictions that enable the sharing of confidential information in a secure manner without compromising that confidentiality.

2. **The Validation and Integrity of the Data**

   Strict access controls are required in order to protect the integrity of the data and guarantee the validity of the results of the research.

   To maintain the credibility and reliability of the results of scientific research, it is essential to exclude the possibility of illegal data changes or tampering at all stages of the research process, including data collection, analysis, and publication.

3. **Incorporation of Instruments and Tools Utilized in Research**

Integration with a variety of research instruments, equipment, and laboratory management software is an essential requirement for access control systems. Problems with compatibility and limitations imposed by technology might make it difficult to develop effective access restrictions, which presents a problem for researchers and administrators.

III. Recommendations for Access Control Procedures in Environments Appropriate for Scientific Research

1. **The Role-Based Access Control (also known as RBAC) system**

   Researchers, laboratory technicians, and administrative staff can all have access to data and resources based on their predefined roles and responsibilities thanks to the implementation of RBAC. This guarantees that each user has the appropriate access rights to accomplish the duties that have been assigned to them while still ensuring the integrity and security of the data.

2. **The Encryption of Data and the Storage of Secure Data**

   The protection of research data against unwanted access, interception, or data breaches is aided by the utilization of powerful encryption methods for sensitive data and the implementation

of secure data storage mechanisms. A complete access control strategy should always include encrypted storage systems and secure data transmission protocols as two of its most important components.
3. **Ongoing Compliance and Security Audits at Regular Intervals**

The maintenance of access control measures that are both effective and in accordance with regulatory requirements requires routine security audits and compliance checks to be carried out. In order to maintain a high level of data protection and research integrity, periodic evaluations are helpful in identifying vulnerabilities, addressing any security gaps, and addressing potential vulnerabilities.

IV. Applications of Access Control in the Real World in the Field of Scientific Research

1. **Research in the Field of Biomedicine**
   Controlling who has access to sensitive patient data, clinical trial results, and genetic information is absolutely necessary in the context of scientific research, because this data must be safeguarded. Only authorized individuals will be able to access and evaluate sensitive medical data if stringent access restrictions are put into place to achieve this.
2. **Research and Experimentation Conducted in Laboratories**
   Access control is a method used in laboratories to govern who can enter different areas of the facility, including research equipment and experimental data. Organizations are able to safeguard the integrity of experimental processes and results by implementing access controls on laboratory doors, data storage facilities, and research instruments. These controls prevent illegal access and ensure the security of stored data.
3. **Research on the Environment and the Accumulation of Data**
   The collecting of sensitive ecological data is a common component

of environmental research and includes things like climatic monitoring, studies of biodiversity, and evaluations of the influence of human activities on the environment. Controlling who has access to sensitive environmental data helps to ensure that only authorized researchers and field workers are able to access and examine that data. This helps to prevent unauthorized changes or the inappropriate use of scientific findings.

4. **Institutions of Higher Education and Research**

Access control mechanisms are utilized in academic research institutes with the purpose of safeguarding intellectual property, research grants, and secret research data. Universities and other research organizations can protect significant research outputs and keep a competitive edge in the academic community by putting in place role-based access controls and secure data storage systems.

V. **Emerging Patterns and Prospects for Access Control in Scientific Research**

1. **The Use of Blockchain Technology to Ensure the Integrity of Data**
   The application of blockchain technology in settings designed for scientific study has the potential to improve both the integrity and the security of data. The immutability and traceability of research data can be ensured by using access control systems that are based on blockchain technology. These systems offer tamper-proof data storage, secure data sharing, and visible audit trails.
2. **Systems for Controlling Access Based on Biometrics**
   In the context of scientific research, the incorporation of biometric access control technologies, such as fingerprint recognition and iris scanning, provides an additional layer of protection. Access control is improved with biometric authentication because it provides a more secure and trustworthy method of user

identification. This in turn reduces the likelihood of illegal access or data breaches occurring.

3. **Solutions for access control driven by artificial intelligence**

Access control solutions that are powered by AI are able to conduct user behavior analysis, discover anomalies, and proactively identify potential security issues in scientific research contexts. AI-driven access control systems can provide real-time threat detection and adaptive security measures to secure research data and resources by employing machine learning algorithms and data analytics. This enables the systems to provide a higher level of protection.

Chapter 6

Secure Data Processing and Analysis

In this day and age of digital technology, data has evolved into a highly prized commodity. It provides the energy necessary for decision-making, propels innovation, and serves as the foundation for many elements of our day-to-day lives, including healthcare, finance, transportation, and entertainment. Having said that, this extensive reliance on data does bring with it a significant risk, and that concern is data security. The importance of securing this information cannot be overstated in light of the increasing number of data that is being generated, processed, and evaluated. Processing and analyzing data in a secure manner is a multifaceted problem that necessitates a method with a similar breadth of scope. This essay digs deep into the complexities of this industry, examining its significance, fundamentals, and best practices, as well as upcoming technological developments.

The Importance of Keeping Processing and Analysis of Data Private and Secure

Security of Private and Confidential Information

A large number of datasets contain sensitive and secret information, including personal identity details, financial records, and proprietary corporate data. It is possible that if this information were to get into the wrong hands, terrible results would follow. The processing of this sensitive data in a secure manner assures that it will continue to be kept confidential and safe.

Compliance with Regulations

Strict data security measures are mandated by a number of rules and laws, including the General Data Protection Regulation (GDPR) in the European Union and the Health Insurance Portability and Accountability Act (HIPAA) in the United States. It is possible to incur significant penalties and face other legal repercussions if you do not comply with these requirements. Processing personal information in a safe and secure manner is necessary in order to fulfill these legal duties.

Both Trust and Reputation Are Vital

Customers and users are required to have faith in the companies that handle their data.

A breach of an organization's data security can cause irreparable harm to its reputation and erode faith in the company. Processing and analysis of client data in a secure environment are an absolute necessity for retaining customer confidence.

Integrity of the Data

The correctness and completeness of the data being processed are prerequisites for successful data analysis. Secure data processing helps to ensure that the data are not altered in any way, which in turn helps to ensure that the findings of analysis are accurate.

Advantage in the Competition

A significant competitive advantage can be gained by companies that perform very well in the areas of secure data processing and analysis. They are able to reassure their customers that the confidentiality of their data is maintained, which may result in an increase in the number of customers and business partners.

Principles Governing the Safe and Secure Processing and Analysis of Data

The Encryption of Data

The process of transforming data into a code in order to prevent unauthorized access is referred to as data encryption. It is a fundamental method for protecting data both while it is being transferred and when it is being stored. The protection of sensitive information relies heavily on cryptographic protocols like the Advanced Encryption Standard (AES), among others.

Management of Access

Data access can be restricted through the use of access control methods, which take into account user roles and permissions. Sensitive information should be accessible to no one but those specifically authorized to view it. Authentication of users, role-based access control (RBAC), and various other authorization mechanisms are all viable methods for accomplishing this goal.

Reduced amount of data

A fundamental tenet of data security is that just the bare minimum of data that is required for analysis should be gathered and stored. The less data that is kept, the less likely it is that there will be a security breach. It is important to eliminate unnecessary data as soon as possible.

The process of anonymizing data

The removal of personally identifiable information (PII) from datasets is the process referred to as anonymization. It enables enterprises to conduct data analysis while also protecting the privacy of individuals. In order to accomplish this goal, methods like as tokenization and pseudonymization are utilized.

Safe and Sound Transfer of Data

The exchange of data between different systems and across networks occurs often. Protocols for the secure transport of data, such as HTTPS and SSH, guarantee that data will keep its confidentiality even while in transit. Virtual Private Networks, sometimes known as VPNs, are frequently utilized to establish encrypted lines of communication.

Auditing and monitoring on a regular basis

It is vital to do ongoing monitoring and auditing of the workflows used for data processing and analysis. Real-time monitoring makes it possible to identify potentially malicious behaviors or security breaches, enabling prompt corrective action.

Management of the Data Lifecycle

It is necessary to manage data over its entire lifecycle, beginning with its generation and continuing through its storage and eventual erasure. It is vital to implement policies for the retention of data and to dispose of data in a secure manner once it is no longer required.

Methods of Securing the Processing and Analysis of Data Best Practices

Combining industry-recognized best practices with the use of cutting-edge technologies is required to guarantee the confidentiality of data processing and analysis.

Classification of the Data

Start off by separating the data into categories according to how important and sensitive they are. This helps prioritize security measures, ensuring that the most important data receives the best level of protection possible, and it also helps keep track of which actions have been taken.

The Encryption of Data

Use encryption for data both while it is stored and while it is in transit. Put in place robust encryption techniques, ensure that encryption keys are kept up to date, and remain vigilant regarding security flaws.

Safe Places to Store Information

Make use of safe storage options, such as encrypted file and database management systems. Back up your data on a regular basis to protect it from being lost in the event that your security is compromised.

Controls For Gaining Entry

Install reliable techniques for access control, such as authentication, role-based access control (RBAC), and multifactor authentication (MFA). Check to see that each user has the bare minimum amount of access necessary for their position.

Patch Management on a Regular Basis

Maintaining an up-to-date software and system with the latest security updates is essential.

Software flaws can be exploited by bad actors, which is why applying patches as soon as possible is absolutely essential.

Instruction for Workers

Provide employees and members of a team with training on the best practices for data security. Education can help reduce the likelihood of breaches occurring due to human error, which is a common source of data loss.

Plan for Dealing with Emergencies

Create a detailed incident response strategy that specifies how you proceed in the event of a data breach or other security incident. A prompt and efficient response can lessen the amount of damage and cut down on downtime.

Backups of one's data

Data should be backed up on a regular basis and the process of restoring it should be tested to verify that data can be accessed in the event that security is breached or data is lost.

Evaluation of the Safety of the Vendors

If the processing of data involves third-party providers, you should investigate their data protection procedures. Make sure that the level of data security that they use is on par with that used by your firm.

Examination of the Safety

It is important to perform security testing on a regular basis, which should include vulnerability assessments and penetration testing, in order to locate and address any vulnerabilities in the data processing and analysis infrastructure.

New technologies for the processing and analysis of confidential data

Encryption Using Homomorphic Functions

Homomorphic encryption makes it possible for data to be encrypted while the processing of the data continues. This technology makes it possible to do secure data analysis on encrypted data, thereby protecting users' privacy and keeping personal information secret.

Differentiated Confidentiality

The process of adding noise or randomness to data is known as differential privacy. This helps to safeguard the privacy of individuals while the data is being analyzed. It offers a method that is rigorous in terms of mathematics for quantifying and controlling the privacy assurances provided by a system.

Chain of blocks

The ledger used to store data can be decentralized and is incorruptible thanks to blockchain technology. For the sake of securing data and preventing tampering, it is utilized in applications such as management of supply chains and healthcare.

The Secure Multi-Party Computation, or SMPC, protocol.

The use of SMPC makes it possible for many parties to jointly compute a function over their inputs while maintaining the confidentiality of those inputs. This technology makes it possible to conduct safe collaborative data analysis without disclosing the data that is being analyzed.

Architecture based on zero trust

The Zero Trust security model operates under the presumption that no person or entity, be they internal or external to an organization, can be trusted by default. In order to prevent unauthorized access to the data, it uses continuous authentication and access controls.

Using Artificial Intelligence and Machine Learning to Spot Anomalies

A growing number of organizations are turning to artificial intelligence and machine learning in order to spot anomalies. These technologies have the ability to recognize anomalous patterns and behaviors, which can serve as an early warning sign of a security breach.

Safe for Quantum Computing Encryption

The development of quantum computing poses an increasingly serious challenge to the security of today's encryption protocols.

Encryption algorithms that are resistant to quantum attacks are now in the process of being developed.

Safe and sound enclaves

In order to provide an isolated environment for the processing of sensitive data, hardware-based secure enclaves like Intel's SGX are utilized. They provide a high level of defense against access by unauthorized parties.

Concerns and Things to Take Into Account

Striking a Balance Between Usability and Security

It might be difficult to find a happy medium between the need for data protection and the need to make data easily accessible. There are times when stringent security measures might hinder productivity and the overall user experience.

Worries Regarding Privacy

The legislation governing privacy are getting tougher, and individuals are becoming more aware of the rights they have regarding the privacy of their data. While organizations are collecting and analyzing data, they are required to negotiate these concerns.

Shifting Nature of Dangerous Situations

The dangers posed by cyberattacks are constantly adapting. In order to protect themselves from new and developing dangers, organizations need to modify the security mechanisms they have in place.

The Amount of Data and How Fast It Moves

The sheer volume and velocity of data being generated in today's world might make it difficult to safeguard information and process it in an effective manner. For the purpose of managing these data flows, scalable solutions are required.

Regulations on Data Transfers Across Borders

Companies with a global presence are required to manage the intricate web of data protection rules that exist in many nations. It can be a challenging endeavor to successfully comply with these requirements while still collecting and analyzing data in a secure manner.

Traditional Methods and Equipment

There are still many companies that rely on outdated computer systems and software, which may not be as secure as more current alternatives. The process of migrating to platforms with increased security can be time-consuming and expensive.

In this day and age, the processing and analysis of data in a safe environment are of the utmost importance. The enormous volume of data that is generated and processed each day brings with it a host of opportunities as well as hazards. When data security is a top priority for an organization, not only are they protecting themselves from potential harm, but they also gain a competitive advantage by earning the trust of their customers and partners.

Organizations are able to improve their data security posture by adhering to concepts such as data encryption, access control, and data minimization, as well as by following best practices such as frequent patch management and employee training. In addition, they are able to keep ahead of the curve in the rapidly developing field of data security by making use of developing technologies such as homomorphic encryption, blockchain, and secure enclaves.

In spite of the difficulties and factors to be considered in secure data processing and analysis, the ongoing development of technologies and practices in this field ensures that businesses can proactively protect their data assets and embrace the enormous potential that data offers in a world that is driven by data.

6.1 Data Anonymization and Pseudonymization

In this day and age of big data, protecting people's privacy and the confidentiality of sensitive information has evolved into an extremely important problem. The protection of people' right to privacy in conjunction with the maintenance of the data's utility for analysis poses a substantial issue for the organizations that are currently collecting and analyzing enormous volumes of data. Anonymization of data and pseudonymization of data are two significant strategies that might be used to address this difficulty. While at the same time enabling companies to leverage the power of data for a variety of analytical objectives, these approaches play an essential part in the protection of sensitive information. This article investigates the ideas of data anonymization and pseudonymization, going into their definitions as well as their methodology, as well as the benefits and difficulties associated with using these practices.

Acquiring Knowledge about Data Anonymization

The process of changing or eliminating personally identifying information (PII) from datasets is known as data anonymization. This makes it so that it is no longer feasible to correlate data with particular individuals. Anonymizing data serves multiple purposes, the most important of which is to safeguard the privacy of individuals while maintaining the data's value for the purposes of investigation and study. Data anonymization helps to ensure that the identities of individuals are never revealed, hence reducing the likelihood of inappropriate disclosure or use of the information.

Various approaches to the anonymization of data

To speak in broad strokes:

The act of substituting specific values with values that are either more general or less precise is known as generalization. For example, using age ranges instead of specific ages (such as 25-30 years) or substituting specific locations with broader geographical areas (such as a state or country) rather than using exact ages.

The practice of repressing:

Suppression involves completely eliminating certain data components from the dataset in their entirety. Using this procedure, sensitive information is removed, and it is ensured that it cannot be connected to any individual that is included in the dataset.

To cause turbulence in:

The process of injecting noise at random or significantly modifying the values of data points is called "perturbation," and it is done to prevent individuals from being identified. This approach safeguards the personal information of individuals without compromising the statistical features of the data.

Covering Up Data:

The process of masking data entails substituting the original data with data that is accurate but fictional. This method protects sensitive data from being seen by unauthorized parties while preserving the material's overarching structure and file format in its entirety.

Anonymization of Data Has Its Benefits

Protection of Personal Information

Data that has been anonymized helps safeguard the privacy of individuals by prohibiting the identification of particular people from within datasets. This is absolutely necessary in order to maintain ethical data handling practices and conform to the legislation governing data protection.

Maintaining Conformity with Regulations:

The General Data Protection Regulation (GDPR) in the European Union and the Health Insurance Portability and Accountability Act (HIPAA) in the United States are two examples of data protection standards that can be complied with by companies thanks to anonymization. The protection of personally identifiable information is required by these standards, and there are severe consequences for failing to comply with them.

Sharing of Information and Working Together:

Sharing data that has been anonymized with third parties allows for increased opportunities for collaboration and study while simultaneously maintaining the privacy of individuals' information. This supports data-driven innovation as well as the sharing of information across a variety of different fields.

Risk Reduction Strategies:

Anonymizing data allows enterprises to reduce the risk of data breaches and illegal access, protecting them from the possibility for adverse legal and reputational repercussions.

The Handling of Ethical Data:

Adopting data anonymization methods is a great way for businesses to demonstrate their commitment to ethical data handling and responsible data stewardship, which in turn helps to build confidence among their customers and other stakeholders.

Acquiring Knowledge of Pseudonymization

The process of substituting or encrypting identifying data with fictitious identifiers, sometimes known as pseudonyms, is an example of the data de-identification technique known as pseudonymization. Pseudonymization, in contrast to anonymization, enables data to be re-identified through the use of supplementary information that is stored in a separate location. This gives authorized parties the ability to re-associate the pseudonyms with the original data.

This method achieves a compromise between the usefulness of data and the protection of individuals' privacy. As a result, it enables businesses to undertake studies while simultaneously protecting the anonymity of individuals.

Pseudonymization Strategies and Methodologies

Code breaking:

Pseudonymization relies heavily on encrypted data as its primary protection mechanism. Utilizing cryptographic techniques, the process involves converting the data into a format that is unreadable. It is only possible to restore the data to its original form for authorized persons that have access to the decryption keys.

Tokenization refers to:

Tokenization refers to the process of replacing sensitive data with tokens that are not sensitive. These tokens are created at random and have no inherent value; as a result, it is difficult for third parties that are not allowed to access the data to relate them back to the source.

To hash out:

The process of transforming data into values of a set length using hash functions is called hashing. The hashing procedure is irreversible, but it does make it possible to compare data without disclosing the values that were used in the beginning.

Pseudonymization offers a number of advantages.

Utilization of Data:

With the use of pseudonymization, businesses are able to preserve the usefulness of data for purposes such as analysis and research while also protecting the privacy of individuals. The data can still be used for a variety of different analytical functions by authorized parties.

Ability to Perform Re-Identification:

It is possible for authorized parties that have access to the proper keys or information to re-identify the data. This provides the authorized parties with the ability to execute specialized studies or securely link the data to external datasets.

Compliance with Regulations:

Pseudonymization is a technique that helps organizations comply with data protection rules by putting in place the necessary technical and organizational safeguards to protect the privacy of individuals' personal information.

Safe Exchange of Information:

Data that has been pseudonymized can be safely shared with third parties for the purposes of conducting research or working collaboratively. This enables data sharing to take place while protecting the privacy and confidentiality of individuals' information.

Reducing the Danger:

Organizations can limit the risk of data breaches and unauthorized access by employing pseudonymization, which in turn minimizes the potential impact of security incidents on both individuals and the business itself.

Concerns and Things to Take Into Account

Risks Involved in the Re-Identification of Data

In spite of the efforts that have been put into pseudonymization, there is always a possibility of re-identification, especially if further data or additional contextual information becomes available. It is necessary for organizations to conduct risk assessments and manage it appropriately.

Loss of Data:

Anonymization and pseudonymization procedures that are not carried out correctly can result in the loss of important data utility, which in turn reduces the efficiency of analyses and research.

Linking of Complicated Data:

The process of linking pseudonymized data with external datasets can be difficult and time-consuming in certain circumstances, necessitating the utilization of sophisticated data management and integration strategies.

Prerequisites in Terms of Technology:

Implementing successful approaches for data anonymization and pseudonymization frequently involves significant technological infrastructure and knowledge. This can be challenging for smaller businesses or those with limited resources because it requires a higher level of investment.

Compliance with Regulations:

Keeping up with ever-changing data protection standards and ensuring that an organization is in compliance with its many different legal obligations may be a difficult and time-consuming task for organizations.

The Quality and Integrity of the Data:

The methods of data anonymization and pseudonymization might potentially have an impact on the quality and integrity of the data, which can therefore lead to inaccuracies in the analyses and the results of the research if they are not implemented appropriately.

Anonymization and pseudonymization of data are essential methods for striking a balance between the utility of data and the protection of individuals' privacy. These methods allow enterprises to maintain the privacy of individuals and comply with severe data protection rules while simultaneously unlocking the value of data for analysis and research. enterprises are able to develop a solid framework for responsible data handling and strengthen confidence with customers, partners, and stakeholders if they use robust anonymization and pseudonymization procedures and handle the associated problems and considerations.

This allows enterprises to protect sensitive data while maintaining user privacy. Because data will continue to play a critical part in driving innovation and decision-making, the ethical and responsible use of data anonymization and pseudonymization will continue to be necessary for a digital world that is both secure and sensitive to privacy concerns.

6.2 Secure Computation and Cloud Computing

Cloud computing has completely altered the manner in which businesses manage their data and their information technology infrastructure. It delivers a level of scalability, versatility, and cost-efficiency that has never been seen before. On the other hand, because individuals and companies are entrusting the cloud with an increasing amount of sensitive data, concerns over cloud security have become more prevalent. It is vital to use secure computation, a subfield of cryptography, in order to alleviate these worries because it guarantees that data will stay confidential even when it is being processed in the cloud. This article examines the significance of secure computation in cloud computing, as well as its key principles, approaches, and challenges, as well as the opportunities and threats that lie ahead.

The Importance of Keeping Data Private and Secure When Using Cloud Computing

Privacy of Data: When data is handled in the cloud, it may be susceptible to illegal access, which can result in breaches of privacy and data leaks.

Data Confidentiality Confidential data, such as proprietary business information, trade secrets, or personal information, must be kept private at all times, even while they are being stored or processed in the cloud. Examples of such data include trade secrets, confidential business information, and personal information.

Integrity of Data: It is essential to take precautions to ensure that data does not become corrupted while being transmitted to and processed within the cloud. This is necessary in order to forestall any unauthorized or malicious changes.

This issue is addressed by secure computation, which makes it possible for data to be processed in the cloud without disclosing its contents to the cloud service provider or any other unauthorized parties. It provides a variety of cryptographic procedures that can protect data, which makes it an essential component of the ecosystem that underpins cloud computing.

Concepts Fundamental to a Secure Computation

1. **A Computation Method That Protects Individual Privacy:**
   A secure computer system must first and foremost protect users' privacy when processing data. It entails executing computations on data that has been encrypted without first decrypting the data. Because of this, the cloud service provider and any other intermediaries will never be able to access the data in their unencrypted form.

2. **Homomorphic Encryption:**
   The cryptographic method known as homomorphic encryption enables operations to be carried out on data that has been encrypted, resulting in the production of results that are also encrypted. This enables computations to be carried out in a secure manner, as the data continues to be protected even after being processed.

3. **Proofs Requiring No Prior Knowledge:**
   The term "zero-knowledge proofs" refers to a class of cryptographic protocols that enable one party to demonstrate to another party that they are aware of specified information without actually disclosing that information. When confirming specific data attributes, secure computation benefits from having this information.

4. **Computation with Multiple Parties:**

The term "multi-party computation" (often abbreviated as "MPC") refers to a framework that provides numerous parties with the ability to jointly compute a function over their inputs while maintaining the confidentiality of those inputs. It has a high degree of applicability in circumstances involving the collaborative processing of sensitive data.

Methods in the Field of Secure Computation

1. **Fully Homomorphic Encryption, also referred to as FHE:**
   The FHE encryption method is a sophisticated encryption algorithm that supports both addition and multiplication operations on data that has been encrypted. Even though it requires a lot of processing power, it opens the door to a broad variety of secure computations.
2. **Safe Multi-Party Computation (also known as MPC):**
   Through the use of MPC, many parties are able to jointly compute a function over their inputs without the need to expose those inputs themselves. This comes in especially handy when a number of different parties wish to examine their data jointly while yet maintaining their anonymity.
3. **Evaluation of Secure Functions (also known as SFE):**
   SFE makes it possible for one party to safely evaluate a function based on the input of another party without disclosing the information from the first party. It is typically applied in circumstances where one party wishes to safely outsource computing to another party.
4. **Circuits That Are Jumbled:**

The computation of functions can be made more secure with the help of garbled circuits, which disguise the circuit in such a way that the evaluator is able to carry out computations without needing to know the particulars of the circuit.

Concerns Regarding the Securing of Computation When Using the Cloud

1. **The burden of computational work:**
   The processing of data is slowed down by the computationally demanding nature of several solutions for providing safe computation. Finding a happy medium between performance and safety is an ongoing task.
2. **The Management of the Keys:**
   The safe management of encryption keys is a fundamental component of secure computation. The administration of keys is a complicated subject, and the system's integrity can be put at risk by even the smallest breach.
3. **Capacity for Use:**
   A secure computation typically requires the use of complicated cryptographic protocols, some of which may not be easy to understand. A big difficulty is to retain a high level of security while simultaneously simplifying the user experience.
4. **Capacity to Grow:**
   Implementing efficient protocols and infrastructure can be difficult, but doing so is necessary for scalable safe compute, which is necessary when dealing with huge datasets or complex tasks.
5. **Capability of Interoperability:**

The challenge of ensuring the compatibility and interoperability of various secure compute tools and platforms can be a barrier, which slows down the process of adopting them.

Prospects for the Future and Possible Applications

1. **Protecting Users' Privacy Through Machine Learning:**
   Protecting sensitive training data in machine learning models with the help of secure computing approaches is becoming more and more common. This makes it possible for organizations to work together and construct models without having to share raw data.

2. **The Sharing of Healthcare Information:**
   Safe computing makes it possible for healthcare practitioners to safely share patients' medical records with one another while protecting patients' right to confidentiality. This is especially important for the overall improvement of the quality of healthcare.
3. **Safe and Reliable Contracting of Computer Work:**
   It is possible for businesses to safely outsource processes that need a significant amount of processing power to the cloud while still protecting the privacy and security of their data.
4. **Banking and other Financial Services**
   In the financial industry, secure computation is valuable for ensuring the safe exchange of data and the conduct of analytics while adhering to stringent regulatory standards.
5. **Voting Methods That Are 100% Safe:**

The use of secure computation in voting systems can make it possible to vote securely from a distance while yet allowing individuals to maintain their privacy.

Within the world of cloud computing, secure computation is an essential enabler for maintaining the confidentiality and safety of data. The significance of utilizing methods of safe computation is becoming more and more apparent as businesses continue to use cloud computing and entrust sensitive data to the care of third-party service providers. The use of these cryptographic methods permits the processing of secret data while simultaneously assuring that the cloud provider and any other parties not allowed to access the data are unable to do so.

In spite of the difficulties that are connected with computing overhead, key management, and usability, secure computation offers a tremendous amount of potential for the future. This potential ranges from privacy-preserving machine learning to safe data sharing in healthcare and financial services. The field is likely to play a vital role in resolving the growing security problems in the digital age as it continues to evolve. This will enable enterprises to fully leverage the promise of cloud computing while also protecting sensitive information.

6.3 Ensuring Data Security in Data Analytics

Data analytics has evolved to the point that it is now an essential tool for businesses that want to gain actionable insights and make intelligent choices. However, as the amount of data and the types of data that can be collected continue to grow, guaranteeing data security in the field of data analytics has developed into a crucially important necessity. For the purpose of preventing unauthorized access, data breaches, and the inappropriate use of sensitive information, it is vital to protect data throughout the entirety of the analytics lifecycle, from collection to interpretation. This article digs into the most important techniques and best practices for maintaining effective data security in data analytics. It addresses the issues that exist and emphasizes how important it is to protect data in this day and age of increased access to insights.

Understanding the Importance of Data Security in Analyzing Data

Maintaining confidentiality requires taking measures to prevent sensitive information from falling into the wrong hands and ensuring that only authorized workers are able to access and examine the data.

Integrity: Maintaining data integrity during the analytics process ensures that the data will continue to be true and unaffected, hence protecting the analytical results' ability to be relied upon.

Availability: Ensuring that data is available ensures that authorized users may access the data whenever it is required, which promotes the efficiency of processes involving data analytics.

Data analytics must have key strategies in place to guarantee the privacy of the data

1. **The Encryption of Data:**
   It is possible to prevent unauthorized access to sensitive information by implementing encryption mechanisms for data both while it is at rest and while it is in transit. The use of robust

encryption algorithms in conjunction with safe key management is an essential part of this strategy.

2. **Regulation of Access:**
Only authorized workers should be able to access and manipulate data while the analytics process is being carried out. This can be ensured by implementing tight access controls, which may include role-based access and multi-factor authentication.

3. **Data Covering and Confidentialization:**
Protecting the privacy of individuals and preventing the exposure of personally identifiable information are two benefits that come from masking and anonymizing sensitive data prior to its analysis. This helps to lower the danger of data breaches.

4. **Safely Sharing Information:**
By utilizing safe data sharing techniques, such as encrypted communication channels and secure file transfer protocols, one may ensure that data is securely exchanged with authorized parties, hence reducing the likelihood of data being intercepted or accessed without authorization.

5. **Routine Inspections of the Security Measures:**
The implementation of timely security enhancements and solutions is made possible for businesses by conducting routine security audits and assessments, which help uncover vulnerabilities and weak points in the data analytics architecture.

6. **Instructional Programs and Occupational Awareness:**
A security-conscious culture can be fostered within an organization by providing staff with education on data security best practices and the potential dangers connected with data analytics. This can help reduce the possibility of security breaches within the business that are the result of human error.

7. **Safekeeping of Information:**

Data can be protected from illegal access or alteration by using secure data storage solutions, such as encrypted databases and secure cloud storage. This ensures that the data's integrity and confidentiality are maintained.

Data analytics presents a number of difficult challenges regarding the protection of data

The complexity of the data sources might make it difficult and time consuming to integrate and secure data coming from a variety of sources with varied levels of security needs.

Volume and Velocity of Data Handling massive amounts of data in real-time analytics can put a burden on an organization's existing security infrastructure and present issues in terms of ensuring that data is secured in a timely manner.

Data Quality and Integrity It is essential to ensure the quality of the data as well as its integrity throughout the entirety of the analytics process in order to get correct insights. A careful balance must be struck between preserving the quality of the data and putting in place security precautions.

Rapidly Changing Threat Landscape Because of the ever-changing nature of cybersecurity threats, businesses are required to always upgrade their security protocols in order to keep one step ahead of any potential vulnerabilities or hazards.

Compliance with Regulations The process of adhering to data security regulations and compliance standards, such as the General Data Protection Regulation (GDPR) and the Health Insurance Portability and Accountability Act (HIPAA), can be challenging for data analytics. Organizations have to ensure that their security measures are in line with the requirements set forth by regulators.

In the realm of data analytics, the protection of data is of the utmost importance, as it is the cornerstone of the confidence, dependability, and legitimacy of analytical findings.

During the process of analytics, firms are able to protect sensitive information and prevent illegal access, manipulation, or exposure of data if they use robust security techniques such as encryption, access limits, and frequent security audits. In spite of the challenges that are posed by the complex data landscape and the evolving cybersecurity threats, a proactive approach to data security in data analytics is crucial for businesses to harness the full potential of data-driven insights while maintaining the confidentiality, integrity, and availability of their data assets. This is the case even though the complex data landscape and the evolving cybersecurity threats pose challenges.

Chapter 7

Insider Threats and Social Engineering

Because of the tremendous value that data and information have in today's world, the protection of these assets has become an issue of the utmost importance for both individuals and businesses. Insider attacks and social engineering stand out as two of the most pernicious dangers to the integrity of a company's data because of the stealth with which they operate. This in-depth analysis goes deep into the complexities of both social engineering and insider threats, illuminating their definitions, underlying goals, common strategies, and the weaknesses they take advantage of. In addition, we will examine real-world instances and the junction of these dangers, talk about detection and preventive techniques, and ultimately, think about the future of insider threats and social engineering in a digital ecosystem that is constantly changing.

Comprehending the Dangers Posed by Insiders
Various Forms of Dangers Posed by Employees

Malicious insiders are people who actively abuse the access rights they have to the organization for the purpose of making personal benefit or causing the company harm. Theft of data, fraud, or even sabotage could be the result of their acts.

Insiders Who Are Negligent Although negligent insiders do not have the intention of causing harm, the acts or inactions they take can nonetheless result in a breach of security. Employees who accidentally divulge confidential information or who are duped by social engineering techniques fall into this category.

Compromised Insiders are those who work inside an organization and whose credentials or access permissions have been stolen by criminals from the outside. In order to penetrate networks and pose as legitimate users, attackers may utilize login credentials that have been stolen or coerced from other users.

The Reasons Behind the Danger Presented by Insiders

Gains in Financial Standing: The desire for personal gain motivates a significant number of dishonest insiders. They may steal confidential information, intellectual property, or trade secrets with the intention of selling them on the dark web or to competitors.

The desire for retribution can motivate disgruntled workers to engage in illegal activities such as sabotage or data theft in order to exact their punishment on their employer for what they perceive to be injustices committed by the company.

Beliefs in Ideology or Politics: Certain insiders' actions can be attributed to ideological or political causes. They may have the intention of advancing a specific cause, ideology, or group, frequently through the unauthorised exposure of data or the disruption of operations.

Negligent insiders may mistakenly release sensitive information owing to carelessness or a lack of understanding, even though they may not have any malevolent intent to do so. This is an example of opportunism.

Extortion or Blackmail: Compromised insiders could become the victims of extortion or blackmail, which would force them to help external threat actors in compromising the security of their organization.

Engineering of Societies

What exactly is the term "social engineering"?

The practice of social engineering is a sort of psychological manipulation that makes use of people's natural tendencies in order to acquire illegal access to computer networks, data, or sensitive information. It entails coercing persons into divulging confidential information or carrying out activities that undermine security. Attacks based on social engineering rely on human psychology and frequently take advantage of trust, curiosity, anxiety, or urgency to achieve their goals.

Methods Typically Employed in Social Engineering

Phishing: Phishing attacks involve sending false emails or messages that appear to be from trusted sources, persuading recipients to click on dangerous links, download infected files, or expose personal information. Phishing assaults are also known as spear phishing or email phishing.

The term "pretexting" refers to an attack technique in which an adversary concocts a made-up scenario or pretext in order to solicit confidential information from a target. In order to accomplish this goal, it may be necessary to assume the identity of a trusted individual, such as an IT specialist or a fellow employee.

Baiting: Baiting attacks are those that allure users with the promise of something desirable, such as a free software download or a reward, in order to seduce them into completing acts that compromise security, such as installing malware. Examples of desirable things include a free software download and prizes.

The act of physically following an authorized individual into a secure place is what is known as "tailgating." Tailgating is illegal. An unlawful entry is gained as a result of the attacker taking advantage of the human propensity to hold doors open for other people.

Quid Pro Quo: Attacks that take the form of a "quid pro quo" offer something of value in exchange for confidential information. An adversary might, for instance, pretend to be a member of the technical support staff and offer assistance in exchange for login credentials.

The Point Where Social Engineering and Insider Threats Intersect

The realms of social engineering and insider threats frequently overlap, producing a terrain that is both perilous and difficult to navigate from a cybersecurity standpoint. The combination of the privileged access provided by an insider with the psychological manipulation strategies of social engineering can have disastrous effects on companies.

Examples taken from the real world

The danger posed by this intersection has been highlighted by a number of high-profile occurrences. One situation that comes to mind is that of Edward Snowden, who worked as a contractor for the National Security Agency (NSA) in the United States. Snowden is an example of a malevolent insider who took advantage of his position to access sensitive material and expose it to the public. His activities were motivated by both his ideological ideas and a desire to expose the surveillance techniques run by the government. The case of Edward Snowden demonstrates how an insider might use their position to carry out a massive data breach by exploiting their privileges.

In a different incident, which occurred in 2013, when Target was the victim of a data breach, the perpetrators employed social engineering to gain access to the credentials of an HVAC contractor.

Because of this compromised insider, the attackers were able to get access to the point-of-sale systems at Target, which eventually led to the theft of credit card data for millions of customers. In order to obtain access to the organization's computer systems, the attackers took advantage of human trust as well as the vulnerability of the contractor.

Opportunities for Risk in Security

Because of the trust that companies have in their workers and contractors, those individuals are frequently granted access to sensitive information and systems. This trust can be abused by dishonest insiders, while social engineers take use of people's trust in order to trick them.

Lack of Awareness: The dangers that are linked with the use of social engineering techniques aren't always brought to the attention of insiders and employees. They run the risk of being tricked by phishing emails or pretexting scams without even realizing it.

Inadequate Training: A large number of companies do not have thorough training programs in place to educate staff members about the dangers posed by social engineering. Because of this, they lack the resources necessary to notice and respond to attacks of this kind.

mistake Caused by Humans Both social engineering and insider threats frequently involve human mistake as a contributing factor. Social engineering strategies take advantage of the mistakes made by careless insiders and use them to their own advantage.

Observation and Preventative Measures

It is necessary to use a multi-pronged approach that includes both detection and prevention techniques in order to effectively mitigate the risks that are connected with insider threats and social engineering.

Detection of Dangers Posed by Employees

User and Entity Behavior Analytics (UEBA): UEBA systems monitor user behavior and look for anomalies that could be signs of malicious insider activity. This involves monitoring logins and data transfers for anything that seems out of the ordinary and tracking patterns of data access.

Access Controls: Make sure that personnel have the bare minimum of privileges required to carry out the responsibilities of their jobs by putting in place tight access controls. Maintain a regular review schedule and remove unauthorized access as necessary.

Continuous Monitoring: Ensure that user activities, particularly those of privileged account holders, are continuously monitored. This can be helpful in identifying suspicious or unlawful activities in a timely manner.

Auditing and Logging: Make sure to keep detailed logs of what each user does and how they gain access. These logs have the potential to give critical evidence in the event of an incident and act as a deterrent to possible dangers posed by insiders.

Reducing the Impact of Social Engineering

Employees should receive frequent training from their employers on how to recognize and respond appropriately to social engineering attacks as part of an organization's security awareness training program. In this session, you should learn how to identify phishing emails, how to authenticate the identities of those making information requests, and how to comprehend the consequences of revealing too much information.

systems for Email Filtering and Anti-Phishing Deploy email filtering systems that are able to identify and isolate phishing emails. These solutions employ a wide variety of methodologies to perform analyses on incoming emails and locate potential security risks.

Multi-Factor Authentication (MFA): Multi-Factor Authentication (MFA) adds an additional layer of protection by forcing users to give several forms of authentication. Users must supply a password, a username, and a security key. Even if they are able to gain the login credentials for an account, this makes it more difficult for attackers to breach the account.

Plan for Responding to Incidents You should devise a comprehensive plan for responding to incidents that covers processes for dealing with security incidents, including social engineering assaults. This plan needs to incorporate tactics for communication, containment measures, and legal issues.

Implementing Transparent Data Handling, Access, and Information Sharing rules and Procedures for Security It is important to put in place transparent data handling, access, and information sharing rules and procedures for security. These policies need to lay out a structure for security and define the repercussions for those who break the policies.

The Prospects of Social Engineering and Insider Attacks in the Future

AI and Machine Learning: As social engineering attacks get more sophisticated, cybercriminals will increasingly rely on artificial intelligence and machine learning to build their schemes. Attacks that are driven by AI can adapt to their targets in real time, making them more difficult to detect.

IoT Vulnerabilities: The increasing number of devices connected to the Internet of Things (IoT) exposes new attack surfaces for both social engineering and insider attacks. As a necessary component of their overall security plans, organizations need to address these vulnerabilities.

Problems Associated with Remote Work: In the wake of recent world events, there has been a significant uptick in the use of remote work arrangements, which has resulted in an increase in the number of potential safety problems. It is possible for malicious insiders or social engineers to compromise systems and data by taking advantage of the remote work environment.

Changes in Regulation The way in which companies respond to episodes of social engineering and insider threats will be influenced by the constant evolution of rules governing data privacy and security. It's possible that compliance requirements will become stricter.

Collaboration in Cybersecurity: In the fight against constantly emerging insider threats and social engineering approaches, organizations and cybersecurity specialists will increasingly work together to exchange threat intelligence and best practices.

Two of the most serious difficulties that the field of cybersecurity faces today are social engineering and the exploitation of insiders. Organizations have a responsibility to recognize that the two risks can interact with one another, producing a synergistic effect that can result in data breaches, financial losses, and reputational damage. It is vital to take a multi-faceted approach in order to effectively counteract these dangers, which includes raising user awareness, implementing technical solutions, and developing a robust incident response plan. When we look to the future, we see that the techniques used by malicious insiders and social engineers will also evolve along with the progression of technology. When it comes to protecting the precious data and information they possess, organizations need to maintain a state of vigilance while also being flexible and proactive.

7.1 Identifying Insider Threats

Insider attacks are a serious obstacle for businesses of all sizes in today's increasingly complex cybersecurity world. The proper identification of these dangers is absolutely necessary in order to protect the honesty and confidentiality of sensitive data and information. It is crucial to recognize potential insider threats as soon as they emerge in order to avert potential data breaches, financial losses, and reputational harm. Insider threats might originate from workers, contractors, or business partners. In this essay, essential tactics for spotting insider threats are dissected, and insights into the signs that might assist businesses in recognizing insider threats and effectively mitigating their effects are provided.

Comprehension of the Characteristics of Dangerous Insiders

Because insider threats can take many different forms, it might be difficult to identify them using typical security measures by themselves. These dangers are frequently brought about by people who are permitted to access the computer systems, data networks, or other infrastructure of an organization. They can be roughly divided into three categories: malevolent insiders, negligent insiders, and compromised insiders. malevolent insiders are the most dangerous type.

Contaminated Informants

Insiders that have bad intentions intentionally abuse the access credentials they have in order to engage in damaging activities within a business. Theft of sensitive data, intellectual property, or financial information with the purpose of making personal gain or causing harm to the company is an example of one of these acts. Malicious insiders may exhibit strange behavioral patterns, such as attempts to gain illegal access, unexpected data transfers, or attempts to circumvent security systems. These behaviors can be indicators of a potential breach.

Insiders Who Don't Play Nicely

An organization's security posture might be unintentionally compromised by careless employees who work there, even if such employees aren't acting maliciously. Their activities are frequently the consequence of negligence, a lack of knowledge, or inadequate training in the protocols for maintaining security. Data leaks or breaches may occur unintentionally as a result of careless actions taken by company employees, such as clicking on malicious websites, mishandling sensitive information, or falling prey to social engineering.

Insiders Who Have Been Compromised

Compromised insiders are a unique category of risks that occur when outside actors get access to an insider's credentials or exploit their weaknesses in order to breach an organization's computer systems. Compromised insiders can also be referred to as compromised employees.

Because compromised insiders may unwittingly allow unwanted access to sensitive data or networks, it is vital to discover any strange activities or behaviors linked with their accounts. This can be done by monitoring their activity and looking for patterns that are out of the ordinary.

Identifying Potential Dangers from Within Your Organization: Key Strategies

User Behavior Analytics (UBA) should be implemented.

Monitoring and analyzing user actions and behavior patterns is what User Behavior Analytics (UBA) is all about. The goal of UBA is to find anomalies in user behavior that may be an indication of potential insider threats. UBA solutions make use of algorithms for machine learning in order to determine baseline user behaviors and identify any deviations from these norms. UBA is able to detect suspicious acts, such as attempts to gain unauthorized access, unexpected data transfers, or irregular login patterns, by continuously evaluating user activities. This gives security teams the ability to analyze and quickly respond to any issues that are discovered.

Audit your security on a regular basis.

Conducting routine security audits is a key proactive measure for spotting potential risks coming from within an organization. An organization's whole security architecture, including network systems, data repositories, and access restrictions, is evaluated thoroughly during these audits. Security teams are able to spot any discrepancies, unauthorized activity, or policy violations that may indicate the presence of insider threats when they do an assessment of data handling methods, evaluate user authorization, and examine access logs.

Put in place access controls that are unambiguous.

It is essential to set up strong access controls if one want to prevent the possible effect that could be caused by insider threats. By putting into practice the concept of least privilege, companies may make certain that their workers and other insiders only have access to the resources that are required for them to fulfill the responsibilities that have been assigned to them. By taking this strategy, the danger of unauthorized data access is reduced, as is the potential damage that hostile or compromised insiders can wreak on the organization.

Encourage the Development of a Security Conscious Culture

It is of the utmost importance, in the process of the early detection of insider threats, to cultivate a culture of security awareness among employees and insiders. Individuals can be educated about the hazards associated with insider threats, the necessity of preserving sensitive information, and the best practices for spotting and reporting suspicious activity if comprehensive security awareness training programs are provided.

The entire security posture of a business can be improved if employees are encouraged to remain watchful and to report any unexpected behaviors or security events.

Keep an eye on all the data accessing and transferring activities.

The identification of any unlawful or suspicious actions that may indicate the presence of insider threats requires continuous monitoring of data access and transfer operations. Organizations are able to spot any aberrant patterns, unexpected data retrieval, or unwanted data exports if they keep track of data access logs, monitor file transfer activities, and use data loss prevention (DLP) solutions. Because this monitoring is proactive, security teams are able to react quickly to any potential security breaches or data leaks that were caused by employees within the company.

Establish Training and Awareness Programs for Employees

Organizations must to give serious consideration to instituting specialized insider threat awareness programs, in addition to standard training on security awareness. Education of employees about the many types of insider threats, the warning indicators of potentially hostile acts, and the right channels for reporting any suspicious behaviors or security events might be the primary focus of these programs. A culture of openness and accountability may be fostered within a company if employees are made aware of the possible dangers posed by insider threats. This will encourage workers to maintain vigilance and take preventative measures when it comes to protecting the assets of the organization.

The identification of potential insider dangers calls for a multidimensional strategy that integrates stringent security precautions, proactive monitoring, and all-encompassing user awareness training programs. Organizations are able to drastically reduce the risks provided by hostile insiders, negligent employees, or compromised persons if they have a grasp of the many sorts of insider threats and put efficient procedures for detection into place. In order to keep a secure and resilient cybersecurity posture, it is vital to maintain constant monitoring, perform routine security audits, and encourage the development of a robust security culture. Organizations have the ability to effectively reduce potential risks and protect their precious assets from unauthorized access or exploitation if they make the identification of insider threats a priority in their risk management strategies.

7.2 Preventing and Mitigating Insider Threats

Insider threats, which can come from individuals who are malevolent, negligent, or compromised, represent a substantial risk to the overall well-being of businesses as well as the data security of those organizations. The importance of identifying these dangers cannot be overstated; nevertheless, preventing them from materializing in the first place is an even more fruitful course of action.

This article investigates best practices for preventing and minimizing insider threats, with the goal of assisting companies in taking preventative measures to protect their valued assets and in preserving a healthy cybersecurity posture.

The Importance of Comprehending the Dangers Posed by Insiders

Contaminated Informants

A malicious insider is a person who works within an organization and uses their privileged access to do damage to the company. Theft of data, unauthorized access, sabotage, or fraud are all possible outcomes of their acts. It is essential for effective preventative and mitigation strategies to have an understanding of the motivations underlying hostile insider threats, such as the desire for financial gain, vengeance, or ideological ideals.

Insiders Who Don't Play Nicely

In spite of the absence of ill will on their part, negligent insiders pose a threat to the integrity of the security system because of their carelessness, lack of knowledge, or inadequate training. They are frequently vulnerable to social engineering attempts, and as a result, they inadvertently divulge critical information or make other errors with the data. It is essential to the preventative process that these vulnerabilities be addressed.

Insiders Who Have Been Compromised

Individuals whose credentials or access permissions have been hacked as a result of external actors are referred to as "compromised insiders." Attackers may employ a variety of strategies to intimidate or trick these insiders into helping them gain unauthorized access to the network. Vigilance is required, along with the monitoring of their accounts for any unusual activity, in order to locate compromised insiders.

Best Practices for the Prevention of Dangers Posed by Employees

1. **Vetting potential employees and doing history checks on them**
   Start the preventative process by doing exhaustive employee screenings and checking employees' backgrounds. It is possible for companies to lessen the likelihood of hiring people who have

a past of bad behavior or who are susceptible to being swayed by outside forces if they conduct thorough background checks on potential employees throughout the hiring process.

2. **Formulate and Disseminate Policies That Are Crystal Clear Regarding Security**

   Establish security policies and processes that are both transparent and all-encompassing. Make sure that all of your staff members, independent contractors, and business partners are aware of the standards that are expected of them when it comes to the management of data, accessing systems, and maintaining security regulations. These policies ought to place an emphasis on the repercussions that accompany policy infractions.

3. **Education and a Consciousness of Safety Measures**

   It is important to educate personnel about the dangers posed by insider threats, hence it is important to invest in regular training and security awareness initiatives. Instruct them to spot phishing attempts, teach them social engineering techniques, and impress upon them the need of protecting sensitive information.

4. **Restrict Access to Privileged Areas**

   Adhere to the principle of least privilege, also known as PoLP, which states that individuals should only be granted access to the resources that are essential to performing their jobs. This decreases the likelihood of malicious insiders abusing their access permissions and places a cap on the amount of harm that they may cause as a result of doing so.

5. **Strict Regulation of Entry Points**

   Install stringent access controls such as role-based authorization and two-factor authentication, also known as 2FA and RBAC. These precautions create an additional layer of protection and ensure that persons have access only to the information that is necessary for the job they are performing.

6. **Maintaining a Constant Watch**

   Maintain a constant vigilance over user activity, paying specific attention to those users who have privileged access. Maintain a close eye on the patterns of data access, attempts at logging in, and data transfers, looking for any anomalies or strange behaviors that would suggest the presence of an insider threat.

7. **Programs to Raise Awareness of Dangers From Within**
   Organizations ought to have not only general security awareness training but also specialized programs focusing on the threat posed by insiders. By educating workers on the many types of insider threats, warning signals, and reporting procedures, these programs help to cultivate a culture of alertness inside an organization.
8. **A plan for dealing with incidents**

Create a detailed incident response plan that explains the processes that should be followed when dealing with occurrences involving insider threats. This plan ought to incorporate communication methods, containment measures, and legal considerations in order to respond to breaches in security in a prompt and efficient manner.

Best Methods for Countering the Dangers Posed by Employees

1. **Detection at an Early Stage**
   When potential insider dangers are discovered earlier rather than later, the amount of damage they can do is reduced. Maintain constant surveillance over user behavior as well as activity on the network in order to detect any signs of abnormalities or unauthorized access. The use of user and entity behavior analytics, often known as UEBA, can be quite helpful in locating unexpected trends.
2. **Support for Employees**
   It is important to investigate the reasons behind insider threats, particularly those that are caused by problems in the workplace or the individual's personal life. It is important to avoid employees' complaints from becoming more serious by providing them with

counseling and other forms of support when they may be going through difficult times.

3. **Taking Legal Action**
   If it becomes necessary, include legal counsel and the appropriate authorities in the investigation. Incidents involving insider threats may involve illegal activity, and hence, legal steps may be required to successfully neutralize the threats.

4. **Placement in Quarantine and Isolation**
   In the case that an insider threat is discovered, the impacted systems or data should be isolated to prevent additional damage. Limiting the threat's reach can be accomplished by isolating compromised accounts or networks.

5. **Data Loss Prevention (DLP), also referred to as:**
   Implementing data loss prevention (DLP) systems that monitor and restrict data movement is an effective way to ensure that sensitive information is not readily stolen by dishonest employees working within the company. The use of DLP solutions allows for the detection and prevention of illicit data transfers.

6. **An Investigation in a Timely Manner**
   Investigate events of possible insider threat as soon as possible to determine their breadth and impact. Details of the occurrence need to be analyzed, proof needs to be gathered, and the level of the compromise needs to be determined.

7. **Exchange of information**
   During instances involving an insider threat, communication is absolutely necessary. Make sure that all key stakeholders, such as management, legal teams, and affected parties, are notified in a timely and suitable manner.

8. **Repair and Restoration of Damage**

After the insider threat has been located and countered, the next step is to concentrate on eliminating the weaknesses that made it possible for the incident to take place in the first place. In order to forestall situations of a similar nature in the future, security measures, rules, and procedures should be evaluated and improved.

The process of preventing and managing the effects of insider threats is an ongoing one that calls for a combination of efficient security measures, comprehensive training, and a culture that encourages constant awareness. Organizations are able to drastically decrease their exposure to the risks associated with insider threats provided they have a solid understanding of the nature of these threats, have implemented the best practices for prevention, and have a well-defined plan for mitigation.

To protect their sensitive data, financial assets, and reputation in today's complicated cybersecurity world, businesses need to place a priority on both prevention and mitigation. Insider threats can be effectively controlled with an approach that is both proactive and adaptable. This enables organizations to concentrate on their primary goals while still maintaining a secure and resilient cybersecurity posture.

7.3 Social Engineering Attacks and Countermeasures

In the field of information technology and cybersecurity, social engineering assaults stand out as being exceptionally sneaky and challenging to fight against. Social engineering is a form of hacking that, in contrast to more conventional hacking techniques, focuses on exploiting flaws in people rather than software or technology. This article digs into the area of social engineering attacks, providing an explanation of their methods and objectives and outlining practical countermeasures to prevent individuals and organizations from becoming victims of these deceptive tactics.

Comprehending Different Methods of Social Engineering Attacks

What exactly is the term "social engineering"?

Social engineering is a sort of psychological manipulation that aims to deceive individuals into revealing sensitive information, doing acts that undermine security, or granting access to protected systems or data. The goal of social engineering is to achieve these goals by convincing individuals that they are acting in their own best interests. In order to successfully con their victims, social engineers frequently make use of human psychology, trust, curiosity, anxiety, and haste. The major objective is to coerce people into behavior that they ordinarily would not engage in if they were thinking rationally and keeping their security concerns in the forefront of their minds.

Methods Typically Employed in Social Engineering

Phishing is an attack method that involves sending misleading emails or messages that look to originate from reliable sources. Phishing attacks are carried out by cybercriminals. The recipients of these communications are often encouraged to download infected files, click on links that could be dangerous, or supply information that could be considered personal or sensitive.

The term "pretexting" refers to an attack technique in which an adversary concocts a made-up scenario or pretext in order to solicit confidential information from a target. This could involve impersonating a trusted individual, such as an information technology specialist, or creating a false identity in order to win people's confidence.

Baiting: Baiting attacks are those that tempt individuals with the promise of something desirable, such as a free software download, a prize, or unique material. Baiting attacks are a form of social engineering. These enticements are used to coerce people into carrying out activities that are detrimental to their security, such as downloading malicious software.

The act of following an authorized individual into a guarded location and taking advantage of the natural desire to hold the door open for others is known as tailgating. Tailgating is a form of physical social engineering that falls under the category of "tailgating."

Quid Pro Quo: An act of espionage known as a "quid pro quo" attack involves the exchange of anything of value for confidential information. An adversary might, for instance, pretend to be a member of the technical support staff and offer assistance in exchange for login credentials.

The Objectives of Engaging in Social Engineering Attempts

Gains in Financial Stability Financial benefits are a primary driver of motivation for many social engineers. They want to conduct fraud using the stolen information or sell it on the black market after they have stolen sensitive data, personal information, or financial details.

Espionage: Actors supported by a state may employ social engineering strategies in order to get access to sensitive government or corporate information for the aim of conducting political, military, or economic espionage.

Theft of Identity: Attackers may try to obtain personal information in order to commit identity theft, which can result in monetary losses and damage to an individual's reputation.

Data Exfiltration: Corporate spies and individuals involved in industrial espionage may employ social engineering as a means to get access to private information, trade secrets, or intellectual property and then exfiltrate it.

Disruption or Sabotage: The goal of certain social engineering assaults is to cause disruption or sabotage to a system, organization, or essential piece of infrastructure. This aim is what motivates some social engineering attacks.

Countermeasures That Are Efficient Against Those Who Engage in Social Engineering

1. **Instruction in the Awareness of Security Risks**
   User education is one of the most important lines of defense against social engineering. It is important for companies to provide frequent security awareness training for their staff and for individuals, since this will better prepare them to identify and counter social engineering attacks. The training should address subjects such as recognizing phishing emails, validating the authenticity of those making information requests, and comprehending the hazards associated with releasing too much personal information.

2. **Anti-Phishing and Email Filtering Software and Services**
   Install effective email filtering technologies that can identify phishing emails and store them in a secure location. Incoming emails are analyzed with these solutions, which employ a variety of approaches, such as content analysis, URL reputation checks, and machine learning algorithms, in order to locate potential security risks.

3. **Multi-Factor Authentication (often referred to as MFA)**
   By forcing users to submit multiple forms of authentication in order to access their accounts, multi-factor authentication (MFA) offers an additional layer of protection. Even in the event that an attacker is successful in acquiring login credentials, multi-factor authentication can make it substantially more difficult for them to breach accounts.

4. **The Policies and Procedures Regarding Safety**
   Establish data handling, access, and information sharing processes that are governed by security policies and procedures that are both clear and comprehensive. These policies need to lay out a structure for security and define the repercussions for those who break the policies. It is expected that workers will be familiar with and compliant with these policies.

5. **A plan for dealing with incidents**
   Create and regularly update an incident response plan that is clear in its articulation of the processes to follow in the event of a security breach, including one caused by social engineering. In order to provide direction for how to respond to attacks of this nature, the plan should include communication methods, containment measures, and legal issues.

6. **Awareness on the Part of Staff**
   In situations where they are confronted with odd requests for information or activities, employees should be encouraged to maintain their vigilance and caution. You should advise them to check the identification of those making information requests,

particularly if the request involves sensitive data or access to system components.

7. **Utilizing Red Teams and Conducting Security Audits**
In order to evaluate an organization's susceptibility to social engineering assaults, red teaming exercises and security audits should be carried out on a regular basis. The purpose of a red team is to test an organization's security policies and employee response to simulated assaults by acting as the organization's adversaries.

8. **A Mock Version of Phishing**
For the purpose of determining how vulnerable employees are to social engineering scams, companies can test their defenses by simulating internal phishing attacks. This can assist identify areas for improvement and aid in the customization of training programs to address specific areas of weakness.

9. **Ongoing Maintenance, Including Patching and Updates to Software**
Make sure that all of the software and operating systems are periodically patched and updated to address any vulnerabilities that may have been discovered. Using out-of-date software can make it easier for attackers to manipulate users in social engineering attacks.

10. **Mechanisms for Reporting by Users**
Establish channels of communication that are both simple and safe for employees to use when reporting questionable emails, phone calls, or other forms of social engineering. Rapid reporting can assist security teams in promptly responding to potential threats and investigating those threats.

11. **Checks of the Employment History of Workers**

During the employment process, doing exhaustive background checks can assist in identifying individuals who have a history of malicious intent or who are susceptible to being tricked by social engineering strategies.

In the field of cybersecurity, social engineering assaults continue to be one of the most common and dangerous types of threats. They take advantage of human psychology and trust, making it challenging to protect against them via technological means alone. It is vital, in order to protect individuals and organizations from these manipulative attacks, to recognize the reasons behind social engineering, to grasp the common strategies that are used, and to implement effective countermeasures. It is feasible to considerably lower the risk of falling prey to social engineering by combining user education, technical solutions, and a vigilant organizational culture. This will ultimately result in strengthened cybersecurity defenses and the protection of valuable data and information.

Chapter 8

Vulnerability Management and Patching

In the linked and ever-changing digital ecosystem of today, maintaining proper cybersecurity continues to be of the utmost importance. There is an endless number of dangers that can put an organization's data, operations, and reputation in jeopardy, and this is a problem that affects businesses of all sizes. Because vulnerabilities in software and systems give attackers a way in, managing vulnerabilities and applying patches are essential components of any cybersecurity plan.

In this article, we will go into the area of vulnerability management and patching, addressing the core ideas, the issues that are faced, and the best methods for efficiently securing information systems and networks. In addition to this, it investigates the changing nature of vulnerabilities, the function of automation, and the significance of taking a preventative stance with regard to cybersecurity.

1. **A Comprehension of Risk and Vulnerability Management**
   Discovery of Vulnerabilities The first thing that must be done is to look for and record any vulnerabilities that may exist in the hardware, software, and network infrastructure of an

organization. Errors in the programming, incorrect setups, and design defects are some of the ways that vulnerabilities can be introduced into a system.

Evaluation of Vulnerabilities Once vulnerabilities have been discovered, they need to be evaluated in order to establish the severity of their impact and the potential dangers that they pose. When doing this evaluation, penetration testing, vulnerability scanning, and the use of other security technologies are common practices.

Prioritization of Risk: Vulnerabilities are rarely on par with one another in terms of severity or immediacy. When it comes to vulnerability management, teams need to establish priorities for which vulnerabilities need to be fixed first based on criteria such as the potential impact of the vulnerability, how easy it is to exploit, and the value of the assets that are at risk.

The term "remediation" refers to the process of reducing or removing vulnerabilities using a variety of techniques, such as installing system patches, re-configuring computer networks, or putting in place compensatory controls. In order to shorten the exposure window, prompt cleanup is absolutely necessary.

The management of vulnerabilities is an ongoing process that requires continuous monitoring. Organizations have an ongoing need to check their computer systems for newly discovered security flaws and to confirm that vulnerabilities that have already been patched do not reappear.

2. **The Significance of Patch Management**

Protection Against Known Threats Researchers in cybersecurity as well as threat actors are constantly looking for flaws in software. Organizations can protect themselves against known dangers and reduce the chance of being exploited if they implement updates as soon as they are made available.

Compliance: Many legal frameworks and industry standards require businesses to ensure that their software is always up-to-date and includes any necessary security patches. Failure to comply may result in financial fines and harm to one's professional reputation.

Improved Stability and Performance: In addition to repairing security flaws, patches can also improve the overall stability and performance of software. Failure to apply patches might result in malfunctions of the system, lost time, and a reduction in production.

Reduced Attack Surface Consistently applying patches helps to protect against known flaws, which results in a reduced attack surface. This is especially significant in settings that include systems that are connected to the internet or that have essential infrastructure.

3. **Obstacles Confronted When Managing Vulnerabilities and Applying Patches**

    Complexity and scale: Because large enterprises have broad and different IT ecosystems, it can be difficult to identify, assess, and remediate vulnerabilities across all assets. This presents a challenge for those responsible for security at these firms. When working with hybrid and multi-cloud setups, the level of complexity increases significantly.

    Establishing a Priority for Patches It might be challenging to decide which vulnerabilities should be addressed first. When deciding whether or not to apply fixes, the possible impact on business operations must be evaluated against the danger provided by the vulnerability.

    Constraints on Resources: Many businesses face the challenge of limited resources, which can impede efficient vulnerability management and patching operations. These resources include trained staff and financial budgets, respectively.

    Legacy Systems: Legacy systems, which are frequently found in critical infrastructure and older businesses, may no longer receive vendor support or security updates. Legacy systems can also be vulnerable to cyberattacks. Because of this, reducing vulnerabilities in such systems presents a difficult challenge.

Software Provided by a Third Party: Organizations frequently use software and components provided by third parties, which can lead to the introduction of security flaws over which they have no control. It can be difficult to coordinate with different third-party vendors to obtain fixes.

Testing of Patches: Before delivering patches, it is standard practice for enterprises to undertake testing to guarantee that the updates will not interrupt mission-critical systems. Because of the potential for this process to be time-consuming, the installation of security updates may be delayed.

Zero-Day Vulnerabilities: Some vulnerabilities are not made available to the public until they have been actively exploited. These vulnerabilities are known as zero-day vulnerabilities. There is minimal time for organizations to respond and implement patches for these vulnerabilities.

User Awareness: Even when patches are readily available, users may put off installing them or completely avoid doing so. This human aspect has the potential to expose individuals to vulnerabilities that are already known.

4. **Industry Standard Procedures for Patching and Vulnerability Management**

   Management of Inventory and Assets: Ensure that an accurate inventory of all of your hardware and software assets is kept at all times. For effective risk management, it is vital to have a good understanding of what you have.

   Conducting Regular Vulnerability Scans and Assessments It is important to perform regular vulnerability scans on both your network and your systems. To determine the order of priority for the repair actions, evaluate the severity and impact of each vulnerability.

   Establish a Reliable Patch Management Framework It is important to implement a reliable patch management framework, which should contain procedures for locating, testing, deploying, and confirming fixes.

Automated Patching: In order to streamline patch management, implement automated solutions. This is especially important for updates that are considered routine or non-critical. Automation can shorten the window of vulnerability, freeing up workers to focus on more important responsibilities.

Prioritizing Vulnerabilities Based on Risk It is important to prioritize vulnerabilities based on the risk appetite of the organization as well as the possible impact on essential business processes. Take into account the dangers and regulations that are relevant to your sector.

Testing of Patches Conceive of and implement an organized testing procedure for patches in order to reduce the possibility of unforeseen consequences. Testing should be designed to be as similar to the production environment as is practically achievable.

Communication with providers It is important to keep an open line of communication with software providers in order to be updated about newly released fixes and vulnerabilities. You might want to think about developing a relationship with the security response team of a vendor.

User Education: Educate end users on the significance of patching, as well as the risks involved with failing to maintain current software versions. Encourage them to perform the patch installation as soon as possible.

Plan for Responding to Incidents It is important to have a plan for responding to incidents in place so that you can handle instances in which vulnerabilities are exploited before patches can be released.

Continuous Monitoring: Make use of security information and event management (SIEM) systems and other intrusion detection technologies to keep an eye out for any signals that an exploit has been used or that the system has been compromised.

5. **Changing Face of Vulnerabilities in the Environment**

   IoT and Embedded Systems: The increasing prevalence of Internet of Things (IoT) devices and embedded systems opens up a new battleground in the battle against security flaws. These gadgets frequently have inadequate precautions against potential dangers and may not be kept up to date with the latest security patches.

   Attacks on the Supply Chain Attackers are increasingly focusing their attention on the software supply chain, which puts software upgrades and distribution mechanisms in jeopardy. The organizations' software sources need to be thoroughly investigated, and the updates' integrity has to be verified.

   Environments Hosted in the Cloud The cloud infrastructure comes with its own unique set of security flaws, such as the potential for misconfigurations, data disclosure, and unwanted access. A distinct strategy is required for effective vulnerability management when working in the cloud.

   Learning Machines and Artificial Intelligence: As machine learning and artificial intelligence systems become more widespread, cybercriminals are exploring new ways to exploit them. It's possible that the vulnerabilities in these systems could have far-reaching repercussions.

   Exploits Discovered on Day Zero Zero-day vulnerabilities continue to be a significant source of risk. Even before updates are available, organizations have a responsibility to build measures for identifying and mitigating the effects of zero-day attacks.

6. **Automation in Risk Assessment and Vulnerability Management**

   Scan for Vulnerabilities Automated vulnerability scanning programs can regularly assess systems, find vulnerabilities, and report the results, decreasing the amount of manual effort that is

required.

Patch Deployment Automation can distribute patches to a predetermined subset of systems based on predefined rules and testing findings, avoiding the need for manual involvement. Patches can be deployed to a system at any time.

Integration of Threat Intelligence: Automation can consume threat intelligence feeds to keep current on emerging threats and enable proactive vulnerability management. This is made possible by the integration of threat intelligence.

Incident Response: Automated incident response systems have the ability to detect and react to potential dangers in real time, which enables quick corrective measures to be taken.

Reporting on Compliance Automated tools can be used to generate compliance reports, which assists firms in demonstrating their conformance to applicable regulatory and industry standards.

Even though there are a lot of advantages to using automation, you still need to be careful when doing so. Human monitoring is still necessary, particularly in circumstances in which significant judgments must be made or when dealing with novel risks.

7. **Approaches That Are More Proactive Rather Than Reactive**

Continuous Monitoring: In order to stay one step ahead of newly surfaced dangers, companies continuously test and inspect their computer systems for security flaws.

Patching on a Regular Basis: Patches are administered as soon as possible, frequently in a well-orchestrated manner, in order to reduce the amount of time that an individual is exposed to a risk.

In risk assessment, vulnerabilities are rated according to the potential damage they could do, with consideration given to both the goals of the business and the regulations that must be followed.

Users and workers receive education on the significance of maintaining security and applying patches, which helps to reduce vulnerabilities that are caused by human error.

On the other hand, using a reactive approach means addressing vulnerabilities and deploying updates only after an incident or security breach has already taken place. This strategy has a higher level of risk and has the potential to cause considerable harm to an organization's operations as well as its reputation.

Management of vulnerabilities and installation of security patches are essential elements of contemporary cybersecurity tactics. Organizations need to adopt a proactive strategy to discovering, analyzing, and remediating vulnerabilities in their information systems and data in order to secure their information systems and data. Automating processes and adhering to best practices in vulnerability management are necessary for companies in order to overcome challenges such as complexity, limited resources, and constantly evolving threats.

In a landscape of vulnerabilities that is always shifting, it is essential to maintain a lead over the competition. It is imperative that organizations have contingency plans in place to address newly discovered vulnerabilities and growing dangers. Effective ways for controlling vulnerabilities and distributing updates are going to need to be developed as technology continues to advance at a rapid pace.

In today's increasingly interconnected world, businesses can protect their digital assets and reduce the risks posed by vulnerabilities by adhering to best practices, embracing automation, and cultivating a culture of security awareness.

8.1 Identifying and Prioritizing Vulnerabilities

In this ever more linked world, where technology is firmly ingrained in practically every aspect of our lives, the necessity to identify vulnerabilities and prioritize them has become of the utmost importance. There is a wide variety of possible dangers that can befall individuals, businesses, and even organizations nowadays. These dangers can take the form of cyberattacks or even physical breaches. As a result, it is absolutely necessary to devise robust strategies that not only detect deficiencies but also effectively prioritize them in order to distribute resources in the most effective manner. This essay looks into the important facets of finding and prioritizing vulnerabilities in modern systems, highlighting the need of taking a proactive and all-encompassing approach to the protection of digital infrastructures.

The Detection and Characterization of Weaknesses:

The first step in strengthening any system is becoming aware of the weaknesses it currently possesses. The first step in this procedure is to conduct a thorough investigation of all of the potential weak points, including both technical and non-technical issues. Outdated software, unpatched systems, insufficiently secure authentication procedures, and vulnerability to malware are all examples of potential technical weaknesses. On the other side, non-technical vulnerabilities can be the result of human error, inadequate training, bad security standards, or even physical security gaps. These vulnerabilities can be exploited in a variety of ways. The identification procedure needs to be comprehensive, meaning that it should take into account every potential entry point via which an adversary could abuse the system.

The identification procedure would not be complete without the routine and comprehensive completion of security audits. These audits may include everything from code reviews and risk assessments to vulnerability inspections and penetration testing. Automated scanning technologies can also be of assistance in the detection of common technological vulnerabilities; nevertheless, one should not place sole reliance on these tools because they may not uncover threats that are more complex or subtle.

The implementation of a reliable reporting mechanism that encourages individuals to report vulnerabilities they encounter and that helps to foster a culture of transparency and collaboration in the process of maintaining security is also quite important.

Vulnerabilities are prioritized in the following order:

As a direct result of the ever-increasing complexity of today's computer systems, it is not unusual for multiple vulnerabilities to be discovered all at once. Therefore, setting priorities is absolutely necessary in order to properly manage limited resources and fix the most important issues first. It is common practice to believe that the most efficient method for prioritization is a risk-based approach, which takes into account both the potential impact and the chance of exploitation. Security teams are able to assign priorities appropriately by first determining the possible amount of damage that could be caused by a vulnerability and then determining the probability that it will be exploited.

It is imperative that critical vulnerabilities, the exploitation of which could result in severe repercussions such as data breaches, financial losses, or system outages, be fixed as quickly and as urgently as possible with the utmost priority. When prioritizing vulnerabilities, the focus should not be limited to the technical issues; rather, it should also take into account the impact on the business as well as the compliance requirements. For example, a vulnerability that could result in non-compliance with data protection legislation or industry rules should be given high attention, regardless of the severity of the vulnerability from a technical standpoint.

In addition, the process of prioritization should be dynamic and responsive, taking into consideration the ever-evolving threat landscape as well as the constantly shifting nature of vulnerabilities. To guarantee that resources are distributed in the manner that is both the most effective and the most efficient, it is imperative that priorities be re-evaluated and adjusted on a continual basis. It is absolutely necessary for several departments within an organization, such as information technology, security, and business divisions, to work together in order to appropriately analyze the possible impact that vulnerabilities may have on various aspects of the organization.

Techniques for Efficient Risk Management:

It is vital to design thorough mitigation methods once it has been determined which vulnerabilities exist and how they should be addressed. This entails putting into action a variety of technical controls, security policies, and training programs with the goal of addressing the identified gaps. Important technological controls like as patch management, regular software updates, and the adoption of effective authentication methods are able to greatly lower the danger of exploitation.

In addition, the education and training of employees plays a critical part in limiting the risks that are caused by human error. The likelihood of there being a breach in the organization's internal security can be considerably reduced by fostering a culture of security awareness within the company. An efficient security awareness program needs to have a number of essential components, including clear security policies and procedures, regular training sessions, and simulated phishing exercises.

In addition, it is necessary to devise a strategy for dealing with vulnerabilities that have already been exploited, as this is a vital step. This strategy should include procedures for containment, eradication, and recovery, as well as a post-incident evaluation to identify lessons learned and improve future response efforts. Also included in this plan should be a post-incident review. It is important to perform regular testing of the response plan, either through simulated exercises or tabletop drills, in order to help ensure that it will be effective in actual situations.

The process of identifying and ranking vulnerabilities is continual and complex, and it requires a methodology that takes into account a variety of factors. Organizations are able to drastically minimize their susceptibility to cyber threats and other vulnerabilities if they cultivate a culture of security awareness, use robust assessment and prioritizing procedures, and deploy complete mitigation strategies. In this day and age, where digital resiliency is of the utmost importance, proactive and strategic vulnerability management is not only a must but also an essential part of an effective cybersecurity posture.

8.2 Patch Management Strategies

It is impossible to place an adequate amount of emphasis on how important patch management is in the context of cybersecurity. Maintaining a robust patch management plan is critical for the protection of digital systems against potential vulnerabilities. The threat landscape is always shifting, and cyberattacks are becoming more sophisticated, so this is especially important. Patch management is a core component of an organization's overall security posture, since it works to ensure that software vulnerabilities are swiftly recognized and remedied as soon as they are discovered. This detailed tutorial looks into the complexities of patch administration, examining topics such as the relevance of taking a proactive approach, the difficulties connected with implementation, and best practices for effective patch management tactics.

Acquiring Knowledge of Patch Management:

The process of collecting, testing, and implementing code updates in already existing software is what is known as patch management. These code changes are installed to remedy vulnerabilities, flaws, or performance concerns. Software vendors are the ones responsible for releasing these patches as a response to the discovery of vulnerabilities that could possibly be exploited by hostile actors.

The major goal of patch management is to guarantee that systems are equipped with the most recent security updates and fixes. This will, in turn, reduce the risk of exploitation while also maintaining the software's integrity and functionality.

A thorough patch management strategy goes beyond merely installing updates; rather, it entails a methodical and preventative approach to monitoring software vulnerabilities, analyzing the impact of patches, and distributing them in a timely and effective manner. Performing these tasks in such a way as to minimize downtime and maximize productivity is the hallmark of an effective patch management strategy. A digital system's level of security can be improved through effective patch management, which also reduces the amount of time the system is offline, boosts its overall performance, and ensures that it complies with all applicable regulatory standards and industry best practices.

The Importance of Taking a Preventative Approach to Patch Management:

It is impossible to place enough emphasis on the significance of proactive patch management in light of the ever-changing nature of today's threat landscape, in which cyber-attacks are growing more complex and widespread. Hackers frequently take use of software flaws that are already known to the public in order to obtain illegal access, steal sensitive data, or disrupt operations. As a result, maintaining frequently updated software that includes all of the most recent patches is essential in order to reduce the likelihood of potential security breaches and the loss of data.

In addition, proactive patch management assists in staying ahead of new threats and reduces the window of opportunity for hackers to exploit vulnerabilities. This is because it cuts down on the time it takes to apply patches. businesses are in a better position to strengthen their defenses against the ever-changing strategies utilized by threat actors if they routinely monitor vendor releases and security advisories. This allows the businesses to quickly detect and remedy any vulnerabilities. Patch management that is proactive is not just a reactive measure; rather, it is a proactive posture that indicates a commitment to rigorous cybersecurity standards and risk reduction.

Concerns Regarding the Implementation of Patch Management:

In spite of the fact that it is of the utmost significance, organizations frequently face considerable obstacles when attempting to effectively adopt patch management systems. The sheer number of software that is used within a company is one of the key obstacles that must be overcome. Managing patches for a wide number of operating systems, applications, and devices may be a challenging and resource-intensive operation, particularly for large businesses that have heterogeneous IT infrastructures.

In addition, the issue presented by the need to strike a balance between the requirements for patching and the need to maintain operational continuity is a significant one. The application of updates without conducting the necessary testing might result in disruptions to the system or compatibility issues, which may result in lost time and productivity. When it comes to successful patch management, one of the trickiest yet most important aspects is finding a balance between the necessity for rigorous testing and the urgency of patch deployment.

In addition, it can be difficult to ensure consistent patch management across a wide variety of devices, such as servers, workstations, and mobile devices. The scope of patch management has expanded in recent years as a result of trends such as the rise of remote work and the proliferation of mobile devices in the workplace. As a result, it is now necessary to take a comprehensive approach that covers all endpoints, irrespective of their location.

Recommended Methods and Procedures for Efficient Patch Management:

Management of All Assets, Including Software and Hardware It is critical to have an accurate inventory of all software and hardware assets in order to have effective patch management. When an organization has an accurate inventory, it is able to identify all of the software programs and devices that need frequent patching. This makes it possible for the company to take a more methodical and structured approach to the deployment of patches.

Risk Assessment and Prioritization: When it comes to prioritizing fixes, it is absolutely necessary to conduct a comprehensive risk assessment in order to identify essential systems and vulnerabilities. Organizations are able to prioritize the deployment of patches depending on the level of risk that they provide to the overall security posture. This is accomplished by conducting an analysis of the possible impact of a vulnerability as well as the likelihood that it will be exploited.

Testing and Validation: Before distributing patches throughout the entirety of the network, it is essential to perform exhaustive testing and validation to guarantee that the upgrades will not cause incompatibilities with any of the preexisting software or hardware. Setting up a separate testing environment that is an exact replica of the production environment can assist in locating and resolving any potential problems that may arise before fixes are applied to the live system.

Utilizing Automation Tools and Scheduling frequent Patch Deployments The utilization of automation tools and scheduling frequent patch deployments can help to streamline the process of patch management and reduce the amount of manual intervention that is required. Automated patch management solutions are able to scan for vulnerabilities, apply patches, and provide reports in an efficient manner. As a result, these solutions can reduce the administrative burden and ensure that timely updates are applied throughout the whole network.

Change Management and Documentation: In order to keep a transparent and accountable environment, it is vital to implement a comprehensive change management procedure that documents all patch distribution actions. The documentation should include specifics such as the reason for the patch, deployment timelines, testing results, and any modifications that were made to the system configurations. This will allow businesses to trace the patch management process and effectively execute post-implementation reviews.

Continuous Monitoring and Reporting: Organizations are able to notice any anomalies or unsuccessful patch installations in a timely manner if they implement continuous monitoring and real-time reporting methods into their infrastructure. It is essential to monitor the efficacy of updates as well as the impact they have on the operation of the system in order to identify any lingering vulnerabilities or issues that may require additional attention.

Employee Awareness and Training: It is necessary to educate employees about the need of timely patching and the potential hazards associated with unpatched systems in order to establish a culture inside the firm that is security conscious. Employees can be helped to understand the relevance of patch management in the context of maintaining a safe digital environment by participating in regular training sessions and awareness activities.

Patch Management Should Be Integrated Into Every Comprehensive Security Framework:

Patch management is not something that should be considered in a vacuum; rather, it should be incorporated as a fundamental part of an all-encompassing cybersecurity framework. Patch management is an essential component of a comprehensive cybersecurity strategy that include a mix of preventative, investigative, and corrective actions. One of the most important roles that patch management plays is in the preventative portion of the strategy. The overall resiliency of the organization's cybersecurity posture can be improved by integrating patch management with other security measures such as network segmentation, access controls, encryption, and threat intelligence.

In addition, for the successful deployment of an all-encompassing cybersecurity framework, communication between several departments, such as information technology, security, and operations, is absolutely necessary. When patch management strategies are aligned with larger organizational goals and broader security objectives, this guarantees that the patch management process is integrated easily into the entire risk management strategy.

It is very necessary for businesses that want to protect their digital assets and keep their operations resilient to put in place a comprehensive patch management plan in this age of digital technology, when the complexity and frequency of cyber attacks are continuing to increase.

Organizations are able to efficiently manage and install patches by adopting a proactive strategy, addressing key implementation issues, and following to best practices. This reduces the risk of potential vulnerabilities and strengthens their defenses against a wide variety of cyber threats. Underscoring the significance of routine software maintenance in the never-ending quest for digital safety is the necessity of a patch management strategy that is both comprehensive and integrated. This strategy acts as a cornerstone in the larger cybersecurity landscape.

8.3 Zero-Day Vulnerabilities and Their Implications

The prospect of cyberattacks looms big in the hyperconnected digital world of today, where people's reliance on technology has reached an all-pervasive level. Zero-day vulnerabilities stand out as some of the most insidious threats and difficult ones to combat among all of these potential dangers. These vulnerabilities are defects in software that are exploited by malicious actors before the program developer or the security community becomes aware of them. We will investigate the nature of these threats, the reasons behind the allure of zero-day vulnerabilities, the risks they bring, and the tactics for both detection and mitigation in this all-encompassing study of zero-day vulnerabilities and their repercussions.

Comprehending the Concept of Zero-Day Vulnerabilities

A zero-day vulnerability, often known as a "zero-day," is a software flaw, security loophole, or vulnerability that is unknown to the program seller or developer. The term "zero-day" is commonly used interchangeably with the term "zero-day vulnerability." It is referred to as a "zero-day" vulnerability because, after a vulnerability has been exploited in the wild, there are no more days in which the vendor may address the vulnerability and patch it. In its most basic form, it is a security flaw for which there is no previously developed fix, which leaves systems open to attack and at danger of being compromised.

There is a wide variety of software that contains zero-day vulnerabilities, including operating systems, web browsers, plugins, programs, and even hardware. These flaws can be exploited by hackers. These vulnerabilities may have been caused by coding faults, design flaws, or other unforeseen difficulties within the product. They can be exploited by hostile actors for a variety of objectives, including gaining unauthorized access, running arbitrary code, or planting malware.

The Appeal of Vulnerabilities with Zero-Day Countdowns

For a number of different reasons, zero-day vulnerabilities hold a distinct attractiveness for both cybercriminals and individuals representing nation-states.

1. **The Elements of Surprise and Stealth:** Zero-day vulnerabilities give attackers an advantage that is one of a kind since they exploit flaws that have never been discovered before. This gives them the element of surprise. Because of this, it is extremely challenging for security measures to detect zero-day attacks and respond appropriately to them.

2. Greater possibility for Attackers Compared to previously discovered flaws, for which patches are already available, zero-day vulnerabilities provide attackers with a greater possibility for success. This time frame can be anywhere from a few days to a few weeks, depending on how long it takes for the vulnerability to be found and a patch to be developed.
3. **No Known Mitigation:** In contrast to known vulnerabilities, which can frequently be fixed by applying patches, updates, or adjusting security configurations, zero-day exploits typically don't have any known remedies that may be used to fix them. This indicates that even after a zero-day vulnerability has been exploited, it is still possible for it to pose a threat until a fix is created and installed.
4. **Greater Potential for Exploitation:** The value of zero-day exploits frequently resides in their capacity to compromise a wide variety of targets, as they are frequently relevant to widely used software and systems. This is one reason why they are so valuable. Because of their adaptability, assailants could be motivated by a wide variety of goals when they launch an attack.

The Consequences of Having Zero-Day Vulnerabilities

1. There Is a Restricted Amount of Time to Respond The restricted amount of time that is available to respond is the most immediate and important implication of zero-day vulnerabilities. As software providers have no prior knowledge of the vulnerability, they have no lead time to prepare patches. This means that the window of opportunity for attackers is almost endless.
2. **The possibility of exploitation:** Zero-day vulnerabilities have the potential to be exploited for a variety of unethical reasons. Among these include the unlawful accessing of data, the theft of identity, the compromising of systems, and the distribution of malware. The damage that could occur is extensive and can take

many forms, ranging from lost money to the disclosure of private information.
3. Data Breach Potential Zero-day vulnerabilities can be exploited to get access to systems or apps that store sensitive data, which may result in data breach potential. The theft of sensitive personal, financial, or corporate information can lead to significant monetary losses, serious legal repercussions, and irreparable harm to a company's brand.
4. Dangers to National Security Beyond the concerns of individuals and businesses, zero-day vulnerabilities can be used as tools in cyberespionage, cyberwarfare, and other state-sponsored activities. There is a possibility that governments and other nation-state actors are stockpiling zero-day exploits in order to hack the systems of their enemies, which could have geopolitical repercussions.
5. **Monetary Losses:** There are frequently significant expenditures involved in the process of mitigating the impact of zero-day vulnerabilities. This includes recovering from any security breaches that may have occurred as well as developing and delivering updates. Because of this, companies may be subject to financial penalties, increased legal expenses, and a decline in productivity.
6. **Advantage in a Competitive Environment:** There are situations in which zero-day vulnerabilities can be weaponized to provide one organization with an advantage in a competitive environment over another. For instance, a firm may take advantage of a zero-day vulnerability in order to acquire access to the intellectual property of a competitor, which would provide the company with an unfair advantage in the market.

Dealing with Zero-Day Vulnerabilities Presents Difficulties

1. A lack of awareness Because zero-days are vulnerabilities that have not been made public, it can be incredibly challenging to determine whether or not they are being exploited. This lack of

knowledge presents a huge obstacle, both in terms of detecting the problem and finding a solution to it.
2. The Risk of Rapid Proliferation Once a zero-day vulnerability has been identified and exploited, there is a risk that it may rapidly spread across a variety of attack vectors. Exploits and attack methods can rapidly spread throughout a system, causing extensive damage.
3. The requirement for a considerable investment of time, skill, and testing resources is a characteristic of the process of developing patches for zero-day vulnerabilities. The requirement for a prompt reaction might put a strain on the capabilities of an organization.
4. **Coordination of Efforts:** Addressing zero-day vulnerabilities frequently calls for strong coordination of efforts between impacted businesses, security professionals, and software suppliers. It is impossible to find a solution in a timely manner without effective communication and teamwork.
5. Victims Who Are Unknown Many zero-day exploits are designed to target a diverse group of possible victims. It's possible that organizations have been penetrated without ever realizing it, which makes identification and response all the more difficult.
6. Difficulties in Attribution It might be difficult to determine the identity and motivations of attackers who take advantage of zero-day vulnerabilities. Understanding the danger situation and coming up with appropriate responses both require attribution in order to be successful.

Reducing the Effects of Zero-Day Vulnerabilities

1. Implement comprehensive cybersecurity procedures, such as frequent updates, strong authentication, and access controls. This is the first item on the Security Hygiene checklist. Even if zero-day

vulnerabilities are exploited, following these best practices will reduce the amount of damage an attacker can cause.

2. IDS and IPS stand for "intrusion detection systems" and "intrusion prevention systems,"

    respectively. In order to monitor network traffic and identify potential threats, implement intrusion detection and prevention systems (IDS and IPS). These technologies can assist in identifying potentially malicious actions and can send out warnings in the event of zero-day attacks.

3. **Vulnerability Scanning:** Conduct routine vulnerability scans and tests on all of your computer systems and software applications. Even though this won't stop zero-day exploits, it will help detect and fix known vulnerabilities that could be used in conjunction with zero-day exploits.

4. Patch Management Ensure that a complete and up-to-date patch management process is always in place. In order to reduce the attack surface, it is vital to stay up to date with fixes for vulnerabilities that are already known about, even if zero-day vulnerabilities are found.

5. **Network Segmentation:** If you want to minimize the lateral movement of attackers, you should segment your network. If a zero-day vulnerability is exploited on one part of the network, the problem can be controlled and kept from propagating to other parts of the network.

6. **Intelligence on Threats:** If you want to be informed about new threats and vulnerabilities, you should subscribe to feeds and services that provide intelligence on threats. Because of this, corporations may find it easier to take a more proactive approach to their defensive efforts.

7. **Security Awareness Training:** Train personnel to identify suspicious actions and to report them. The ability to detect threats early on can assist companies in reacting more quickly to zero-day attacks.

8. Developing a Comprehensive Plan for Handling Incidents The eighth step is to develop a comprehensive plan for handling incidents, which includes processes for handling potential security breaches, including those using zero-days.
9. **Collaborative Partnerships:** Establishing contacts with cybersecurity organizations, governmental agencies, and industry peers to exchange knowledge and resources for combating zero-day threats is an important step in the process of building collaborative partnerships.

The landscape of cybersecurity is marked by a number of critical challenges, one of the most prominent being zero-day vulnerabilities. They are difficult to anticipate, difficult to identify, and have the potential to cause considerable harm to individuals, companies, and even governments. Organizations need to embrace a proactive and diversified approach to security that combines robust security procedures, effective monitoring, and strong incident response capabilities in order to successfully limit the effects of zero-day vulnerabilities. While it's possible that zero-day vulnerabilities will never be completely eradicated, having a security posture that is well-prepared and resilient will help minimize the damage they cause and improve overall cyber resilience. In the ongoing fight against this elusive and ever-evolving danger, vigilance, collaboration, and a commitment to best practices are critical components of a successful strategy.

Chapter 9

Secure Collaboration and Data Sharing

In this day and age, when data is the lifeblood of organizations and individuals alike, it has become of the utmost importance to collaborate and share data in a secure manner. The ability to communicate information in a frictionless manner while maintaining its confidentiality is fundamental to modern civilization because it paves the way for increased productivity, creativity, and global connectivity. However, along with this convenience comes an inherent issue, and that is figuring out how to protect both the integrity and the secrecy of the data that is being exchanged. This essay digs into the significance of data sharing and cooperation in a secure environment, as well as the primary obstacles and potential solutions, as well as the changing landscape of digital security.

The Importance of Working Together and Sharing Information in a Safe Environment

Providing Assistance with Business Operations

The success of modern businesses depends heavily on the availability of safe methods for employees to work together and share information. Companies are becoming more open to the concept of remote work and distributed teams, and because of this, they require a robust infrastructure for team collaboration. It is essential for the success of a company's efficiency and continuity of operations that employees, contractors, and business partners effectively share data.

Collaboration platforms such as Microsoft Teams, Slack, and Zoom have recently seen a meteoric rise in popularity. These tools enable teams to connect with one another and share information in real time. The ease of use of these technologies, on the other hand, is accompanied by concerns, such as the possibility of data breaches and illegal access. As a result, establishing secure cooperation is essential for companies to protect sensitive information and keep their edge in the market.

Promoting Creative Efforts

Environments that encourage collaboration are frequently conducive to the growth of innovation. Secure data sharing encourages innovation in a variety of contexts, including collaboration between research institutions on the pursuit of scientific breakthroughs and between software engineers working on open-source projects. When people working together have faith that their proprietary information and research will be kept secret, they are more likely to openly discuss ideas and conclusions.

Personal Convenience and Discretion are Priorities

On a more personal level, the sharing of confidential information is not confined to the usage of businesses or institutions. People today exchange a vast array of personally identifiable information, ranging from images and texts to financial data and medical records, thanks to the proliferation of digital technology. A basic component of both privacy and security is the ability to exercise control over who can access and make use of the data.

Challenges Facing Efforts Made to Securely Collaborate and Share Data

Data Security Flaws

The risk of data breaches is among the most serious obstacles to overcome in the field of data sharing. These occurrences take place when third parties that should not have access to sensitive information do so. The repercussions can be catastrophic, including monetary losses, damage to reputation, and legal responsibilities.

Data breaches can be caused by a variety of vulnerabilities, including having weak passwords, using unpatched software, or being the victim of social engineering. It is possible for employees, even those with good intentions, to mistakenly leak critical data, which highlights the necessity of rigorous security procedures.

Worries Regarding Privacy

Increased legislation, such as the General Data Protection legislation (GDPR) in the European Union and the California Consumer Privacy Act (CCPA), is one factor that is contributing to the growing worry around the privacy of one's data. The collection, use, and dissemination of personal information are all subject to stringent constraints imposed by these legislation.

It can be difficult to strike a balance between the benefits of data sharing and the requirement to protect the privacy rights of individuals. In order to stay compliant and keep their consumers' trust, organizations need to successfully navigate this complicated landscape.

Security for Collaborative Work Tools

The very tools that are supposed to make collaboration easier can potentially pose a threat to one's privacy and safety. Cybercriminals frequently focus their attention on these sites, taking advantage of weaknesses or employing social engineering strategies in an attempt to gain unauthorized access to user accounts. During the COVID-19 epidemic, for example, the widespread use of video conferencing capabilities revealed a number of vulnerabilities in the system's security.

In addition to ensuring the safety of their data, companies also have a responsibility to protect the collaborative tools their employees utilize. Keeping software up to date, educating employees on how to see and respond to possible risks, and implementing multi-factor authentication and encryption are all necessary steps in this process.

Threats From Within

Even though risks from the outside, such as hackers and malicious software, are well known, threats from within a company can be just as harmful. When employees or trusted partners have access to sensitive data, there is a risk that the data will be mishandled or exposed, either purposefully or unintentionally. In order to protect against risks posed by insiders, it is necessary to put in place access controls and monitoring procedures.

The Answers to Your Problems with Secure Collaboration and Data Sharing

A code or cipher

Encryption is a fundamental data security principle that should never be overlooked. The process of encrypting data entails transforming the data into a code in order to prevent unauthorized access. There are a number of distinct varieties of encryption, the most common of which being symmetric and asymmetric encryption. In the former, only one key is required for encryption and decryption, whereas in the later, two keys are required: one for encryption and the other for decryption.

End-to-end encryption, also known as E2E encryption, is particularly important for the secure sharing of data. Data is encrypted on the sender's end using end-to-end encryption, and the data can only be decoded on the receiving end by the intended recipient. Even the company that is providing the service that is facilitating the communication is unable to view the contents of the data. This strategy assures that the data will continue to be kept confidential even in the event that the communication route is breached.

Controls For Gaining Entry

Access controls are absolutely necessary for restricting the number of people who can view shared data. A system known as role-based access control, or RBAC, delegate privileges to individuals within an organization according to the role that they play within that organization. For instance, human resources staff may have access to employee records, while software developers may have access to repositories of source code. By using RBAC, organizations may ensure that only those individuals who require access to certain data can gain that access.

In addition, the access controls must to be examined and updated on a consistent basis. The access permissions of workers should be promptly modified or canceled whenever employees leave the organization or change responsibilities within the organization. This lowers the possibility that unauthorized access will be gained.

Platforms for the Secure Sharing of Files

There are several different platforms that specialize in safe file sharing. These platforms provide functions like as safe cloud storage, access controls, version control, and audit trails. Dropbox Business, Box, and Microsoft OneDrive for Business are a few examples of similar services.

These platforms frequently combine encryption with access controls to produce a safe setting for the exchange of data and documents. In addition to this, they typically comply with data protection requirements, which reduces the workload associated with compliance for enterprises.

The acronym VPN stands for "virtual private networks."

Virtual private networks, or VPNs, allow users to connect their devices to remote servers in a

secure and encrypted manner. This technology is often used to safeguard data while it is being transferred from one location to another. It is especially helpful for distant workers who need to access confidential company data while they are connected to public networks.

However, because not all virtual private networks (VPNs) offer the same level of protection, selecting a reliable VPN service is really necessary. In addition, companies need to make sure that their remote employees are taught on the best practices for using virtual private networks (VPNs), such as the importance of avoiding accessing public Wi-Fi for sensitive work.

The acronym MFA stands for "multi-factor authentication."

Users are required to present not one, but at least two different forms of identity before being granted access to a resource protected by multi-factor authentication (MFA).

Something that the user knows, such as a password, and something that the user possesses, such as a mobile device on which to receive a one-time code, are often required for this.

Even if a malicious actor manages to obtain the user's password, multi-factor authentication (MFA) is an effective approach to prevent unwanted access to data and accounts. MFA is currently a possibility with the majority of the main online services, and it should be strongly pushed for use with both personal and business accounts.

The Changing Face of Safer Coordination and Information Exchange

The technology behind blockchain and distributed ledgers

The use of blockchain, which is a decentralized ledger system, has become increasingly popular as a safe method of sharing data. The basic tenets of blockchain technology, namely immutability, transparency, and decentralization, combine to create a powerful tool for ensuring the confidentiality of shared work and data. Automating and securing data-sharing operations can be done with the help of smart contracts, which are contracts that can execute themselves and have their conditions encoded directly into code.

The management of supply chains and healthcare are two examples of industries that could

benefit greatly from utilizing blockchain technology because of the importance of data sharing among various stakeholders. Transparency and trust between parties are increased as a result of the provision of an immutable record of the data.

Model of Security Based on Zero Trust

As more and more businesses become aware of the need to rethink their strategy regarding cybersecurity, the zero-trust security model is becoming increasingly popular. This paradigm operates under the presumption that no one, whether they are a member of the organization or not, should be trusted automatically. Instead, trust is built by the rigorous verification of identities and the ongoing surveillance of behaviors.

Before allowing users, devices, or applications access to resources, businesses must first validate their identities in order to comply with the zero-trust architecture standard. In addition to that, it involves the persistent monitoring and inspection of traffic in order to identify and respond to any dangers.

AI and ML (machine learning and artificial intelligence)

The fields of artificial intelligence (AI) and machine learning (ML) are currently being utilized in an effort to increase data sharing's level of safety. Artificial intelligence can examine massive databases to search for anomalies that may point to a security issue. Machine learning algorithms can "learn" from previous data to better anticipate and thwart potential attacks.

Security systems that are powered by AI have the ability to automatically detect and respond to security issues in real time, which cuts down on the amount of time and resources needed for threat mitigation. In addition, authentication systems that are powered by AI can offer adaptive security by modifying users' access privileges according to user behavior and other risk factors.

Secure cooperation and the sharing of data are vital to modern society, as they simplify company processes, propel innovation, and make it possible for individuals to enjoy more comfort. On the other hand, robust security measures are required because the risks of data breaches, worries about privacy, and insider threats are on the rise.

Encryption, access controls, secure file sharing platforms, virtual private networks (VPNs), and multi-factor authentication are some of the most important solutions that may be used to address these difficulties. Emerging technologies such as blockchain, the zero-trust security model, and AI are further boosting security measures and redefining the way we approach data sharing as the digital world continues to grow.

In a world that is more interconnected and in which data is recognized as a valuable resource, maintaining the data's integrity and secrecy remains a key issue. Individuals and companies are able to confidently navigate the digital age with the knowledge that their data is adequately safeguarded if they adopt these security measures and continue to educate themselves on the ever-evolving threats and technology.

9.1 Secure Collaborative Tools and Platforms

In the fast changing modern workplace, secure collaborative tools and platforms are now an absolute necessity for both businesses and individuals. Because of the capabilities provided by these digital technologies, teams are able to collaborate effectively regardless of physical location. On the other hand, given the growing reliance on these tools, it is impossible to gloss over the extremely important matter of security. In this post, we will discuss the necessity of secure collaboration tools and platforms, the changing environment of remote work, as well as the critical security considerations that should be made when utilizing these technologies.

The Importance of Private and Trusted Cooperative Applications and Platforms

Enabling Workforces Around the World

These days, a company is not limited to operating out of a single office or physical location. Because of globalization and developments in technology, it is now possible to recruit workers from all over the world who possess a wide range of skills. The foundation of this workforce consists of trustworthy collaboration tools and platforms, which make it possible for companies to draw on the skills of individuals located all over the world.

These platforms make it possible for teams to collaborate effectively, regardless of whether they are working on project management, software development, content creation, or customer service. This is true even when members of the team are located in various time zones. This versatility is especially beneficial in times of crisis, such as the

COVID-19 epidemic, when working from a remote location became a requirement.

Improving One's Productivity

Productivity can be increased with the help of collaborative tools since they offer a centralized digital workspace where members of a team can connect with one another, share documents, and collaborate in real time. Work processes can be streamlined with the use of features such as instant messaging, video conferencing, and document sharing, which also reduces the need for face-to-face meetings and email correspondence.

In addition, a multitude of collaborative tools include integrations with other productivity apps, so producing a streamlined workflow that saves time and cuts down on the number of mistakes made. This interconnection is extremely useful for firms who want to operate as effectively as possible.

Increasing Interdepartmental Cooperation Through Facilitation

The members of a team who are working on the same project within the same department are not the only ones who can collaborate well. Cross-functional collaboration is essential to the success of many firms. This type of cooperation sees workers from many teams or departments working together to accomplish a common objective.

Tools and platforms that are secure for collaboration provide an environment that is both safe and effective for working across functional boundaries. They make it possible for diverse teams to share information, resources, and knowledge with one another, which ultimately drives creativity and the solution of problems.

The Evolving Terrain of Work Done From a Distance
The Growth of Work Done From Home

The traditional office-based work model is going through a considerable shift, which has been largely expedited by the epidemic caused by COVID-19. Many companies have successfully adapted to distributed workforces, including those that were previously opposed to the idea of remote labor. As a direct consequence of this, many business sectors have moved away from viewing remote work as an option and instead view it as a typical style of conducting business.

This transformation is being driven in large part by the development of secure collaborative tools and platforms. They make it possible for workers to work away from the office while preserving productivity, cutting costs connected with office space, and offering a better work-life balance all at the same time. In addition, the use of these tools is essential to guaranteeing that working remotely is both safe and productive.

The Work Model Based on Hybridization

The hybrid work paradigm has become increasingly prevalent in the world that has occurred after the epidemic. This strategy allows employees to select when and where they work, giving them the flexibility to work either in the office or remotely. For the purpose of providing support for this flexible approach and enabling smooth transitions between physical and digital work environments, organizations are investing in secure collaborative tools.

The hybrid approach gives workers the freedom to choose the working environment that is most suited to the tasks they need to complete. Because members of a team need access to the same resources and collaboration skills, regardless of where they are physically located, it is crucial to have frictionless and secure collaborative tools at your disposal.

Important Factors to Consider Regarding Safety

The Encryption of Data

When using collaborative tools and platforms, maintaining data security is of the utmost importance. The use of encryption safeguards data both while it is being transmitted and while it is being stored. By encrypting the data and transforming it into a code that can only be deciphered by the recipient for whom it was intended, it prevents illegal access.

End-to-end encryption, often known as E2E encryption, is an especially safe method. The data is encrypted on the sender's end using end-to-end encryption, and the only person who can decrypt it is the recipient of the message. Even the company that is providing the service that is facilitating the communication is unable to view the contents of the data.

Management of Access

It is essential to have access control methods in place in order to determine who can view shared information. A system known as role-based access control, or RBAC, delegate privileges to individuals within an organization according to the role that they play within that organization. This limits access to the data to only those individuals who are required to have it as part of their obligations.

Additionally, access restrictions should undergo routine reviews and be kept up to date. The access permissions of workers should be promptly modified or canceled whenever employees leave the organization or change responsibilities within the organization. This helps limit the possibility of access being gained by an unauthorized party.

Authentication Methods and Protocols

For the purpose of determining whether or not a user is who they claim to be, it is essential to use authentication procedures such as multi-factor authentication (MFA). Users are required to present not one, but at least two different forms of identity before being granted access to a resource protected by multi-factor authentication (MFA).

Even if a hostile actor has obtained the user's password, multi-factor authentication (MFA) is still able to effectively prevent unwanted access to data and accounts. The multi-factor authentication (MFA) option is now provided by the majority of the main online services, and its adoption should be advocated for both personal and business accounts.

Awareness Training on Safety and Security

Human error frequently constitutes one of the cybersecurity industry's most vulnerable points. It

is possible for employees to unintentionally undermine data security if they have not received appropriate training in the best security procedures. As a result, businesses ought to make investments in the form of security awareness training for their staff members.

This training ought to address things like identifying phishing attempts, coming up with robust passwords, and comprehending the significance of data security. Employees are kept on their toes against constantly emerging security threats through the provision of regular refresher training.

Updates to the Software on a Regular Basis

Updates to collaborative tools and platforms are frequently released in order to address any security flaws that may have been discovered and to enhance their functionality. If you don't keep these programs' versions up to date, fraudsters may be able to exploit any vulnerabilities that exist in them. As a result, enterprises ought to make the quick application of software patches and updates a priority.

Safe and Sound File Sharing

A crucial component of collaboration tools is the ability to share files in a secure manner. It guarantees that sensitive documents and information are exchanged only with the appropriate individuals while also preventing unauthorized access to those documents and information. Platforms such as Dropbox Business, Box, and Microsoft OneDrive for Business are intended to provide secure cloud storage, version control, access controls, and audit trails for their users.

Continuous Keeping an Eye On

A preventative method of ensuring safety is to perform continuous monitoring. Monitoring network traffic, user activity, and system records in order to identify and respond to potential threats in real time is an essential part of this process. Continuous vigilance enables organizations to notice security events and take corrective action before those occurrences might result in substantial damage.

Secure collaborative tools and platforms have become an absolute necessity for today's modern workforce. These tools and platforms enable effective communication and cooperation among distributed, hybrid, and global teams. The security of these technologies is of the utmost significance as the nature of work continues to undergo continuous transformation.

Encryption of data, access control, authentication systems, security awareness training, frequent software upgrades, secure file sharing, and continual monitoring are all priorities that organizations need to make in order to protect sensitive information and keep their work environments safe and productive.

In this day and age, the capacity to collaborate safely is not just an organizational requirement, but also a critical factor in determining a company's level of competitive advantage. Individuals and businesses are able to confidently exploit the power of secure collaboration tools and platforms, which results in increased productivity and innovation. This is made possible by adopting these security measures and remaining updated about new risks.

9.2 Secure Data Sharing Practices

Sharing information is an essential part of modern life, both on a personal and a professional level, given the increasingly interconnected nature of our society. The interchange of data is necessary for a variety of activities, including file sharing in the office, sending private communications, and working together on projects. On the other hand, while it is convenient to share data, doing so brings with it the duty of keeping it secure. This article examines the significance of data sharing in a secure manner, as well as best practices, technologies, and tactics that contribute to the maintenance of data confidentiality.

The Importance of Communicating Information in a Risk-Free Manner

Facilitating Collaborative Work

The safe exchange of data is absolutely necessary for teamwork. Teams and people in the workplace regularly need to communicate with one another and share papers, information, and insights in order to be productive. Tools for collaboration, data storage on the cloud, and communication platforms are the pillars upon which modern digital collaboration is built. These elements make it possible for teams working from different locations to communicate with one another and share data in real time.

In addition, the exchange of data encourages innovative thinking. To make progress in their fields, researchers, scientists, and engineers frequently collaborate to share their data and conclusions. Concerns about data breaches or the inappropriate use of data could hinder innovation if it were not possible to share data in a secure environment.

Improving the Experience of the Customer

A large number of companies now collect and keep customer data in order to provide individualized services and suggestions for their clients. The safe exchange of data is essential to the development of a streamlined and individualized experience for the customer. Sharing data can assist businesses in better understanding the preferences, behaviors, and requirements of their customers, which can in turn lead to improvements in the quality of products and services offered.

Nevertheless, any improper use of or breach of this sensitive data can have significant effects, including damage to one's reputation as well as legal repercussions. Therefore, the implementation of safe data sharing policies is absolutely necessary in order to preserve the trust and confidence of customers.

Maintaining Confidentiality

Sharing data in a secure manner is essential for protecting the privacy of individuals as well as their personal information. The disclosure of personally identifiable information, such as financial records or medical history, is frequently required in order to complete transactions or get access to services. In situations like these, the transmission of private information securely is not just an issue of convenience, but also of protecting one's privacy and building confidence.

Best Practices for the Safe Exchange of Information

The Encryption of Data

Encryption of data is absolutely necessary for any kind of safe data sharing. It guarantees the confidentiality of the data throughout both the transmission and the storage processes. The process of encrypting data entails transforming it into a code that can only be decoded by a recipient who has been specifically allowed to do so.

End-to-end encryption, also known as E2E encryption, provides an extra layer of protection. Data is encrypted on the sender's end using E2E encryption, and the data can only be decoded on the receiving end by the receiver. Even the service providers who are helping to facilitate the data transmission do not have access to the data's actual content.

Robust Controls Over The Access Points

Controls over who can access information that has been given are an absolutely necessary component. A system known as role-based access control, or RBAC, delegate privileges to individuals within an organization according to the role that they play within that organization. This limits access to the data to only those individuals who are required to have it in order to fulfill their job tasks.

Controls on access must to be evaluated and modified on a consistent basis. The access permissions of workers should be promptly modified or canceled whenever employees leave the organization or change responsibilities within the organization. This lowers the possibility that unauthorized access will be gained.

The acronym MFA stands for "multi-factor authentication."

Users are required to present two or more pieces of identity before being granted access using multi-factor authentication (also known as MFA), which adds an additional degree of protection to the system. Something that the user knows, such as a password, and something that the user possesses, such as a mobile device on which to receive a one-time code, are often required for this.

Even if a malicious actor manages to obtain the user's password, multi-factor authentication (MFA) is an effective approach to prevent unwanted access to data and accounts. MFA is currently a possibility with the majority of the main online services, and it should be strongly pushed for use with both personal and business accounts.

Platforms for the Secure Sharing of Files

Platforms for the secure sharing of data provide users with a specialized setting in which to safely exchange files and documents. These platforms typically combine encryption tools with access control mechanisms in order to produce a secure environment for the exchange of information. Dropbox Business, Box, and Microsoft OneDrive for Business are a few examples of similar services.

These platforms not only protect the data, but they also frequently comply with data protection rules, thereby minimizing the compliance load that is borne by enterprises.

Backing up and restoring of data

Data sharing must always be accompanied by a solid plan for backing up and restoring lost or damaged information. Accidents, malfunctioning hardware, and security breaches are all potential causes of data loss. Maintaining frequent backups of your data helps ensure that it can be restored even in the most catastrophic of circumstances.

The data for a backup should be kept in a safe location, apart from the data for the primary copy. The use of cloud-based backup systems is becoming increasingly common since they offer redundancy and are simple to recover from.

Awareness Training on Safety and Security

Human error is frequently one of the weakest links in the chain of data protection. It is possible for employees to unintentionally undermine data security if they have not received appropriate training in the best security procedures. As a result, businesses ought to make investments in the form of security awareness training for their staff members.

Training should cover a variety of issues, including how to identify phishing efforts, how to generate secure passwords, and how to comprehend the significance of data security. Employees are kept on their toes against constantly emerging security threats through the provision of regular refresher training.

Data Labeling and the Classification Process

Classification and labeling of data are absolutely necessary in order to differentiate between the various forms of data and implement the proper safety precautions. Not all data should be treated with the same degree of caution, and it is necessary to classify it according to how important it is and how dangerous it could be.

For instance, sensitive personal information ought to be designated as "confidential" and given the utmost level of protection possible. The efficient allocation of resources and the prioritization of security measures are both facilitated for businesses by data classification.

Instruments and Methods for the Safe Exchange of Information
The acronym VPN stands for "virtual private networks"

A Virtual Private Network, or VPN, encrypts and creates a secure connection between a user's device and a remote server. VPNs are also known as tunneling protocols. Virtual private networks, or VPNs, are frequently used to encrypt data while it is being sent from one location to another. This is especially useful for remote workers who need to access sensitive information across public networks.

However, because not all virtual private networks (VPNs) offer the same amount of protection, selecting a reliable VPN service is essential. In addition, companies need to make sure that their remote employees are taught on the best practices for using virtual private networks (VPNs), such as the importance of avoiding accessing public Wi-Fi for sensitive work.

The technology behind blockchain and distributed ledgers

The use of blockchain technology has become increasingly popular as a trusted method of information exchange. The openness, immutability, and decentralization that are inherent to blockchain technology make it a very robust solution for the secure sharing of data. Automating and securing data-sharing operations can be done with the help of smart contracts, which are contracts that can execute themselves and have their conditions encoded directly into code.

The management of supply chains and healthcare are two examples of industries that could benefit greatly from utilizing blockchain technology because of the importance of data sharing among various stakeholders. Transparency and trust between parties are increased as a result of the provision of an immutable record of the data.

Solutions for Data Loss Prevention (also known as DLP)

Data Loss Prevention (DLP) solutions are intended to monitor, detect, and prevent the loss or exchange of data in an illegal manner. They assist firms in making certain that sensitive data does not leave the organization without the appropriate authorization being granted first.

DLP systems have the ability to automatically classify and secure sensitive data, as well as monitor data movement across networks, endpoints, and cloud services. They can also enforce security standards. When working in situations with complicated requirements for data sharing, they play an essential part in the protection of the data.

Sharing information in a way that is both private and professional can benefit greatly from the use of encryption technology. Because data breaches and misuse can have serious implications, including financial losses, reputational harm, and legal liability, it is impossible to overestimate the value of ensuring that data is protected.

It is of the utmost importance to put into effect best practices such as data encryption, stringent access controls, multi-factor authentication, secure file sharing platforms, data backups, security awareness training, and data classification. The use of virtual private networks (VPNs), blockchain technology, and data loss prevention solutions are just some of the technologies and techniques that might further improve data security.

Not only are secure data sharing procedures a matter of compliance in this day and age, but they also serve as a testimonial to an organization's commitment to preserving sensitive information. In an era in which data is both a valuable asset and a privacy problem, secure data sharing practices are a matter of both. Individuals and organizations are able to confidently navigate the digital landscape if they adopt these practices and make use of the right tools. This gives them the peace of mind that comes from knowing that their data is secure.

9.3 Data Sharing Agreements and Data Access Control

Sharing data has grown both more commonplace and essential in today's world, which is characterized by data-driven decision making and increased global connectedness. Data is routinely shared for a wide variety of reasons, ranging from business partnerships to research collaborations, and it is done so by individuals, organizations, and institutions. On the other hand, this convenience poses significant concerns over the privacy and safety of data. In order to address these issues and ensure that sensitive information is effectively protected, data sharing agreements and rigorous data access control systems are crucial components. This article delves into the significance of data sharing agreements, data access control, and best practices, as well as their respective roles in the protection of sensitive information.

The Importance of Entering Into Agreements to Share Data Specifying One's Duties and Obligations

Data sharing agreements are papers that are legally enforceable and serve the purpose of defining the duties and responsibilities of the parties participating in the process of data sharing. In these agreements, the data that is being provided, the reason that it is being shared, as well as the terms and conditions under which the data can be accessed and used, are all spelled out in plain detail.

Agreements on the exchange of data serve to prevent misunderstandings and disagreements between the parties involved by providing for the clear delineation of roles and expectations. They serve as a legal framework that ensures all parties will adhere to the agreements that have been agreed upon.

Who Owns the Data and How It's Used

The determination of who owns the data and who has the rights to use it is of the utmost significance when it comes to data sharing. In most cases, agreements on the sharing of data will detail who the data belong to, as well as who has the authority to use the data and for what objectives. These agreements assist avoid disagreements and potential legal challenges that are related to intellectual property and data ownership.

In addition, data sharing agreements typically include sections that explain the acceptable use of the data that has been shared. For instance, certain data may be provided for the sole purpose of conducting research, while other data may contain particular limits on its usage, such as clauses requiring that it not be used for commercial reasons or disclosed to third parties.

Observance of all applicable laws and standards

In the current regulatory context, data sharing frequently requires compliance with a variety of rules and regulations, such as the General Data Protection Regulation (GDPR) in Europe or the Health Insurance Portability and Accountability Act (HIPAA) in the United States. Examples of such laws and regulations include the GDPR and HIPAA, respectively. By helping to verify that all parties are in compliance with these legal and ethical standards, data sharing agreements play an important role.

These agreements provide a method for data controllers and processors to define how they will handle and protect data in a manner that is compatible with legal and ethical requirements in a way that is consistent with how they will handle and protect data.

Data sharing agreements allow both transparency and accountability through the detailed documentation of the aforementioned activities.

Reduced Exposure to Danger

The exchange of data is not without its associated dangers. Agreements to share data are an indispensable instrument for mitigating risk in this day and age of widespread data breaches and cyberattacks. They explain the obligations for alerting impacted individuals as well as the relevant authorities, as well as specify how the parties will manage data breaches and other security issues.

Data sharing agreements typically include stipulations on liability and indemnification, both of which are important considerations in the event that a data breach or unauthorized use of data results in a dispute or legal action. These agreements function in the capacity of insurance, assisting the parties involved in successfully allocating and mitigating risks.

Guidelines for the Execution of Successful Data-Sharing Agreements

Clarify the Definition of Data

A clear and precise definition of the data that is going to be shared should be included in a well-written agreement for its sharing. Specifying the type of data (such as personal, financial, or medical information), the format (such as structured or unstructured data), and any particular identifiers or categories that require protection are all part of this step.

Function and Range of Coverage

The objective of the data sharing as well as its parameters should be outlined in the agreement. What are you planning to do with the information, and for how long will it be shared with others? If you want to prevent others from using data in inappropriate ways, you should make the restrictions and limitations clear.

Ownership of Data and Other Forms of Intellectual Property

Clearly define who owns the data and who has rights to the intellectual property. This involves determining who owns the data that is being shared and who retains ownership over works that are produced from the data, such as articles or products based on research.

Protection of Information and Encryption of Data

Include a discussion of the safeguards that will be put in place to protect the data that has been disclosed. To guarantee that the data is kept private and secure, the protocols for encrypting it, controlling who can access it, and otherwise protecting it should be described.

Observance of all Relevant Legal and Ethical Requirements

Indicate how the sharing of data will comply with the relevant rules and regulations, such as those pertaining to the protection of personal data, as well as ethical standards. This involves laying out the procedures for acquiring the relevant consents and permissions, as well as the systems for reporting and handling any breaches or non-compliance that may occur.

The Process of Keeping and Erasing Data

Provide details regarding the length of time that the data that has been shared will be stored, as well as the conditions under which it will either be erased or given back to the original owner. It is absolutely necessary to have solid data retention policies in place in order to stop unwanted data access and usage.

Roles and Responsibilities Regarding the Sharing of Data

Make sure that the duties and obligations of each party that is participating in the data sharing are very clear. All data controllers, data processors, and any other third-party service providers are included in this category. The obligations and responsibilities of both parties should be outlined in the agreement.

The Importance of Having a Data Access Control System

Controlling and limiting who has access to particular pieces of data or resources is the process known as data access control (DAC). The protection of sensitive information relies heavily on the implementation of this fundamental component of data security, which is an essential part of the whole system. The following are some of the most important reasons for its significance:

Avoid Gaining Access Without Permission

Through the implementation of data access control, unauthorized people are prevented from accessing sensitive information. It is possible for companies to reduce the likelihood of data breaches or leaks by ensuring that only authorized workers are able to see or edit data. This can be accomplished by installing stringent controls.

Observance of the Rules and Regulations

Controlling who can access the data is absolutely necessary in order to be in compliance with data protection standards. In order to comply with regulations such as GDPR, businesses are required to restrict access to individuals' personal data and guarantee that only those with an appropriate reason can view it. Should you fail to comply, you risk incurring significant penalties.

Maintain the Privacy of Sensitive Information

A large number of businesses deal with sensitive information on a regular basis, which may include trade secrets, financial data, or proprietary research. Data access control contributes to the protection of this sensitive information by restricting the individuals within the organization who are permitted to access it, in addition to recording both access and usage of the data.

Protection against Data Loss

Controlling who has access to the data can reduce the risk of data being stolen or lost. It is possible for businesses to lessen the likelihood of inadvertent data leakage by imposing restrictions on the individuals who are authorized to download, copy, or transfer company information.

Methods of Data Access Control That Are Most Effective
RBAC stands for "role-based access control"

Access Granted Based on Roles Access to data can be effectively managed through the use of control. It does this by assigning permissions to individuals based on the position that they play within an organization. For instance, human resources staff members might have access to employment records, while software developers might have access to source code repositories. This restricts the information that individuals can access to only that which is relevant to the duties associated with their jobs.

The acronym MFA stands for "multi-factor authentication"

Users are required to present two or more pieces of identity before being granted access under multi-factor authentication, which adds an additional degree of protection to the system. Something that the user knows, such as a password, and something that the user possesses, such as a mobile device on which to receive a one-time code, are often required for this. MFA is a strong mechanism for validating the identity of users and preventing illegal access. MFA stands for multi-factor authentication.

Audit Trails (plural)

Audit trails are logs that document when and by whom specific data was accessed. Monitoring data access, identifying unauthorized activity, and keeping tabs on changes to sensitive information are all made possible for enterprises by implementing audit trails. This aids in the identification of security issues and the timely mitigation of hazards.

The principle of least privilege

The concept of providing users only the minimum amount of access necessary for them to carry out the duties assigned to them is known as the least privilege principle. By ensuring that users only have access to the information that they require and nothing more, it decreases the danger of data being exposed either unintentionally or maliciously.

Continuous Keeping an Eye On

Controlling access to the data should involve continual monitoring of both the activity of users and the traffic on the network. Because of this continual awareness, companies are better able to spot possible risks and react to them in the moment.

A code or cipher

Encryption of data, and particularly encryption from beginning to end, is absolutely necessary for the protection of data both while it is in transit and while it is stored. It guarantees that the data will continue to be protected and unreadable even in the event that unwanted access is gained.

For the purpose of protecting sensitive information in this day and age, when data sharing has become an inherent part of modern life, data sharing agreements and data access control are very necessary. The legal basis for defining obligations, safeguarding data ownership, and ensuring compliance with laws and regulations is provided by data sharing agreements in the form of a contract. Among the best practices are explicitly identifying data, establishing roles and duties, resolving issues of data ownership and intellectual property, implementing data security measures, and specifying purpose and scope.

The control of data access is equally essential since it helps avoid data loss, safeguards personal information, assures compliance with legislation, and prevents illegal access. Role-based access control (also known as RBAC), multi-factor authentication (also known as MFA), audit trails, adhering to the principle of least privilege, continuous monitoring, and encryption are some of the best practices for controlling data access.Organizations, institutions, and individuals can navigate the environment of data sharing with confidence if they adopt these practices and methods and know that sensitive information will continue to be protected and that privacy and security concerns will be effectively addressed.

Chapter 10

Incident Response and Data Breach Recovery

The protection of data is of the utmost importance in this day and age, when it serves as the very foundation of modern businesses. In spite of an organization's best efforts, data breaches and security events can still take place, which could result in substantial harm to the organization's reputation, finances, and even legal repercussions. It is crucial to have a solid incident response plan in place, as well as a clear strategy for recovering from a data breach, in order to reduce the likelihood of these hazards occurring. This in-depth study digs into the realm of incident response and data breach recovery, examining the significance of these processes as well as their fundamental steps, recommended procedures, and the role that technology plays in preserving information and guaranteeing the continuity of corporate operations.

The Significance of Being Quick to Respond to Incidents Locating Dangers and Taking Precautions Against Them

A methodical strategy to resolving and managing security breaches or other incidents that may have an effect on an organization's information systems is what we mean when we talk about "incident response." It plays a critical part in identifying possible dangers and minimizing their effects before those prospective threats may develop into severe security lapses.

Organizations are able to develop defined methods for monitoring and identifying security incidents if they execute an incident response strategy. This enables them to respond quickly, minimizing the potential damage, and protecting sensitive information from being exposed to the greatest extent possible.

Keeping Private Information and One's Good Name Safe

Breach of data can result in the loss of sensitive information, as well as financial and reputational fallout for a business. By demonstrating a dedication to the protection of users' personal information and data, a business can defend its reputation with the support of an effective incident response strategy.

A prompt and well-managed incident response can also help confine the impact of a security breach, stopping it from spreading throughout the business or causing additional damage. This can be accomplished by preventing the breach from occurring in the first place.

Compliance with Regulations

Having a good incident response strategy is essential for compliance in an environment that is heavily regulated and where the regulations governing data privacy and security are getting increasingly strict. Organizations are required to have data breach response plans in place by a number of regulations, including the General Data Protection Regulation (GDPR) in the European Union and the Health Insurance Portability and Accountability Act (HIPAA) in the United States.

If you do to comply with these regulations, you may face legal repercussions as well as financial penalties. Not only is having an effective incident response strategy a recommended best practice, but in many instances, it is also a legal necessity.

The Significance of Recovering Lost or Stolen Data
Trying to Keep Financial Losses to a Minimum

Data breaches can result in considerable financial losses for its victims due to factors such as the cost of restoring lost data, paying legal settlements, and losing business. A data breach recovery strategy that is well-structured helps firms reduce these losses by handling the breach effectively, reducing the damage, and returning to normal operations as quickly as feasible.

Regaining the Trust of Our Customers

When trying to recover after a data breach, it is not enough to simply solve the technical flaws; you also need to work on rebuilding confidence. Customers, clients, and other stakeholders require reassurance that the company is committed to protecting their privacy and the data they provide, as well as that their data is secure.

A reliable plan for recovering after a data breach should include a communication plan that acknowledges the issue in an open and honest manner and describes the efforts taken to prevent the breach from happening again. This proactive strategy can assist in the rebuilding of trust and the maintenance of strong relationships with partners and customers.

Eliminating Future Occurrences

Beyond addressing the immediate repercussions of a data breach, a complete plan for recovering from a data breach goes further. In addition to that, it contains measures that can be taken to stop instances of the same kind from occurring in the future.

Organizations are able to lessen the likelihood of another security breach occurring if they conduct an investigation into the underlying factors that led to the initial incident and then take steps to amend existing practices in order to strengthen their defenses against potential threats. This method that looks into the future is necessary in order to guarantee the long-term safety and resiliency of an organization's information systems.

Important Stages in the Reaction to an Incident

A preparatory step

Create a plan for dealing with unexpected events

The first thing that should be done in response to such occurrence is to prepare. The development of a well-documented incident response plan, which lays out the procedures and responsibilities for reacting to security occurrences, should be a must for organizations. This plan should be adapted to meet the specific requirements of the company, and it should include information on how to get in touch with the incident response team, as well as details on data classification and preset procedures for responding to incidents.

Gather an Emergency Response Team together

When it comes to organizing the response to a security problem, having an incident response team on hand is absolutely necessary. This team often consists of members who have expertise in a variety of fields, including information technology (IT), law, public relations, and compliance. Training and regular drills are two ways that a team can better prepare itself to respond quickly and effectively in an emergency situation.

Determine Who Does What and Why They Do It

The tasks and responsibilities of each individual participant in the incident response team has to be made perfectly clear. In the event of an incident, this guarantees that tasks are distributed and carried out in an effective manner.

Observation and Investigation
Finding Out What Happened

During the detection phase, an organization will monitor its networks and systems for any indications that a potential security breach may have occurred. This can be accomplished with the help of automated security solutions like intrusion detection systems (IDS) and security information and event management (SIEM) systems, in addition to the incident response team's manual monitoring of the network's activity.

Conducting Research on Occurrences

The incident response team should conduct an investigation into a potential event as soon as it is discovered in order to assess the type and level of the threat. This may involve conducting an investigation into the cause of the incident, determining the impact it had, and locating systems or data that were compromised.

Elimination and Containment of the Threat

The practice of containing

After it has been established that there has been an incident, the organization must move promptly in order to bring the situation under control. This may involve isolating systems that have been infiltrated, disabling accounts that have been compromised, and stopping the problem from spreading further.

Complete extermination

After the threat has been contained, the incident response team must then begin working to

eliminate it. Performing this step may require locating and eliminating harmful code, vulnerabilities, or access points that are not authorized. The objective is to guarantee that the problem has been thoroughly fixed and that all of the systems are protected.

Recuperation and Reflections on the Experience

Return to normalcy

During the recovery stage, the primary objective is to resume business as usual. This includes restoring the systems that have been compromised, verifying their security, and making sure that they are completely functional. During this phase, organizations should also think about their protocols for data backup and recovery in the event of a disaster.

Experience and its Fruits

It is essential to carry out a post-incident investigation once the problem has been rectified in order to comprehend what transpired and the factors that led to its occurrence. This research assists businesses in determining where they have room for improvement in terms of their security posture and developing better incident response protocols.

Transmission of Information and Reporting

Throughout the entirety of the incident response process, clear and concise communication is of the utmost importance. Notifying those who have a stake in the matter, such as customers, employees, and regulatory agencies, when necessary is part of this. Additionally, the incident response team have to put together incident reports in order to document the incident, the measures taken in reaction to it, and the lessons gained.

The Very Best Methods for Handling Emergencies
Examine and Bring the Plan Up to Date

Tabletop exercises and simulations should be used on a regular basis to test the incident response plan. This helps to ensure that the team is ready to respond successfully in the event of a genuine occurrence. In addition, the strategy needs to be revised on a regular basis in order to include previously gained knowledge and adjust to newly emerging dangers.

Working Together and Coordinating Efforts

A successful reaction to an incident requires close cooperation and coordination not only among the members of the team but also among the various stakeholders. In order to facilitate effective teamwork in the event of a crisis, organizations must to cultivate cultures of open communication and openness.

Classification of the Data

Helping to focus response efforts is a clear categorization and classification of data depending on how sensitive the data is and how important it is. Because not all data is equally valuable, it is necessary to have a solid grasp of what is in jeopardy in order to arrive at sound decisions in the event of an incident.

Safe copies of data

The process of data, system, and configuration recovery can be simplified by performing backups on a regular basis. On the other hand, backups should be kept in a safe location and tested on a regular basis to ensure that they can be depended upon in the event that something goes wrong.

Compliance Requirements in Addition to Legal Considerations

Make sure that the plans and activities you have in place to respond to incidents meet all of the legal and regulatory requirements. It is absolutely necessary for compliance and risk management to have a solid understanding of the legal obligations and reporting requirements associated with data breaches.

Key Steps in the Recovery Process after a Data Breach

Isolate Systems That Are Affected

Isolating the impacted systems in order to avoid additional harm and access by unauthorized parties is the first stage in recovering after a data breach. For this purpose, the compromised systems may need to be taken offline or disconnected from the network.

Hold the Breakout in Check

After the security breach has been located, companies need to act to secure the area. Performing this step entails locating the source of the security breach, plugging any vulnerabilities found, and preventing any further unwanted access.

Conduct a Needs Analysis.

The extent of the damage that was caused by the breach should be evaluated by the organizations. This includes locating the data and systems that have been compromised and gaining a grasp of the impact on the individuals who have been impacted as well as the company as a whole.

Notify Those Who Are Affected

Organizations may be required to tell affected parties, such as customers or workers, of a

breach in their security, depending on the legal obligations that are in place and the nature of the breach. The communication should be open and transparent, and it should also include direction on how to keep personal information secure.

Recuperate and Put Back Together

In the recovery phase, you will work to return disrupted systems and data to their original, unaffected states. Because of this, it's possible that the software will need to be reinstalled, patches applied, and security measures verified.

Put into action improvements to the security system

One of the most important components of recovering from a data breach is locating the security flaws that allowed the breach to occur and fixing those flaws in order to avoid a similar breach from happening in the future. Patching software, tightening access limits, and improving monitoring and detecting capabilities are all potential steps in this direction.

Observe and Perform Tests

After recovering from a data breach, companies should continue to monitor systems and undertake regular testing to verify that security measures are effective and that no new vulnerabilities have surfaced. This is to ensure that no new vulnerabilities have been introduced.

Recommended Procedures for the Recovering of Lost or Stolen Data

Swiftness as well as effectiveness

The ability to quickly and effectively recover from a data breach is essential. The longer it takes to recover from a breach and get it under control, the more harm it is likely to inflict. In light of this, companies ought to place a high priority on swift response and recovery operations.

Openness and honesty

When recovering from a data breach, transparent communication is absolutely necessary. Organizations have a responsibility to communicate honestly with affected parties and stakeholders about data breaches, the impact of the breach, and the efforts being taken to remedy the breach. Restoring confidence and preserving a good reputation are both facilitated by transparency.

Compliance with the Law and Regulations

Make sure that the efforts to recover from a data breach comply with all of the applicable legal and regulatory standards. The rules and regulations that pertain to data breaches must be followed by organizations, including the obligations for reporting and notifications to authorities as well as individuals who have been affected by the breach.

Regular Advancement in Quality

The recovery from a data breach should not be considered the end of the tale. The lessons that can be learned from the security breach should be used by organizations to continuously improve both their security posture and their incident response protocols. The organization's security defenses can be found to have vulnerabilities and flaws if they are subjected to testing and reviews on a regular basis.

The Part That Technology Plays

Technology plays an essential part in both the reaction to incidents and the recovery from data breaches. The following is a list of important technology components that could help improve these processes:

IDS stands for "intrusion detection system"

The use of intrusion detection systems is absolutely necessary in order to identify security breaches in real time. The intrusion detection system (IDS) can examine the network traffic and system logs for unexpected activity or recognized threat signatures. When the IDS has been properly set, it is able to send alerts and start response actions whenever it identifies potentially malicious behavior.

SIEM Systems are abbreviated for Security Information and Event Management

SIEM (Security Information and Event Management) systems offer a single platform for collecting and analyzing data about security from a variety of sources. These systems can assist organizations in correlating data from a variety of logs and sources, which enables the identification of possible issues and the provision of helpful insights for incident response.

Solutions for Data Loss Prevention (also known as DLP)

Monitoring and safeguarding data while it is both in motion and at rest or while it is being used is what data loss prevention (DLP) systems do. They are able to contribute to both the incident response and the data breach recovery processes by helping to identify and prevent unwanted data access, sharing, or movement.

EDR stands for "endpoint detection and response"

EDR solutions focus on detecting and responding to security issues on endpoints, such as individual devices and servers. These endpoints can be anything from a computer to a mobile device. They enable swift action to be taken in response to potential threats and provide insights into the activities and behaviors of endpoints.

Solutions for Backup and Recovery in the Event of a Disaster

The recovery after a data breach cannot be attempted without regular backups as well as options for disaster recovery. These solutions assist organizations in restoring their data and systems to a condition that existed before to the breach, which helps to reduce the amount of downtime experienced and the amount of data that is lost.

Forensics Equipment

Investigating and evaluating security incidents is made easier with the help of forensics technologies. The incident response teams can collect evidence, track down the source of a breach, and comprehend the impact of the breach with the assistance of these tools. An in-depth forensic investigation is absolutely necessary in order to comprehend the specifics of a security breach and the remedial actions that must be taken.

The recovery from data breaches and the reaction to incidents are both key components of the cybersecurity strategy of a company. Not only are they reactive measures, but they are also proactive techniques to reduce the impact of security incidents, thereby protecting an organization's reputation as well as its revenue.

A methodical approach to locating, containing, and reducing the impact of potential dangers is required for incident response. Preparation, detection, analysis, containment, recovery, and communication are the primary focuses of this strategy. The testing of the incident response plan, the promotion of collaboration and coordination, the classification of data, the implementation of safe backups, and the verification of compliance with legal and regulatory standards are all examples of best practices.

Equally important is the process of recovering from a data breach, which should center on reducing financial damages, restoring consumer trust, and preventing future occurrences. This procedure includes isolating the compromised systems, bringing the security breach under control, determining the extent of the damage, alerting those who were affected, and installing new security measures. The best practices for recovering after a data breach include acting quickly and effectively, maintaining transparency, complying with applicable laws and regulations, and seeking continual improvement.

In order to support incident response and data breach recovery efforts, technology, such as intrusion detection systems, SIEM systems, data loss prevention solutions, endpoint detection and response, backup and disaster recovery solutions, and forensics tools, plays an essential role.

Organizations that place a priority on incident response and data breach recovery are better positioned to protect sensitive information and assure the continuity of their business operations in an environment where the risks to information security are constantly developing. They are able to confidently traverse the complicated world of cybersecurity if they utilize technology and embrace best practices.

10.1 Developing an Incident Response Plan

Data security is of the utmost importance in the linked world of today. Any company, regardless of its size, runs the risk of experiencing a cybersecurity incident, which might include anything from a data breach to malware assaults and even more. The creation of an incident response plan is a preventative approach that enables organizations to better prepare for and react to security issues. This article investigates the significance of incident response plans, the primary stages involved in creating one, best practices, and the role that technology plays in the protection of digital assets.

The Importance of Having a Plan in Place for When an Incident Occurs

Readiness for Contingencies Regarding Safety and Security

Plans for responding to incidents are preventative actions that are aimed to assist organizations in being ready for potential security breaches. Having a well-defined plan in place ensures that an organization is ready to respond quickly and efficiently in the event that a security issue occurs. This is preferable to the alternative of reacting to occurrences on an ad hoc basis.

Reducing the Amount of Damage

One of the most important advantages of having incident response plans is the possibility that they will reduce harm. Organizations are able to reduce the extent of the harm caused by security breaches if they respond to occurrences in a quick and effective manner. It is possible that as a consequence of this, financial losses, reputational harm, and regulatory implications will all be mitigated.

Observance of the Rules and Regulations

The General Data Protection Regulation (GDPR) in Europe and the Health Insurance Portability and Accountability Act (HIPAA) in the United States are two examples of laws and regulations that are particularly stringent with regard to the protection of personal information and are in effect across a variety of sectors and areas. In order for companies to comply with legislation concerning the notification and reporting of data breaches, these regulations frequently demand that companies have incident response plans in place.

Management of One's Reputation

The manner in which a company handles a breach in its security can have a substantial effect on the reputation of that firm. The successful execution of an incident response plan not only indicates a commitment to security but also has the potential to assist in the restoration of trust among customers, partners, and other stakeholders. On the other hand, if the incident is not handled properly, it can result in reputational harm that lasts for a long time.

Important Measures to Take Before Creating an Emergency Procedure

1. **Define the Objectives and the Scope of the Project**
   It is vital to identify the objectives and scope of the incident response plan before beginning the road of constructing the plan itself to respond to an incident. Determine what it is you want to accomplish with the plan, as well as the many kinds of emergencies that it will cover. Think about the particular requirements of the company as well as the dangers it faces.

2. **To put together an incident response team**
   The plan revolves around an incident response team as its central component. Gather together a team of specialists that are equipped with the experience and expertise required to deal with a wide range of security breaches. Professionals in information technology, people with expertise in law and public relations, those who specialize in compliance, and so on could all be members of the team.

3. **Construct a Policy for Responding to Incidents**
   The policy should provide an overview of the organization's position on incident response, highlighting the significance of immediate reporting as well as the duties and responsibilities of the incident response team.

4. **Create an Incident Response Plan as the fourth step**
   The incident response plan is a thorough document that explains the steps that need to be taken in the event that a security incident takes place. It ought to include the entirety of the incident response lifecycle, from the initial discovery to the final lessons learned and recovery.

5. **Classification and Prioritization of Incidents**
   Determine the criteria that will be used to categorize and rank the severity of occurrences, as well as the possible impact they could have on the company. During incident response, this classification helps effectively distribute resources to meet the needs of the situation.

6. **Develop Procedures for Dealing with Incidents**

   In this section, you will outline the step-by-step procedures that will be followed for the various sorts of occurrences. The procedures should address how to detect incidents, how to control them, how to eliminate threats, how to restore systems and data, as well as how to communicate with stakeholders.

7. **Practice and Examination**

   Tabletop exercises and simulations should be used on a consistent basis to test the incident response plan. Training the incident response team guarantees that they will be adequately prepared to carry out the strategy as intended. Testing helps reveal aspects of the plan that need to be improved upon as well as flaws.

8. **The communication plan**

   Create a communication plan that will alert stakeholders and the general public in the event that a security incident takes place. In order to effectively manage the organization's reputation, this strategy ought to incorporate sample documents for incident notifications and public relations initiatives.

9. **Documentation and Reporting constitute the Ninth Step.**

   Define the documentation and reporting requirements for incident response in a clear and concise manner. Logs, event reports, and post-incident analyses are all included in this category. For the sake of gaining a deeper comprehension of the events that transpired and enhancing response protocols, accurate recording is critical.

10. **Evaluate and Make Changes**

It is important to evaluate and update the incident response plan on a regular basis to ensure that it continues to be relevant and is aligned with the needs of the organization as well as the ever-changing threat landscape.

Guidelines for the Construction of an Effective Incident Response Plan

Adjust Your Goals to Fit the Business's

Check to see that the organization's overarching business goals and the amount of risk it is willing to take are reflected in the incident response strategy. This congruence makes it easier to justify investments in security and preparedness for responding to incidents.

Determine Who Does What and Why They Do It

Make sure that the duties and responsibilities of each member of the incident response team are defined in a way that is easy to understand. To effectively respond to an incident, it is necessary to have a solid understanding of who is responsible for what.

Collaborate and talk to one another

Develop a spirit of cooperation and openness to communication throughout the organization. For a rapid and well-coordinated response to any security issue, effective communication is absolutely necessary.

Regular Practices and Examinations

It is essential to test and practice the incident response strategy in order to guarantee that it is both practical and effective. Conduct simulations on a regular basis in order to identify aspects of the strategy that could use improvement.

Relationships With Outside Parties

During the incident response process, you should think about how third-party relationships will be managed. This includes communicating with any partners, service providers, or vendors who might be engaged in the issue.

Compliance Requirements in Addition to Legal Considerations

Check to see that the incident response plan complies with all legal and regulatory requirements, such as those pertaining to the notification and reporting of data breaches. To verify that the plan is compliant with the regulations, legal professionals should review it and give their approval.

The Part That Technology Plays

Technology plays an important part in incident response, since it assists organizations in detecting, analyzing, and mitigating security occurrences in an efficient manner. The following is a list of important technological components:

IDS stands for "intrusion detection system"

Network traffic and system activity are continuously scanned by intrusion detection systems for telltale signals of any breaches in network security. IDS can identify illegal access, activity from malware, and other suspicious behavior, and then trigger warnings so that additional investigation can be conducted.

SIEM Systems are abbreviated for Security Information and Event Management.

SIEM systems collect data from a wide variety of sources, such as logs, network traffic, and system activity, and then analyze that data centrally. They offer an all-encompassing perspective of the security events that have occurred and assist in the identification of patterns that may suggest security issues.

Solutions for Data Loss Prevention (also known as DLP)

DLP solutions can monitor and secure data while it is being used, while it is at rest, and while it is moving. They contribute to the prevention of unwanted data access and exchange, which makes them essential instruments in the incident response process.

Platforms for Responding to Incidents

Platforms for incident response provide a method of managing incidents that is both centralized and automated. These platforms can improve efficiency and collaboration within the incident response team by streamlining incident detection, response, and recovery.

Forensics Equipment

Investigating and evaluating security incidents is made easier with the help of forensics technologies. They contribute to the collection of evidence, the identification of the source of incidents, and the comprehension of the consequences of such episodes. The application of forensic science to post-incident investigations is absolutely necessary.

Solutions for Backup and Recovery in the Event of a Disaster

It is imperative to have regular backups as well as options for disaster recovery in order to recover from any security events. They help restore data and systems to a previous state, before the incident occurred, hence reducing the amount of time that the system is offline and the amount of data that is lost.

The formulation of a procedure for handling incidents is an essential element of the cybersecurity strategy of any firm. It guarantees that the business is ready to respond quickly and efficiently to security crises, reducing harm and protecting digital assets in the process.

Defining objectives and scope, assembling an incident response team, developing an incident response policy and plan, creating incident classification and prioritization mechanisms, developing incident response procedures, testing and training, and defining communication and reporting processes are key steps in the process of developing an incident response plan.

Best practices for developing an incident response plan include aligning the plan with the objectives of the business, defining roles and responsibilities, encouraging collaboration and communication, conducting regular tests and drills, taking into consideration the relationships with third parties, and ensuring compliance with legal and regulatory requirements.

Technology, such as intrusion detection systems, SIEM systems, data loss prevention solutions, incident response platforms, forensics tools, and backup and disaster recovery solutions, plays an essential role in the support of incident response efforts. These technologies assist organizations in effectively detecting, analyzing, and mitigating security incidents. The ability of an organization to respond to incidents and protect its digital assets can be improved through the implementation of best practices and the utilization of technology.

10.2 The Anatomy of a Data Breach

In this day and age of digital technology, it is unfortunately becoming more and more typical for there to be data breaches. It entails gaining unauthorized access to sensitive information, acquiring that knowledge, or disclosing it, all of which can have severe repercussions for both persons and businesses. It is vital to have an in-depth understanding of the fundamental components that make up the anatomy of a data breach in order to successfully reduce the risks that are connected with data breaches. In this post, we will investigate the many factors that can lead to a data breach, such as the attack vectors, breach methods, and potential repercussions.

Vectors of Assault

1. **Scams Using the Email System**
   Phishing attacks are a widespread sort of attack vector in which hackers use misleading emails, websites, or messages to trick individuals into disclosing personal information such as login credentials or financial details. These attacks are carried out via the use of a phishing website.
2. **Malware (adjective)**
   Computer systems are frequently compromised through the deployment of malicious software such as viruses, Trojan horses, and ransomware. Once it has gained access to the system, malware might steal data, cause disruptions, or ask for ransoms.
3. **Dangers Coming From Within**
   Individuals working for or employed by an organization can represent a threat to the company when they steal information or accidentally or deliberately reveal it by abusing the access permissions they have been granted. These people might be employees, independent contractors, or some other trusted personnel.
4. **Attacks Classified as Distributed Denial of Service (DDoS)**
   DDoS assaults cause a network to become overloaded and inaccessible to users because of this. It is possible that these attacks are being used as distractions so that other, more clandestine operations can be carried out in the background.
5. **Documentation that is either Fake or Stolen**

Credentials that are either not strong enough or that have been stolen can allow an attacker to obtain access to systems and data. Attacks using brute force, credential stuffing, or phishing campaigns are all potential vectors for achieving this goal.

Methods for Breaching

1. **Access Granted Without Permission**
   Unauthorized access happens when an attacker takes advantage of a vulnerability in a system or application in order to obtain access to sensitive data or systems without the appropriate authorization.
2. **Theft of Information**
   Theft of data is a typical objective of data breaches, which is when sensitive data, such as personal information, financial data, or intellectual property, is exfiltrated by cybercriminals.
3. **The Manipulation of Data**
   Data may be manipulated by attackers, which may compromise its accuracy or integrity under certain circumstances. This can have severe repercussions for companies and organizations that are dependent on accurate data.
4. **Restitution**
   Ransomware is a type of malicious software that encrypts a victim's data or computer system and then demands a payment from the victim in exchange for the key to decode the data. It is not recommended to pay the ransom because doing so does not ensure that the data will be recovered and instead encourages the hackers to launch other attacks.
5. **Attacks That Are Distributed**

Attackers may use dispersed attack tactics, such as initiating simultaneous attacks from multiple places or devices. This is one example of a distributed attack strategy. Distributed assaults have the potential to overwhelm security protocols and make detection more difficult.

Possible Repercussions

1. **A Decrease in One's Wealth**
   Breach of data security can lead to huge financial damages for enterprises. The costs may include legal fees, regulatory fines, financial compensation to those who were harmed, and expenses linked to the recovery from the breach.
2. **Injury to One's Reputation**
   A damaged reputation is potentially one of the most long-lasting repercussions that can result from a data breach. It can be difficult for businesses to win back the trust of their clients, partners, and the general public.
3. **Repercussions in a Court of Law**
   Data breaches frequently have legal repercussions, particularly when they result in the disclosure of personally identifiable information (PII). It is possible for organizations to be subject to legal action, regulatory inquiries, and compliance fines.
4. **Theft of Identities**
   The aftermath of a data breach can be painful for individuals, as the theft of personal information can lead to identity theft, financial fraud, and mental suffering, among other negative outcomes.
5. **The loss of data**
   Breach of data can result in irretrievable loss of data, which can be especially disastrous for
   businesses that rely on essential information such as research data, customer records, or intellectual property.
6. **Interruptions to the Operations**

The aftermath of a data breach can cause normal operations to be disrupted since firms frequently have to take systems offline in order to investigate and recover from the attack. This downtime can have an impact on production as well as service to customers.

Mitigation and prevention of adverse effects

1. **All-Inclusive Safety and Assurance Measures**
   Protect yourself from malicious software and illegal access by implementing stringent security measures such as firewalls, intrusion detection systems, and antivirus software.
2. **Instruction for Workers**
   It is important to educate staff on best practices for cybersecurity, such as how to identify phishing efforts, how to maintain good password hygiene, and how to comprehend the significance of data protection.
3. **Restrictions on Access**
   Establish stringent access controls to restrict user privileges and guarantee that only authorized people may view sensitive data. This will prevent unauthorized individuals from viewing the data.
4. **Codes and ciphers**
   Encrypt sensitive data while it is being moved around and while it is sitting in storage to prevent unauthorized access to it even if it is obtained by the wrong people.
5. **A plan for dealing with incidents**
   Create an incident response strategy for your firm, and make sure to keep it up to date on a regular basis. This plan should include how your organization will react when security breaches occur. Make sure that the strategy includes mechanisms for communication, legal considerations, and coordination with law enforcement when it is appropriate to do so.
6. **Routine Inspections and Examinations**
   Conduct regular audits and tests of security measures, including simulations of probable security incidents, vulnerability assessments, and penetration testing.
7. **Backing up and Recovering Your Data**

In the event that your organization is compromised, it is imperative that you have your data backed up in a secure location and ensure that your disaster recovery plan is always up to date.

10.3 Data Recovery and Business Continuity

Planning for data recovery and business continuity are important parts of any organization's plan to keep its processes safe, keep its data safe, and make sure it can keep running even when bad things happen. This piece talks about why data recovery and business continuity are important, what their main parts are, what the best practices are, and how technology can help make sure that business operations can keep going even when there are problems.

Why data recovery and business continuity are important

Getting rid of downtime

Unexpected events, like natural disasters, hacking, or broken equipment, can make it hard for a business to run. Downtime can be expensive because it can lead to lost sales, less work getting done, and damage to your image. To keep important processes running and reduce downtime, you need data recovery and business continuity plans.

Keeping data safe

Companies need to keep their info safe because losing it can have very bad effects. Data recovery methods help make sure that data is safe and can be restored if it gets lost. This is true whether the data is customer records, intellectual property, financial data, or other important information.

Compliance with Regulations

There are rules in many fields that say businesses need to have data recovery and business survival plans in place. For those who don't follow these rules, there could be legal and financial implications. Strong plans not only keep a business running, but they also meet government standards.

Managing Your Reputation

A company can keep its good name if it has a good data recovery and business survival plan in place. Customers and other important people in an organization see that it can keep running and look out for their best interests even when things go wrong, that builds trust and confidence.

Important Parts of Business Continuity and Data Recovery
Evaluation of Risk

Make a list of possible risks and threats that could affect your business, like natural disasters, online threats, power outages, or problems with the supply chain. You should do a full risk assessment to find out what weaknesses need to be fixed.

Backing up and recovering data

Set up a strong way to back up your info. Back up important data and processes regularly, both on-site and off-site. For backups, you might want to use cloud-based options. If you lose data, you need clear data recovery steps to get your operations back up and running quickly.

Study of the Effects on Business

Do a business impact study to find out what will happen when operations are interrupted. Figure out which processes, systems, and data are the most important and need to be recovered first. In a strategic way, this study helps decide how to use resources and time.

How to Respond in an Emergency

Make an emergency reaction plan that spells out what needs to be done right away in case of a problem. Make sure that everyone knows what to do in a situation and that there are clear ways for everyone to communicate.

Plan for Business Continuity

A thorough business continuity plan shows how to keep important processes running during and after a disruption. It includes plans for moving to new locations, keeping important processes going, and making sure that important tools are always available.

Training and tests

Test and improve your plans for data recovery and business stability on a regular basis. Make sure that your workers are ready for emergencies by having drills and simulations. Change the plans based on what you've learned and how the risks are changing.

The best ways to recover data and keep a business running
Setting priorities

Figure out which systems and data are the most important and need to be returned first. This makes sure that important tasks can be quickly resumed if something goes wrong.

Getting fired

Make sure that important tools and data are backed up. This means having backup systems or copies of the data on hand at all times to cut down on downtime.

The Conversation

It's important to be able to communicate clearly during a disruption. Set up clear lines of communication and contact lists to keep customers, workers, and other important people in the loop about what's going on and how the recovery is going.

Training for Employees

Make sure that your workers know how to handle emergencies and keep the business running. Employees can handle a change better when they get regular training and awareness programs.

Regular Checks

It is important to try your data recovery and business continuity plans often. By simulating different situations, you can see how well your plans work and find places where they could be better.

Always Getting Better

Always go over and make changes to your plans so they can fit new risks and changing situations. Keep an eye on problems and learn from them to get better ready.

What Tech Does for Us

Technology is an important part of both recovering lost data and keeping a business running. Here are some important technical parts that help with these efforts:

Using the Cloud

When you back up, store, and recover data, cloud-based options offer a safe and expandable space. When you use the cloud, your data is protected and can be accessed even if there are problems with your computer.

Tools for backup and recovery

Set up backup and emergency recovery tools that will do the backups automatically and let you get back to work quickly. Often, these tools come with features like point-in-time recovery and incremental saves.

Using virtualization

Virtualization technology lets businesses make "virtual copies" of their systems. This makes it easier to get back to work after hardware failure or system damage.

Locking up data

Encrypting data makes sure it stays safe while it's being sent and stored. It keeps private data safe from people who shouldn't have access to it.

Access from Mobile and Remote

Include tools that let workers do their jobs from home or use their phones to access important systems and data. This adaptability makes sure that important jobs can keep going even when there are problems.

Alerts and monitoring

Set up monitoring and alerting systems to find problems and possible problems before they

happen. These systems can send out alerts, which lets people quickly deal with new threats.

Data recovery and business stability are important parts of any company's plan to keep operations running smoothly and keep data safe. These plans are important for more than just avoiding downtime and keeping data safe. They are also needed to follow the rules and keep your image in good shape. Organizations can improve their ability to handle changes and keep running important tasks even when unexpected things happen by understanding the key parts, best practices, and role of technology. Data recovery and business continuity plans aren't just backups; they're necessary for long-term success in a business world that is becoming more connected and risky.

Chapter 11

Ethical Considerations in Secure Data Handling

Managing data is an important part of both our personal and work lives in this digitally connected world. Data can be very important because it can hold private information like medical histories, financial records, personal details, and more. As data has become more important, so have the moral issues that come up when it is collected, stored, processed, and shared. This long piece goes into great detail about the tricky subject of ethical data handling. It talks about the problems, the best ways to deal with them, and how technology can help make sure data is handled safely and ethically.

Why ethical data handling is important

Protecting your privacy

Protecting people's privacy is one of the most important social issues that come up when working with data. Data collection can be tied to a person or thing, and if it is handled wrong, it can lead to a privacy breach. To keep people's private information safe and keep their trust, data handling must be done in an ethical way.

Trust and a Good Name

Trust is an important part of any business's relationships with its partners, buyers, and clients. Keeping trust and a good image requires handling data in an ethical way. Data breaches or using data in an unethical way can hurt your image for a long time.

Following the law and regulations

A lot of places have strict laws and rules about protecting data. For example, the General Data Protection Regulation (GDPR) in Europe and the Health Insurance Portability and Accountability Act (HIPAA) in the US are two examples. Ethical data handling is needed to make sure that these legal requirements are met and that no one gets in trouble with the law.

Stopping Discrimination

Dealing with data in an unethical way can keep discrimination and bias going. When data is gathered and used in an unethical way, it can lead to unfair treatment of people based on their race, gender, or age, for example. Ethical concerns try to stop this kind of abuse.

Problems with handling data in an ethical way

Safety of Data

Cyber dangers and data breaches happen all the time, making it hard to keep data safe. Lax security can lead to unethical data treatment, which can lead to data breaches and unauthorized access.

Accuracy of Data

Ensuring the correctness of data is very important. Because it's the right thing to do, validating data stops the spread of fake or misleading information that can hurt people and businesses.

Aware Consent

A key part of handling data in an ethical way is getting educated consent. However, it can be hard to make sure that people know what giving their data means, especially when the terms and conditions are complicated.

Methods for Collecting Data

Data is often gathered in many ways, such as through monitoring and online tracking. Ethical data handling means collecting data in a way that is clear, fair, and respects people's rights and desires.

Best Practices for Handling Data in an Ethical Way

Being clear

Transparency is one of the most important ethical principles for treating data. Organizations should be clear with people about how they gather and use data, so that people know how their information will be used.

Aware Consent

Before you gather and use someone's data, make sure you have their permission. People should have the right to know how their data will be used and be able to give their consent easily and in a clear way.

Minimizing the data

Only gather the information that is needed for the goal. Avoid gathering too much or useless data, as this can make it more likely that someone will misuse the data.

Accuracy of Data

Make sure the info is correct and up to date. Check and fix data on a regular basis to stop the spread of mistakes that could hurt people or businesses.

Steps Taken for Safety

Put in place strong security steps to keep data safe from breaches and unauthorized access. This includes things like encryption, controls on who can access what, regular security checks, and following data protection rules.

Removing an identity

To protect people's privacy, de-identify sensitive information before sharing it. By making data anonymous, businesses can share useful information without putting people at risk of harm.

Policies for keeping data

Set rules for how long data will be kept by making data retention policies. Ethical data handling means getting rid of data when it's no longer needed and making sure it's not kept forever.

Duty to Account

Assign someone in the company the responsibility of handling data in an ethical way. This includes picking a data protection officer or privacy officer to make sure that data protection rules are followed.

Audits and evaluations done regularly

Do regular checks and audits of how data is handled to make sure that they are still following ethical standards and legal requirements.

Thoughts on Ethics in Sharing Data

Giving permission to share data

When businesses share information with outsiders, they should get permission from the people whose information is being shared. This makes sure that everyone knows about and agrees to the plans for sharing info.

Agreements to Share Data

Make sure that your deals with third parties about sharing data are clear and complete. These contracts should spell out why the data is being shared, what kind of data is being shared, and who is responsible for keeping the data safe and private.

Keeping Private Data Safe

When you share information, be sure to identify and protect private data. This could mean using encryption, anonymization, and secure channels to keep critical information from getting into the wrong hands.

What data recipients have to do

Make sure that the people who will be receiving the data know about and follow proper data handling practices. In agreements to share data, make sure that the people who receive it agree to follow privacy and data security rules.

How Technology Affects the Right Way to Handle Data

Technologies that protect privacy

Technologies that protect privacy, like differential privacy and homomorphic encryption, help businesses keep data safe while still getting useful information from it. These tools are very important for handling data in an ethical way.

Locking up data

Encrypting data is one of the most important technologies for keeping data safe. It makes sure that data stays private and safe, even if it is stolen or viewed by people who aren't supposed to.

IAM stands for Identity and Access Management

IAM solutions handle and control who can see and change data. They are very important for making sure that only approved people can access data, which lowers the risk of data being handled without permission.

Tools for managing compliance

Tools made to handle compliance with data protection regulations help businesses keep track of and follow the rules for ethical data handling, which speeds up the compliance process.

Solutions for Data Governance

Data governance solutions help businesses set and follow rules and policies for handling data, making sure it is handled in an honest way and in line with legal requirements.

What You Should Know About Ethics in Artificial Intelligence (AI)

Using artificial intelligence (AI) to handle data comes with its own set of social problems. If AI algorithms aren't built and taught in an ethical way, they can reinforce biases and be unfair to some groups. Important things to think about when dealing with AI data ethically are:

Getting rid of bias

For AI to be ethical, steps need to be taken to find and fix flaws in the data that is used for training and making decisions. To do this, training data needs to be varied, and AI systems need to be constantly checked for biased results.

Ability to Explain

AI models should be clear and easy to understand so that people can see how decisions are made using their data. Making sure that AI systems are open and clear is a basic social issue.

Duty to Account

Companies that make and use AI solutions need to take responsibility for the choices these systems make. This includes dealing with any bad outcomes and giving people who are affected by AI-based choices a way to get help.

In the digital age we live in now, ethical data treatment is a complex problem that is always changing. Protecting people's privacy, keeping faith, following the law, and stopping discrimination are all important reasons to do this. When organizations gather, store, process, and share data, they need to be ethical about it. They should use best practices that encourage openness, informed consent, data minimization, and data accuracy.

Technology, such as privacy-protecting technologies, data encryption, identity and access management, compliance tools, and data governance solutions, is a key part of treating data in an ethical way. When it comes to AI, ethics also matter because bias must be avoided, things must be able to be explained, and people must be held accountable.

Ethical data handling isn't just a matter of following the rules; it's also a basic concept that protects people's rights and dignity in a world that is becoming more and more data-driven. Companies can handle the complicated world of data ethics in an honest and responsible way by incorporating moral standards into their data handling methods and using tech tools that support these ideas.

11.1 Ethical Principles in Data Science and Technology

The subject of data science has become very important in this era of big data and advanced technology. It is changing businesses, economies, and societies in many ways. Because data science and technology have so much power and impact, they need to be developed and used in a way that is ethical. This long piece talks about the moral issues and rules that should guide data science and technology. It stresses the significance of trustworthy data management, AI ethics, privacy, fairness, openness, and the part that ethics plays in the innovation process.

The Need for Ethics

We use data science and technology all the time, from personalized suggestions on streaming services to healthcare tests, financial predictions, and self-driving cars. As decisions are made more and more using data, ethics concerns have never been more important. In data science and technology, ethics are very important for the following main reasons:

Looking out for privacy

Concerns about privacy are raised by the gathering, storage, and study of huge amounts of personal data. Ethical principles help set limits and safety measures to protect people's privacy and make sure their data is used in a good way.

Stopping Discrimination and Bias

Biases in society can be strengthened or kept alive by data and algorithms, which can lead to unfair or biased results. Ethical standards stress the need to fight bias, encourage fairness, and make sure that AI and data-driven systems don't treat people unfairly because of their race, gender, or other traits.

Making sure accountability

It's important to find out who is responsible when things go wrong with data-driven processes. Organizations should follow ethical principles that require them to own up to their actions, give people who were hurt a way to get help, and deal with the effects of mistakes or abuse.

Keeping the trust

Trust is a key part of getting people to use data science and technology. Being ethical builds trust among users, buyers, and the public, which is important for these technologies to be widely used and successful.

Compliance with Regulations

The General Data Protection Regulation (GDPR) in Europe and the Health Insurance Portability and Accountability Act (HIPAA) in the US are two examples of privacy and data protection laws that have been passed in many places and businesses. Ethical principles are in line with these rules, which makes sure that groups follow the law.

Thoughts on Ethics in Data Science

The field of data science collects, processes, analyzes, and makes sense of data in order to gain insights and make smart choices. In data science, ethical issues come up in many forms and during all stages of a data set's life. Here are some of the most important ethics issues in data science:

Getting the Data

Getting informed permission from the people whose data is being collected is the first step in collecting data in an ethical way. It means being clear about how data is used, only collecting as much data as is needed for the intended reason, and keeping private data safe.

Storage for Data

Safely storing info is the right thing to do. Organizations must protect data from breaches and unauthorized access to keep data private and secure.

Studying the Data

When looking at data, it's important to be responsible and avoid bias, discrimination, and wrong interpretations of data. When doing their work, data scientists should think about what their research might mean and try to be fair.

Shared Data

Sharing data with outsiders needs to be clear, with informed consent and data security measures in place. Companies need to take care of their data and make sure it is only used for what it was created for.

Holding on to Data

Setting data retention rules to make sure data isn't kept forever, respecting people's privacy rights, and getting rid of data when it's no longer needed are all ethical ways to handle data.

Duty to Account

People who use data to make decisions and the companies that use them should be held responsible for those choices. Ethical principles say that decisions based on facts should be explained and that mistakes and their effects should be dealt with.

Ethical Guidelines for Creating New Technologies

Ethical concerns are linked to the progress of technology, especially artificial intelligence (AI) and machine learning. Using AI and machine learning techniques for many things, from self-driving cars to predictive analytics, brings up a number of ethical issues:

Fairness and Favoritism

AI systems can reinforce biases that are present in training data. Ethical principles stress the

importance of fairness and the need to fix bias in AI models to make sure that everyone gets the same results.

Openness and being able to explain

It can be hard to figure out how AI systems make decisions because they are often complicated and hard to see. Ethics guidelines support openness and comprehensibility so that people can understand choices made by AI.

Technologies that protect privacy

Differential privacy and federated learning are two technologies that developers should use to protect private data while still getting useful insights.

Being responsible and accountable

AI system developers and groups should be held accountable for what their systems do and decide. Ethics show that AI systems need to be held responsible for their actions and any bad effects need to be fixed.

Moral Guidelines for AI and Machine Learning

When it comes to AI and machine learning, ethical principles are very important for solving hard problems and making sure that these technologies are created and used in a responsible way. Here are some important moral rules for AI and machine learning:

Being fair

In AI and machine learning, fairness is one of the most important moral principles. It means making sure that AI systems don't treat people differently because of their race, gender, or other traits. Unbiased data, balanced training samples, and fair algorithms can all help make things fair.

Being clear

Being open is important for understanding the choices and actions of AI systems. Ethical guidelines say that AI models and algorithms should be clear so that people who are affected by choices made by AI can understand them.

Duty to Account

Making sure that people or groups are responsible for what AI systems do is called accountability. Ethical principles tell businesses they need to be responsible for the results of AI systems and give people who were affected by choices made by AI a way to get their problems fixed.

Private Life

Privacy is one of the most important social issues in AI and machine learning. Companies need to keep people's privacy and personal information safe by using technologies and methods that protect privacy and keeping private data safe.

Quality of the Data and Reducing Bias

Quality data is very important for keeping AI systems from being biased and unfair. Companies should use good data and make sure there is no bias in training datasets and algorithms because it is the right thing to do.

Consent and Making Smart Choices

One of the most important social rules is to get people's permission before collecting and using their data. Ethical standards also stress openness in data practices so that people can make smart choices about their data.

What role does technology play in promoting morals?

Technologies that protect privacy

Technologies that protect privacy, like differential privacy and homomorphic encryption, help businesses keep private data safe while still getting useful information from it. These tools are very important for protecting privacy and data.

Solutions for Data Governance

Data governance tools help businesses set rules and policies for their data and make sure they are followed. They make sure that data is treated in a way that is moral, follows the rules, and is in line with the organization's morals.

IAM stands for Identity and Access Management.

IAM solutions handle and control who can see and change data. They are very important for making sure that only approved people can access data, which lowers the risk of data being handled without permission.

Tools for managing compliance

Organizations can keep track of and follow ethical and legal data handling standards with the help of tools made to handle compliance with data protection regulations. These tools make the process of accountability easier and help businesses do what's right.

Ethical Technology Development and New Ideas

Ethical from the Start

Giving technologies that are "ethical by design" means thinking about ethics from the start of the creation process. Ethical principles should be a top priority for organizations at all stages of growth, from idea to deployment.

Review of Ethics

It is important to do ethical studies of technology and data science projects. Ethical review boards or groups can look at projects to see what ethical problems they might cause and give advice on how to lower those problems and make sure they follow ethical rules.

Participation of Stakeholders

Talking to influencers, like customers, users, and the public, is important to understand what they care about and what they expect from you in terms of ethics. This feedback can help guide the development process and make sure that technology is in line with moral standards.

Taking ethics into account when making decisions

When organizations and tech workers make decisions, they should think about what is right and wrong. As part of judging the effects and meanings of tech and data science projects, moral standards should be taken into account.

Training in Ethics

Ethics training and instruction are very important for people who work on technology. Organizations should give their teams training in ethics and work to create a culture that values ethics and responsible creativity.

The study of data, the creation of new technologies, and the use of AI and machine learning are all based on ethical ideals. When it comes to AI ethics, privacy, fairness, transparency, and the role of ethics in technology innovation, these concepts show how to handle data responsibly.

To protect privacy, stop bias and discrimination, keep people accountable, and build trust, it's important to encourage ethical principles in data science and technology. By following moral guidelines, businesses can handle the complicated world of AI and data-driven decision-making with honesty and duty, making sure that these strong tools help society while protecting people's rights and respect.

11.2 Responsible Data Use and Governance

In this age of digital transformation and data-driven decisions, businesses and societies need to make sure that data is used and governed responsibly. As the amount and value of data grows, so does the need for moral frameworks and governance structures to help with its collection, storage, processing, and sharing. This long piece goes into great detail about the idea of responsible data use and governance. It talks about what it means, its main parts, the best ways to use it, and how technology can help make sure that data management is ethical and lasts.

Why responsible data use and governance are important
How to Handle Data Ethically

Responsible data use and governance put ethics at the top of data management, making sure that data is treated in a way that protects privacy, keeps things open, and stops misuse or unauthorized access.

Privacy and safety of data

The goal of responsible data use and control is to keep data safe from security breaches and protect people's privacy. To protect private data, this includes putting in place strong security measures like encryption, access controls, and data anonymization.

Compliance and Following the Rules

As there are more and more data protection laws around the world, organizations need to make sure they follow the law. This includes the General Data Protection Regulation (GDPR), the California Consumer Privacy Act (CCPA), and other data protection laws that are specific to their industry.

Trust and a Good Name

Following the rules for responsible data use and control builds trust among customers, partners, and the public. Organizations can keep their good name and gain trust from their partners over time by showing they are committed to ethical data practices.

Data practices that last

Responsible data use and control include long-term data management methods that help data stay useful and be used in an honest way. Companies can make sure that data is used in ways that are good for society and the general good by using sustainable data practices.

Important Parts of Data Governance and Responsible Use

Management of Data Privacy and Consent

Data privacy and consent management are important parts of responsible data use and

governance. This makes sure that people have control over how their data is gathered, used, and shared. This means getting people's permission after they've been told about the data methods and respecting their choices about their data.

Steps to Keep Data Safe

Strong data security steps are needed for responsible data use and management. For example, to keep data safe from hackers, illegal access, and breaches, this means putting in place encryption, access controls, firewalls, and intrusion detection systems.

Quality and trustworthiness of data

Keeping the quality and purity of data is an important part of using and managing data responsibly. This means making sure that the data is correct, reliable, and up to date, and taking steps to stop data corruption and mistakes.

Frameworks for Data Governance

For responsible data use and control, it is important to set up complete data governance frameworks. These models spell out who is responsible for what when it comes to data management tasks like data stewardship, data lifecycle management, and data quality assurance.

Management of Compliance

For organizations to use data responsibly and govern it well, they need to follow data security laws and industry-specific compliance standards. This means keeping an eye on and updating data practices on a daily basis to make sure they keep up with legal and regulatory requirements.

Ethical Rules for Handling Data

For responsible data use and governance, it is important to make and follow ethical data handling rules. These policies spell out the moral principles and rules that an organization must follow when managing data. They stress the importance of being open, fair, and responsible.

Accountability and Openness of Data

Promoting openness and responsibility in data is important for managing and using data in a smart way. This includes giving people clear information about data practices so they can understand how their data is used and setting up ways to deal with questions and issues about data.

The best ways to use and manage data responsibly
Set up clear rules for data governance

Make and share clear data governance rules that show the company is dedicated to using and managing data responsibly. These rules should spell out how to handle data, who is responsible for what, and how to make sure that all legal and regulatory requirements are met.

Data privacy by design should be used

Adopt a "privacy by design" method to managing data, which means building privacy and security into products, services, and data systems from the very beginning. This proactive method makes sure that privacy and security of data are important parts of all activities that involve data.

Do regular assessments of the privacy impacts of your data

Do regular data privacy effect assessments to find and reduce possible threats to the security and privacy of data. These evaluations help companies find and fix security holes before they happen and make sure that the way they handle data is in line with legal and moral standards.

Give ongoing training on data security

Give your workers thorough training in data security, and stress how important it is to use and manage data responsibly. Best practices for handling data, security protocols, and procedures for handling sensitive information should all be covered in training. This will give employees the knowledge they need to make smart choices about data security.

Encourage people to use data in an ethical way.

Encourage the company to use data in an ethical way by pushing for open communication, honesty, and responsibility in all activities that involve data. Stress how important it is for all departments and teams to be responsible with how they use and manage data.

Use techniques for data anonymization and pseudoanonymization

To protect people's privacy and confidentiality, use methods like data anonymization and pseudonymization. While still using data for research and insights, these methods help businesses lower the risk of sharing private data.

Regular checks and audits of data

Do regular audits and studies of the data to see how well the ways of handling it are working and find places where they can be improved. These checks help businesses find holes in their data security, make sure they're following data protection rules, and keep the quality and integrity of their data.

Talk to Data Subjects and Stakeholders

Talk to data subjects and partners to build trust and transparency. Ask for feedback, address concerns, and talk freely about how you handle data to show that you are committed to responsible data use and governance.

The Part Technology Plays in Safe Data Management and Use
Technologies for Encrypting Data

Use data encryption to keep private data safe and stop people from getting to it without permission. When data is sent or stored, encryption helps keep it safe by making sure that only authorized users can access and decrypt it.

Mechanisms for controlling access

Set up access control systems to manage and control who can see what data in the company. Organizations can implement data privacy and security policies by limiting access to data to only authorized personnel through role-based access controls and identity and access management (IAM) solutions.

Solutions for stopping data loss (DLP)

Use solutions to stop data loss to keep an eye on, find, and stop the sending or sharing of private data without permission. Data loss prevention (DLP) solutions help businesses find and reduce data security risks, keeping data safe from being exposed by mistake or on purpose.

Using blockchain technology to keep data safe

Look into how blockchain technology can be used to protect data security and openness. Blockchain makes it possible for transactions to be safe, unchangeable, and clear. It also keeps a record of all data trades that can't be changed, which builds trust in how data is handled.

Technologies that protect privacy

Use technologies that protect privacy, like homomorphic encryption and differential privacy, to keep private data safe while still letting you analyze and process it. These tools let businesses learn useful things from data without putting people's privacy at risk.

Ethics Frameworks for Artificial Intelligence (AI)

AI ethics models should be used in the creation and use of AI-driven solutions. AI ethics models help people use AI in a smart way by encouraging fairness, openness, and responsibility in AI algorithms and decision-making processes.

Tools for Data Governance and Compliance

Use data governance and compliance tools to make managing data easier and make sure you're following data security rules. These tools help businesses keep the quality of their data high, make sure they follow data governance rules, and show they are following moral and legal guidelines.

How to Use and Manage Data Ethically in a Global Setting

Diverse and sensitive to culture

Because morals can be different in different places and cultures, think about how to handle facts in a way that is sensitive to and inclusive of different cultures. Companies that do business around the world should be aware of and respect the moral standards and beliefs of different groups and communities.

Transferring data across borders

Take a look at how hard it is to send data across borders, especially in places with strict data protection laws. Make sure that the ways you transfer data, like standard contractual clauses, binding corporate rules, or privacy shield frameworks, are in line with both local and foreign data protection laws.

International Rules for Safeguarding Data

Learn about the OECD Privacy Guidelines and the APEC Privacy Framework. These are international standards and models for protecting data. They set rules for how data should be used and managed on an international level.

Ethics in Data and New Technologies

Keep up with new technologies like bioengineering, quantum computing, and artificial intelligence and how they might affect ethics. As technology changes, new ethical issues may come up, which is why we need to keep talking about and giving advice on ethics.

In the digital age, where data has become a driving force behind innovation and decision-making, it is essential to use and control data in a responsible way. Governance and ethical frameworks make sure that data is treated in a way that protects privacy, keeps things open, and stops it from being misused. Organizations can protect data security and privacy, build trust among stakeholders, and follow the law and regulations by adopting responsible data use and control.

Ethical data management is based on the main parts of responsible data use and governance, such as data privacy, security, openness, responsibility, and long-term practices. Clear data governance policies, data privacy impact assessments, and ongoing data security training are some of the best practices that can help companies put these principles into action.

Technology plays a big part in making sure that data is used and managed responsibly. It provides ways to encrypt data, control access, protect privacy, and keep data security. Using technologies that protect privacy and AI ethics models makes a company's dedication to doing ethical data practices even stronger.

In a global setting, businesses have to deal with different cultures, sending data across borders, and following different rules for protecting data. As new technologies continue to change the world, ethical and long-lasting data management practices will depend on how well we use and control data.

Chapter 12

Future Trends and Emerging Technologies

Technology is about to change everything. New and groundbreaking inventions and advances are about to change businesses, economies, and societies. As we look to the future, we can see that a number of important trends and new technologies are likely to bring about big changes and open up new chances for growth and development. This in-depth piece takes a look at the fascinating world of future trends and new technologies, looking at how they might affect, use, pose problems, and have effects on different groups and stakeholders.

The Speeding Up of Digital Transformation

The Internet of Things (IoT) and Being Connected

People think that the Internet of Things (IoT) will change the way we connect with our surroundings. As more and more devices and sensors are linked, data will be able to be shared easily. This will make processes more efficient, help people make better decisions, and improve user experiences in many areas, such as healthcare, manufacturing, transportation, and smart cities.

5G and the Next Generation of Connectivity

When 5G networks are widely used, they will be able to send data faster, have lower latency, and hold more data. This will open up new options for real-time apps, immersive experiences, and advanced connectivity. The new features of 5G technology will be very helpful for many fields, including entertainment, internet, and self-driving cars.

Using the Edge

Edge computing is going to change how we handle, store, and look at data. Edge computing lowers latency, improves data security, and allows for real-time decision-making by letting data be processed closer to where it is created, at the network's edge. This is especially helpful for applications that need quick responses and high bandwidth, like self-driving cars, smart infrastructure, and augmented reality.

How Artificial Intelligence (AI) and Machine Learning Have Changed Over Time

Progress in AI algorithms

Deep learning and neural networks are two AI methods that are always getting better. This will lead to big improvements in natural language processing, computer vision, and predictive analytics. AI-powered solutions will get smarter, allowing clever automation, personalized suggestions, and self-made decisions in many fields, including retail, healthcare, and finance.

Ethical AI and AI that can be explained

As AI systems spread, explainable AI will become more important to make sure that decisions made by AI are clear and easy to understand for end users and stakeholders. Ethical AI frameworks and rules will be very important for encouraging responsible AI use, reducing bias, and building trust in systems and apps that use AI.

Automation and robotics powered by AI

Robotics and automation driven by AI will change the way we live and work. AI-powered technologies will boost productivity, streamline operations, and make many industries more efficient. This will cause big changes in how things are done and how workflows are organized.

Examples include self-driving cars, robotic process automation, smart manufacturing, and healthcare robotics.

Biotechnology and healthcare innovation coming together
Genes and personalized medicine

As genomics and personalized medicine continue to improve, customized treatment plans and precision therapies will become possible. This will completely change how healthcare is provided and how well patients do. Putting genetic information, bioinformatics, and AI-driven analytics together will help with more accurate diagnoses, targeted treatments, and proactive ways to avoid getting diseases. This will start a new era of personalized healthcare.

New developments in biopharmaceuticals

Biopharmaceuticals, such as gene therapies, RNA-based medicines, and personalized vaccines, are being developed. These will lead to new and innovative ways to treat a wide range of illnesses and medical conditions. Biopharmaceutical innovations will make treatments more effective and targeted, boosting patient reactions and lowering side effects, and speeding up the creation of new treatment methods.

Digital technologies for health care and telemedicine

Widespread use of digital health tools and telemedicine will make healthcare more accessible, get patients more involved, and improve the quality of care. From wearable tech and digital therapies to virtual care platforms and remote patient tracking, digital health solutions will give people the power to take charge of their health and well-being. This will lead to more proactive and preventative healthcare practices.

The Rise of Green Energy and Sustainable Technologies
Solutions for Renewable Energy

Renewable energy sources like solar, wind, and hydroelectric power will become more popular as people become more concerned with sustainability and protecting the earth. As grid integration and energy storage technologies improve, clean energy solutions will be widely used. This will cut down on our reliance on fossil fuels and lessen the effects of climate change.

The circular economy and green technologies

The growth of green technologies and support for a cycle economy will encourage environmentally friendly ways of making things, building things, and managing resources. By using eco-friendly materials and long-lasting production methods, as well as programs to cut down on trash and recycle, green technologies and circular economy ideas will encourage people to be good stewards of the environment and use resources in a smart way.

Smart cities and infrastructure that lasts

Smart towns and sustainable infrastructure will change how cities are planned, how transportation systems work, and how resources are managed. Integrated solutions, like smart grids, energy-efficient buildings, and smart transportation networks, will make cities more resilient, better use their resources, and better places for people and companies to live and work.

What Blockchain and other decentralized technologies can do

Blockchain can be used in finance and supply chain management

Using blockchain technology in banking and supply chain management will change the way transactions are done, make them more open, and make the sending of data safer. From decentralized finance (DeFi) solutions and digital currencies to transparent supply chain tracking and authentication, blockchain applications will make things run more smoothly and make deals safe and quick in many fields.

Government and Decentralized Autonomous Organizations (DAOs)

As decentralized autonomous organizations (DAOs) and decentralized governance models become more popular, they will make it easier for everyone to make decisions and support community-driven projects. Stakeholders will be able to take part in making decisions with DAOs. They will also encourage collaborative innovation and make governance systems more fair and decentralized in many areas, such as finance, governance, and social impact projects.

Digital Safety and Identity

Blockchain technology will be used to make digital identity solutions that will make data more secure, private, and give users more control over their personal information. Digital identities that are safe and can be checked will be made possible by decentralized identity platforms. This will lower the risks of data breaches, identity theft, and illegal access, making the internet a safer and more trustworthy place for everyone.

How Quantum Computing and Quantum Technologies Fit Together

What Quantum Computing Can Do

Quantum computing will change how data is processed, encrypted, and simulated. It will also make it possible to do complicated calculations and solve problems that classical computing systems can't do. There will be big changes in areas like materials science, drug discovery, cryptography, and optimization problems because of quantum computers.

Communication and encryption using quantum fields

Quantum communication and quantum cryptography will make it possible to send and protect private data in ways that are very safe. Quantum key distribution (QKD) and quantum-resistant cryptography will provide security and privacy levels that have never been seen before. They will protect digital messages and private data from hackers and people listening in.

Metrology and Quantum Sensing

Quantum sensing and metrology technologies will make many uses more precise and accurate, such as in navigation, medical imaging, and watching the environment. Quantum sensors, like atomic clocks and quantum magnetometers, will make readings that are very accurate, which will lead to big steps forward in both science and industry.

How space exploration and space technologies have changed over time

Private Space Projects

Private space research companies will keep working to make space travel and exploration more accessible to the public. Space tourism, reusable launch systems, and missions to the moon and Mars will all create new chances for scientific study, resource use, and space-based businesses. This will start a new era of space exploration.

Infrastructure in space

Setting up space-based infrastructure, like mega-constellations of satellites, will improve global communication, remote sensing, and data collection about Earth. These satellite networks will be used for many things, such as connecting people around the world to the internet, keeping an eye on the weather, helping people after disasters, and precision farming.

Exploration and settlement of other planets

Exploration and settlement of other planets will move forward, and trips to the Moon, Mars, and other places will become possible. These projects will lead to improvements in spacecraft technologies, life support systems, and long-term living conditions on other celestial bodies. This makes it possible for people to live on worlds other than Earth.

The Problems and Moral Issues to Think About

As we look forward to the exciting new tools and trends of the future, we need to think about a number of problems and moral issues.

Privacy and safety of data

There are worries about data privacy, security, and safety as more and more technologies are based on data. To solve these problems, we need to gather and use data in an open and honest way, follow strong cybersecurity measures, and handle data in an ethical way.

Ethical AI and Getting Rid of Bias

As AI becomes more a part of our lives, it is important to make sure that it is developed in an acceptable way and that biases are reduced. To handle these worries, AI ethics frameworks, openness, and fairness in AI algorithms will be very important.

Sustainability in the environment

To stop climate change and other environmental problems, we need to switch to clean energy and long-lasting tools. Making sure that resources are managed responsibly, reducing e-waste, and encouraging sustainable practices are all important parts of protecting the environment.

Inclusion in digital

The move to digital shouldn't make digital gaps and differences worse. To keep disadvantaged groups from falling behind, efforts must be made to make sure that everyone has equal access to new technologies and is digitally included.

Internet safety and quantum threats

When it comes to safety, the rise of quantum technologies brings about new problems. To keep

digital messages safe from possible quantum threats, we need cryptography that doesn't work with quantum computers and security methods that don't use quantum computers.

Space Exploration That Is Moral

As we explore and settle in space, it is very important to think about the moral issues that come up when it comes to protecting planets, keeping celestial environments safe, and the rights and duties of spacefaring countries and people.

What Collaboration and New Ideas Can Do for You

It is important for governments, businesses, universities, and foreign groups to work together to solve problems and make the most of new technologies and trends. Sharing knowledge across disciplines, doing study, and making policies will help us figure out how to use new technologies in an ethical and environmentally friendly way.

Entrepreneurship and new ideas are very important for making these tools useful. Startups, research institutions, and organizations that think ahead are the ones who are coming up with and using these new ideas to solve important global problems and open up new possibilities.

A lot of new technologies and trends that are changing things will make the future full of opportunities. These will change industries, social norms, and open up new areas of study. The speeding up of digital transformation, the growth of AI and machine learning, the coming together of biotechnology and healthcare innovation, and the use of environmentally friendly technologies will change the world in ways that have never been seen before.

Coming together of blockchain and decentralized technologies, the strength of quantum computing and quantum technologies, and the progress made in space research and space technologies all look like they will lead to exciting times in the future. To get the most out of these trends and technologies, we will need to deal with the problems that come with them, like data safety and security, ethical concerns, environmental sustainability, and digital inclusion.

To use the transforming power of new technologies and future trends, people must work together, come up with new ideas, and be committed to doing things in an ethical and environmentally friendly way. We can handle the complicated world of tomorrow's technology with purpose and strength if we all work together and take responsible, welcoming actions. This will make the future better for everyone.

12.1 Quantum Computing and Data Security

up many industries. It has the potential to solve hard problems at speeds that were previously unthinkable, but it also poses a major threat to the security of our data. The effects of quantum computing on data security are discussed in this piece, along with the holes it creates and the defenses being created to deal with the quantum threat.

How Quantum Works: Speed and Power

Superposition of Quantum

Bits can be either 0 or 1 in traditional computers. Quantum bits, or qubits, can be in a state that is a combination of the two. This lets them do more than one calculation at the same time. This trait makes some computer tasks go faster.

Entanglement of Quantum

Quantum coupling lets qubits talk to each other so that the state of one qubit affects the state of another. This property makes it easier to solve hard tasks and gives computers more power.

The Quantum Danger to Data Safety

Quantum computers are amazing in how fast and powerful they are, but they also pose a big threat to current data security measures, especially when it comes to encryption. Quantum computers can quickly break traditional encryption methods like RSA and ECC (Elliptic Curve Cryptography) that depend on how hard it is to factor large numbers. They do this by using an algorithm called Shor's algorithm. This algorithm quickly factors out big numbers that are used in a lot of encryption methods, which makes them weak.

Security Flaws in RSA and ECC

RSA and ECC encryption are safe because it is hard to factor big semiprime numbers and they use elliptic curves. Quantum computers, on the other hand, can quickly factor these numbers, which can break the encryption in a few seconds, based on how powerful the quantum machine is.

Concerns about privacy and data exposure

The fact that quantum computing can break encryption could make a lot of data public and raise privacy issues. Quantum computers could put private data like personal data, bank records, and private messages at risk if they get into the wrong hands.

The Danger to Important Buildings

Quantum threats affect more than just personal information. They also affect the safety of important systems like the power grid, financial systems, and the national military. There could be very bad effects if quantum computers are able to break the encryption used in these devices.

Ways to protect yourself from the quantum threat

Because experts and researchers are aware of the possible threats that quantum computing could pose to data security, they are working hard on defenses and post-quantum cryptography to keep data safe in the age of quantum computing.

After quantum cryptography

The goal of the area of study called post-quantum cryptography is to create ways to encrypt data that are safe from quantum attacks. These types of encryption work by solving math problems that are hard for both regular computers and quantum computers.

Cryptography Based on Lattices

Lattice-based cryptography is a method used after quantum computing that depends on how hard lattice problems are. Both classical and quantum computers have a hard time solving these problems. This means that quantum attackers can't break lattice-based encryption methods.

Cryptography based on codes

Coding-based cryptography is another post-quantum method that encrypts data using codes

that can fix mistakes. It takes advantage of the fact that quantum computers still have a hard time reading linear codes.

Polynomial cryptography with multiple variables

Multivariate polynomial cryptography is based on the fact that it is hard to solve sets of multivariate polynomial problems. Quantum attacks can't break this type of encryption because it's hard to figure out the answers to these equations.

Signatures Based on Hash

Hash-based signatures are a way to make digital signatures that can't be read by quantum computers. They use the way cryptographic hash functions work to make signatures that are safe and hard for quantum computers to fake.

Distribution of Quantum Keys (QKD)

A method for safely exchanging cryptographic keys that uses the rules of quantum physics is called quantum key distribution. It's based on the quantum no-cloning theory, which says that you can't exactly copy an unknown quantum state. So, if someone tried to steal the key, it would change its quantum state, which could be used to find out who was listening in.

The Race for Safe Quantum Solutions

As quantum computing gets better, there is more pressure to come up with and use quantum-safe methods. In a world after quantum computing, governments, research institutions, and business leaders are working together to make sure that data is safe. Here are some important steps forward in the search for quantum-safe solutions:

Plans for the whole country

A number of countries have started national projects and study programs to help the growth of post-quantum cryptography and technologies that are safe for quantum computers. These programs give money and resources to speed up research in the area.

Work on Standardization

Standardization groups are working hard to set guidelines for post-quantum cryptography. These standards will help many different fields and uses use encryption methods that are not affected by quantum mechanics.

Implementation of Quantum Key Distribution (QKD)

More and more QKD networks are being used, especially in fields like finance, healthcare, and

government where private communication is very important. The QKD method is a useful way to protect data from quantum threats.

Protocols for Quantum Safety

Quantum-safe methods for secure communication, secure data storage, and secure digital signatures are still being improved. These methods are meant to keep data safe from quantum threats while still working with systems that are already in use.

Getting ready for the future of quantum
Check for Vulnerabilities

Companies should look at their current data security policies and encryption methods to see if they are open to quantum threats. The first step in making a quantum-safe plan is to understand the possible risks.

Quantum-resistant encryption should be used.

You might want to use encryption methods and protocols that are not affected by quantum computing in private systems and interactions. It might take some time to switch to quantum-safe methods, but it is necessary to keep data safe in the long run.

Stay Up to Date

Keep up with the latest changes in quantum computing and security that can't be broken by quantum computers. To make smart choices about data security, you need to be aware of how things are changing.

Plan for Giving Out Quantum Keys

If safe communication is important to you, you might want to use quantum key distribution (QKD) to keep data safe while it's being sent. When it comes to protecting data from quantum threats, QKD is a strong option.

Work with Professionals

Talk to and work with people who are knowledgeable and interested in post-quantum cryptography and quantum security. Talking to people who are working on quantum-safe solutions right now can give you useful information and direction.

Keep an eye on changes to the rules

Keep an eye on how rules and regulations for quantum-resistant encryption change over time. Following new rules will be very important for keeping data safe and following the law.

The Way Ahead

When it comes to data security, quantum computing offers both new possibilities and challenges that have never been seen before. Quantum dangers are on the horizon, but post-quantum cryptography and quantum-safe solutions are being worked on to deal with them. As quantum computing gets better, people and businesses need to change how they handle data and put money into safe data practices so they can confidently and successfully manage the quantum future. We can keep our data and information safe in the age of quantum computing by staying informed, getting ready for quantum-safe solutions, and working together with experts.

12.2 AI and Machine Learning in Data Security

Now that we live in the digital age, data security is very important for both businesses and people. Because of the fast growth of data and the increasing complexity of cyber threats, we need more advanced ways to protect private data. Artificial Intelligence (AI) and Machine Learning (ML) have become very useful tools for data security. They help with proactive defenses and smart danger detection. This piece talks about how important AI and ML are to data security, how they can be used, what problems they can cause, and the future of data protection in the digital world.

The Need for Data Security

Data has become an important part of modern businesses because it helps them run, connect with customers, and make decisions. As the world has become more digital, the amount of data has grown by leaps and bounds. This means that data must be protected from cyberattacks, data breaches, and illegal access.

Traditional ways of protecting data, like routers and signature-based antivirus software, aren't always effective against threats that are getting smarter and changing. In this case, AI and ML really shine because they can offer dynamic and flexible solutions that can keep up with how threats change.

Using AI and machine learning to keep data safe

Finding threats and noticing strange things

AI and ML are very good at finding trends and outliers in very large datasets. They can look at system logs, network traffic, and user behavior to find actions that seem odd. This kind of proactive danger detection lets businesses find and deal with possible threats before they get worse.

Analysis of Prediction

Machine Learning systems can look at past data to guess what threats and weaknesses might happen in the future. By looking for trends in past attacks, businesses can get ready for new security problems.

Analysis of Behavior

AI-powered solutions can set a standard for how users should behave and quickly spot changes from that behavior. This method works especially well for finding insider threats, which are people who have permission to do something but are abusing it.

Stopping Fraud

AI and ML are very important for finding and stopping fraud in the financial industry. They look at transaction data in real time to spot activities that might be fraudulent and stop deals that aren't supposed to happen.

Automation for security

AI can take care of some security jobs automatically, like managing patches and scanning for security holes. Security experts can focus on more difficult security problems when they don't have to do as much work by hand.

Processing of Natural Language

AI can do more than just look at structured data. It can also handle unstructured data like voice and text. This feature is very helpful for filtering emails, finding phishing attempts, and looking through chat logs for possible security risks.

Information about threats

AI and ML can collect and analyze threat intelligence data from many sources, which helps businesses stay up to date on the newest risks and holes.

Response in Real Time

In the event of a security breach, AI can immediately take action, such as cutting off access to systems that are affected or people who have been hacked. This quick response time can help keep a security issue from getting worse.

What AI and ML Can't Do to Make Data Safer

Data Safety

Concerns about privacy can arise from the huge amounts of data that are needed to build AI models. Organizations need to make sure they follow data security rules and protect people's privacy.

Attacks by the Other Side

In adversarial strikes, AI models are changed to give wrong results. Security experts need to make models that are strong enough to resist these kinds of threats.

Bias in Models

AI models can pick up on biases from the data they are trained on. Because of these attitudes, unfair outcomes may happen. When making and testing models, ethical concerns must be taken into account.

Always Learning

In order for AI models to stay useful as threats change, they need to keep learning and adapting. Model upkeep can use a lot of time and resources.

Level of difficulty

Putting AI and machine learning ideas into action can be hard and require specific knowledge and skills. Companies need to spend money on getting the people and tools they need.

Where AI and ML Are Taking Data Security

Security Operations Centers (SOCs) with AI

AI will be very important for making jobs in security operations centers automatic. This will make it easier to find threats, handle incidents, and make decisions more quickly.

Threat Hunting with AI

Artificial intelligence (AI) will be used by security teams to actively look for risks and holes in the security system before they can be used by hackers.

Quantum computing and keeping data safe

Quantum computing is both a risk and a chance for keeping data safe. Quantum computers might be able to break current encryption methods, but AI and ML will be used to make encryption and security systems that can't be broken by quantum computers.

Security with no trust

More people will use the Zero Trust model, which means that all users and gadgets are not trusted until they are proven to be safe. AI will be very important for real-time access control and identification.

Edge AI to Protect IoT

As the Internet of Things (IoT) grows, it brings about new security problems. When Edge AI is put on IoT devices, it will protect data and find threats in real time.

How AI Works

It will be important to make AI that can be explained as models get more complicated. This means AI systems will have to give reasons for the choices they make, especially when they are used in important areas like healthcare and banking.

Compliance with Regulations

As time goes on, data privacy laws will change, making AI and ML's role in compliance even more important. Businesses will have to make sure that their AI programs follow these rules.

Ethics Things to Think About

When AI and ML are used for data security, they must be guided by moral values. When AI makes security choices, there will be a focus on being open, fair, and responsible.

How Human and Machine Intelligence Work Together

The way data protection is changing means that humans and AI-powered systems will need to work together more than ever. Experts in the field bring knowledge, context, and moral judgment to the table, while AI systems offer speed, automation, and more advanced danger detection.

Together, these two things will make the future of data security possible. AI and ML will be used more and more by security pros to look at huge datasets, find oddities, and predict threats. Then, experts will use the information these systems give them to make smart choices.

AI and machine learning are now tools that can't be done without in the area of data security. In a world where the amount and complexity of data are always growing, these technologies allow for proactive danger detection, predictive analysis, and responses in real time.

The future of data security looks bright, even though problems like data protection, adversarial attacks, and model bias need to be fixed. AI and ML will be very important for improving security operations, keeping people safe from new threats, and responding to new rules.

The best way to protect data in the digital age will be for humans and machines to work together. Companies can make their digital fortresses stronger and confidently handle the constantly changing world of data security by investing in the right people, tools, and morals.

12.3 Blockchain and Secure Data Handling

As our world becomes more digital, data security has become very important. People and businesses are looking for good ways to keep private data safe from hackers and people who shouldn't have access to it. Blockchain technology was first created to support cryptocurrencies like Bitcoin. It has since become a powerful way to handle and control data securely. This piece will talk about the connection between blockchain and safe data management, focusing on the main benefits, use cases, and problems that come with this decentralized method of data protection.

How to Understand Blockchain Technology

Decentralization: Blockchain works with a spread-out network of nodes, so it doesn't need a central authority or middleman.

Transparency: All network members can see transactions that are recorded on the blockchain. This makes the network more transparent.

Immutability: A transaction can't be changed or removed once it's been added to the blockchain. This feature makes sure that the info is correct.

Security: Blockchain uses strong cryptography to keep data safe and limit who can see what data.

Pros of Blockchain for Safely Handling Data

Integrity of Data

The ability to keep data safe is one of the best things about blockchain technology. When a transaction is added to the blockchain, it is time-stamped, encrypted, and tied to the block before it. This makes it very hard to change the data. This function is very helpful in places where changing data is very dangerous, like with medical records, legal documents, and managing the supply chain.

Taking away power

Blockchain doesn't need a central authority because it is autonomous. This lowers the risk of a single point of failure. Data is spread out across the network, and to break into the system, someone would have to take over most of the network hubs, which is not possible.

Better security

Blockchain uses cryptography to keep data safe and limit who can see it. To make sure that only authorized users can access and change the data, public and private keys are used to identify users and encrypt transactions. Because it has a strong security infrastructure, blockchain is perfect for uses that need high levels of security, like verifying identities and making financial deals.

Being clear

Everyone in the network can see transactions on the blockchain. This openness can make people more responsible and build trust in many areas, such as supply chain management (so customers can see where goods come from and how they got to them) and elections (so the honesty of the voting process can be checked).

Contracts that work

Blockchain helps the creation of smart contracts, which are deals that carry out themselves based on rules and conditions that have already been set. When certain conditions are met, these contracts automatically carry out actions, so there is no need for middlemen. Smart contracts make sure that everything is safe and clear by automating everything from financial deals to real estate transfers.

How Blockchain Can Be Used to Handle Secure Data

Supply Chain Management: Blockchain can be used to keep track of how things move from being made to being delivered, which makes the process clear and stops fraud.

Identity Verification: Blockchain can make identity verification safe and impossible to change, which lowers the risk of identity theft.

In healthcare, medical information stored on a blockchain can only be accessed by authorized healthcare providers in a way that protects patient privacy.

Intellectual Property: People who make content can use blockchain to prove who owns something and protect their intellectual property rights.

Financial transfers: Blockchain makes it possible for safe and quick financial transfers, which lowers the risk of fraud and makes everything clear.

Voting Systems: Blockchain can make voting systems more reliable, which makes it harder to change the results of an election.

Problems and Things to Think About

Scalability: One big problem that blockchain networks still have is scalability. Some of them have trouble handling a lot of operations quickly.

Consumption of Energy: Proof-of-work blockchains, like Bitcoin, use a lot of energy. Consensus methods that are sustainable and use little energy are being looked into.

Interoperability: If two or more blockchain networks can't talk to each other, it can make it harder for data to be sent between them easily.

Problems with regulations and the law: The laws that govern blockchain are still changing, and following the rules can be hard.

User Experience: Blockchain platforms can be hard for people who aren't tech-savvy to understand. Improving the user experience is one way to get more people to use blockchain.

Blockchain technology has changed the way that data can be controlled and handled safely. Because it is decentralized, has features for data consistency, improved security, and is open, it is a very useful tool for situations where keeping data safe is very important.

As blockchain technology improves and solves its problems, it will likely be used in more ways to keep data safe. Accepting blockchain's potential in data management can improve safety, openness, and trust in many areas, eventually changing how we store, share, and handle data in the digital world.

www.ingramcontent.com/pod-product-compliance
Lightning Source LLC
LaVergne TN
LVHW011929070526
838202LV00054B/4559